PLOMBIERES
Secret Diplomacy and the Rebirth of Italy

PROBLEMS IN EUROPEAN HISTORY:
A DOCUMENTARY COLLECTION

PLOMBIÈRES

Secret Diplomacy and the Rebirth of Italy

EDITED BY

MACK WALKER
**Associate Professor of History
Cornell University**

New York
OXFORD UNIVERSITY PRESS
London   Toronto   1968

FOREWORD

Problems in European History: A Documentary Collection has arisen out of a collective teaching experience. The series seeks to take care of a shortcoming which the authors believe persists in college history instruction. Certainly the restricting confines of the traditional textbook have been expanded as numerous collections of "readings" have appeared. But the undergraduate still remains at a distance from the historian's workshop. A compilation of heavily edited "significant documents" does not make for the sense of contact with the past that the study of history ought to promote. And the predigested selections from contending historians, neatly arrayed on either side of "classic" controversies, does not get the student to probe the underlying evidence; in fact, these academic disputations often leave him bewildered.

The conviction that students learned little of the way in which historians actually worked prompted a group of young Harvard historians five years ago to develop a new approach. The course that resulted—Social Sciences 3: Problems in Modern European History—represented an attempt to focus intensively on a small number of problems. Each problem would involve careful analysis of a wide variety of original source material. The student could develop the skills and understanding of historical explanation. In learning to compare evidence, make and test hypotheses, and judge critically earlier accounts, he would encounter some of the prob-

v

lems of historical research as experienced by the working historian.

In Social Sciences 3 eight studies in historical analysis are presented in a year. Our intention here is to make these documentary collections available, not necessarily as a series except in their underlying aim, but as separate problems that can be studied individually in connection with courses in European history. Each book has been edited and introduced with that purpose in mind. Thus the student can wrestle with the problems inherent in historical writing and judgment while he studies intensively a segment of the history of the country or period being taught.

Social Sciences 3 has developed over the past four years through the efforts of our collaborators, who share in the creation of these books beyond what we can gratefully acknowledge. Individual problems were prepared or substantially recast by the respective authors, but each case study was discussed and scrutinized by the entire staff of Social Sciences 3. To all of them, to the Committee on General Education of Harvard College, which has generously given of its time and efforts, and to our students—whose criticisms and suggestions were a fundamental guideline—we extend our thanks.

Cambridge, Mass.   RICHARD BIENVENU
August 1967   JOHN F. NAYLOR

PREFACE

On the aims and scope of the volume

The materials gathered in this volume are almost exactly those from which the Plombières problem has been taught at Harvard since 1962-63. The collection has stood the teaching test in a collegial but decentralized undergraduate course rather well, and there seems little reason to shuffle it. The only important modification has been to add the Historical Introduction. The Historical Introduction is an abridgment of the three lectures given by Professor John Rothney (now of the University of Missouri) to introduce the Plombières problem at Harvard in 1964-66.* It is intended to provide historical context and a kind of *dramatis personae* for study of the Plombières sources. But the documents and readings that make up the body of the volume were chosen and arranged to stand on their own, as nearly as could be managed, so as to allow the greatest possible independence to instructor and student.

The sources were not chosen to represent the most recent or even the most accurate possible portrayal of the Plombières conference and its participants. Of course historical accuracy was an important goal, but the main goal was an effective classroom instrument. Pedagogical concerns were uppermost also in the arrangement of sources. Each group of materials (the five included

*I thank Professor Rothney for his generous permission to use his lecture materials in this way; he is not responsible for the result.—Ed.

in this volume, and pp. 1–113 of Albert L. Guérard's *Napoleon III* [New York, Alfred A. Knopf, 1955]) is meant to serve as the basis for one hour of classroom discussion. In briefing students for the study of this problem my practice has been simply to state, as questions, the principles that guided my selection and organization of materials.

What happened at Plombières; what does one need to know to understand the meeting? (Section I of this volume.)

What kind of political man was Louis Napoleon; what did he think was being done at Plombières? (The Guérard biography cited above, or the Historical Introduction to this volume.)

What kind of political man was Cavour, and what did he think was being done at Plombières? (Section II of this volume.)

What was the international position of the Italian Question under discussion at the Plombières conference? (Section III of this volume.)

What precipitated the meeting, and what does that explain about the form it took, the issues that were raised, and the immediate intentions of the participants? (Section IV of this volume.)

How did the affair turn out? Were the plans of the participants fulfilled in the events? (Section V of this volume.)

Each successive question, and the materials to which it leads, seeks a further dimension for understanding the Plombières event. Within that over-all scheme, the choice is left as nearly open as possible for students and instructors to select and interpret what seems to them the most telling of the evidence presented. There is no denying that a collection of sources, however "primary," is almost as much a product of the editor's own thinking as an essay

or a textbook chapter would be; but the purposes of the volume
are best served where the editor's hand is felt least.

A note on sources

The early editions by Luigi Chiala of *Lettere edite ed inedite di
Camillo Cavour* (6 vols., 1st and 2nd editions, Turin, 1883-87)
reflect Chiala's firm allegiance to Cavour, Piedmont, and Italy.
The most notable effect of his editorial selections and omissions
was to pass over the more ignoble diplomatic practices of Cavour
and his times, but I am not aware of any literal falsifications among
the materials taken from that source, and have used them especially
as evidence of Cavour's general political views and personality.
Domenico Zanichelli's edition of *Gli scritti del Conte di Cavour*
(2 vols., Bologna, 1892) is a collection of published writings.

The publication of the *Textuel procés Orsini* in Turin in 1858
by Jules Favre's secretary, C.-A. Dandraut, is in itself a fact worth
noting. Joseph A. v. Hübner's *Neun Jahre der Erinnerungen eines
Oesterreichischen Botschafters* (2 vols., Berlin, 1904) is a diplomat's chatty diary. Nicomede Bianchi's *Storia documentata della
diplomazia europea in Italia dall' anno 1814 all' anno 1861* (8
vols., Turin, 1865-72) is a very extensive collection of documents
which, of course, is affected by its publication at a time when the
events it treats were very live issues. Franco Valsecchi (ed.),
*L'unificazione italiana e la politica europea dalla guerra di Lom-
bardia, 1854-1859* (Milan, Instituto per gli studi di politica inter-
nazionale, 1939), is an important supplement for the years named.

The publication of the *Carteggio Cavour-Nigra dal 1858 al 1861*
(4 vols., Bologna, N. Zanichelli, 1961; first published in 1926)
added much that the older collections on Cavour had ignored or
evaded, including much material beyond the scope the title indicates. Nigra was Cavour's intimate secretary and aide; and in this
collection appear not only the Cavour-Nigra correspondence, but
other documents written by Cavour and others which had been

omitted or cut in older collections. Here more treatment of personalities appears, and the seamier side of the politics and diplomacy of the time; and this is the source for most of the materials used in this volume to represent the immediate background of the Plombières conference. All translations from the sources cited above, with the exception noted in the text, are by the editor.

Excerpts from three secondary works are reprinted here: John A. R. Marriott's *Makers of Modern Italy* (London, 1931; not the lectures published under the same title in 1901) is in the tradition of British benevolent interest in the Risorgimento. His *The Eastern Question* (4th ed. Oxford, 1940) is a diplomatic narrative with emphasis on the British role. William R. Thayer's *Life and Times of Cavour* (2 vols., Boston, 1911) is a sympathetic account based on the earlier, more favorable published materials.

Bibliography

The following books are noted not as bases for the preparation or the use of this volume but as studies of general interest and relevance to its theme.

Kent R. Greenfield, *Economics and Liberalism in the Risorgimento: A Study of Nationalism in Lombardy, 1814-1848* (rev. ed., Baltimore, 1965).

Edward E. Y. Hales, *Pio Nono, A Study in European Politics and Religion in the Nineteenth Century* (2nd ed., London, 1956).

Denis Mack Smith, *Cavour and Garibaldi, 1860: A Study in Political Conflict* (Cambridge, England, 1954).

Georges Maurice Paléologue, *Cavour*, tr. I and M. Morrow (New York, 1927).

Alan J. P. Taylor, *The Struggle for Mastery in Europe, 1848-1918* (Oxford, 1954).

James M. Thompson, *Louis Napoleon and the Second Empire* (Oxford, 1954).

Theodore Zeldin, *The Political System of Napoleon III* (New York, 1958).

CONTENTS

HISTORICAL INTRODUCTION

1. Background of the Italian Risorgimento, to 1831

On July 20, 1858, the Emperor Napoleon III of France and Prime Minister Cavour of the Kingdom of Piedmont met privately in the resort town of Plombières in eastern France. Their meeting opened the final chapter, one of diplomatic and military action, of the movement Italians call the Risorgimento, the reawakening of Italy as a united national state.

Questions of Italian political destiny had taken shape as a problem of national unity during the preceding two or three generations: the years of the French Revolution, the Napoleonic conquests, and then the efforts of restored European governments led by the Austrian chancellor Prince Metternich to enforce a peace of the *status quo* on Europe. During that period the notion took root that the "natural" condition of peoples was national unity, so that where national unity did not exist, that was because it had been interfered with and suppressed. The *status quo* of Metternich's Europe stipulated a multitude of separate states in Italy and in Germany; and although this situation had existed for centuries, it now came to be looked upon as *dis*unity, a deviation from the norm, an aberration in the path of history. Italians looked for the sources of disunity in the past—not forgetting as they did so that their real objects were the obstacles to Italian unity in the present.

Among the obstacles to unity to be found in the distant past,

3

three related ones deserve special mention: the medieval Holy
Roman Empire, the power of the Papacy, and the individualist
traditions of the Italian towns and principalities. Counterparts or
residues of all these still existed.

The Holy Roman Empire of the German nation had developed
from the efforts of German dynasties to establish sway over Germany and Italy, as successors to the Roman emperors of ancient
times, but through the feudal political apparatus of the Middle
Ages. Because of the inadequacy of the political means available
and because they attempted more than they could achieve, the Holy
Roman Emperors never imposed political unity on Germany or
Italy, much less on both of them together. On the contrary, resources were so slight that they could maintain even their shadowy
position only by setting one locality or group of subjects against
another. Unable to establish unified control themselves, their interest therefore was commonly to foster disunity by preventing
consolidation from within or annexation from without. The Holy
Roman Empire was a defense of Italian and German particular-
ism: that much it was able to do. By the end of the thirteenth
century their efforts for direct control of Italy had ceased. They
had met their match in the Papacy, and in the towns. But neither
of these provided unity either.

The presence of the Papacy at Rome was, rather, a second
obstacle to Italian unity for a number of reasons. Of course it
occupied the historic capital city of the peninsula. But also the
interests of the Popes, Italy's greatest princes, extended far outside
Italy, and their Italian policies were only part of their international
role. The aspirations of the Supreme Pontiffs, like those of the
Emperors, lay beyond their material means. The claims of both
to supremacy over Christian Europe led to irreconcilable conflict
between them. In Italy the partisans of the Pope were called
Guelfs, and the partisans of the Emperor, Ghibellines. But while
the Popes had no overriding interest in unifying Italy themselves,
their need for a secure territorial base from which to carry on

their activities made them unwilling to accept the rise of any secular Italian power which could bring the whole peninsula under its control. The prevention of unity was something they, like the Emperors, could manage.

In the absence of any effective supreme power in Italy, the medieval towns or communes were able to maintain their independence and traditions largely unbroken, and by expanding their influence outside their walls developed into the city-states of Renaissance times. The civic allegiance of a citizen was for his city-state: yet even a Florentine patriot like Machiavelli might see if he chose that small weak states in the long run would be unable to maintain their independence against consolidated monarchies like France and Spain (though the relatively "national" composition of these great monarchies did not seem important until much later). Italy did in fact come piecemeal under the domination of greater European powers. From the sixteenth century through the eighteenth especially, Italy was a cockpit for European war, diplomacy, and dynastic politics. Native Italian civic life stagnated. But the brilliant monuments of antiquity and Renaissance were there to show the achievements of an earlier, freer Italy. The stagnation, it seemed, had come with subjugation by powerful foreigners.

Most historians nowadays would probably say that revival began under the auspices of those very foreign princes, in the late-eighteenth-century era of reform that bears the European label Enlightened Despotism. Enlightened princes furthered economic development, education, and efficient administration—by autocratic means, and in the interest of the state. A body of native Italians grew up who were men of the world. They discovered those ideas of eighteenth-century Europe which were to become the ideology of the French Revolution. An important channel for the communication of ideas and ideals was the Freemasonic lodges, deliberately contemptuous of state boundaries. There men could meet with the like-*minded*, reformist intellectuals

and officials, dissatisfied noblemen, and aspiring businessmen, and deplore the fussy social and political boundaries that kept them apart in the existing order, and that kept new things from happening. The seeds of the Risorgimento were planted in the Freemasonic lodge; but the lodges also created for these ideas a tradition of sectarianism and secrecy.

The moment of opportunity for the men and the ideas represented by Freemasonry began with the era of Revolution in France, cultural bellwether of Europe. But the real impact of the new age on Europe was brought by the person of Napoleon Bonaparte, a Corsican-born general sent to command the French armies fighting Austria in Italy. Bonaparte expelled the petty Italian princes held to be lackeys of the Austrians and established new governments, which were to be not subjects but little sisters of the great French Republic. The new states bore such names as the Cisalpine Republic. New regimes meant new opportunities for men with political ambitions and liberal political ideas. Governments composed of such men joined with the French army and its commander in driving out the rulers of the old Italian states— even the Pope, in 1798—and in such reforms as abolishing feudal privilege and subordinating the Church to the state.

In 1799 there was a reversal, with results that Italian liberals long remembered. In the north, Austrians and Russians counterattacked, and drove the French (Bonaparte was now in Paris) from the peninsula. Without French support the satellite republics collapsed. In the south, the forces of the Bourbon King of Naples, who had taken refuge in Sicily, returned to the mainland as the Army of the Holy Faith, led by the Cardinal Ruffo. These *Sanfedisti* (notably Sicilian bandits and pious south Italian peasants) took bloody reprisals against the Frenchified and atheistical liberal supporters of the Neapolitan Republic, killing four thousand of them, mostly from the educated middle class of the towns.

But Bonaparte, once he had achieved mastery in France, returned to Italy. By 1809, the man who was now Emperor Napoleon I had brought all Italy under his control, direct or indirect.

About a third (including Turin, where Camillo di Cavour was born in 1810) was annexed to France. Another third, the Kingdom of Italy, was administered in the name of its king—Napoleon himself—by a viceroy who was Napoleon's stepson. And the southern third, a Kingdom of Naples, was entrusted to a French field marshal who had begun as an innkeeper's son: Joachim Murat, now King Joachim I.

Napoleon's ensuing exactions of blood and treasure from Italy were commensurate with his ambition to conquer and control Europe. Italian soldiers behind their red, white, and green tricolor made the terrible marches to Madrid and Moscow. Yet the period of his rule was a dynamic and for many people a liberating one. Efficiently organized administration and police cleared the tangle of civic privilege and petty bullying. Tariff barriers separating the hodgepodge of old principalities disappeared, opening new horizons to the businessmen of the former communes. And even though the Napoleonic governments of Italy were satellites of France, they brought opportunity to the new men composing them —the "career open to talent"—which had usually been denied by the old regime and which they and others like them did not forget when it was denied again, by the governments restored after Napoleon's fall in 1814–15.

In Italy as elsewhere in Europe, the Revolution and Napoleon had been a double stimulus for the idea of nationality and unity. The brilliant example of the French nation one and indivisible came together with nationalist rejection of the French invader— something that could lead to serious political ambiguity. Resentment of a powerful and patronizing foreign conqueror might take the name of Italian national consciousness. And yet after all it was that conqueror who had driven out the Austrians and their princely lackeys. It was Napoleon who had let new air into Italian civic life, shaking up and breaking up the old regime, and Napoleon who had created, by his rule and in the Kingdom of Italy, something more like an Italian national state than had ever been seen, and a harbinger of what a revolutionary age might bring.

In his struggle against Austria and the old European political
system he had created a freer, more nearly united and nationally
conscious Italy. Here we are still speaking, of course, of the small
minority of the Italian population who were literate and politically
alive to such questions and who were not, like most of the clergy
and many others, adherents of the old regime or simply indifferent.
In 1815 such men were few, in Italy and in the councils of
Europe, and the problems of Italian nationality became a matter
for pondering, as dreams of the past blended into dreams of the
future; for the European system established at Vienna in 1814–15
gave them no greater role.

At Vienna the great powers handed Italy back to the dynasties
which the Revolution and Napoleon had overthrown—which
meant, in political fact, back to Austria and its conservative Prime
Minister, Metternich. Explicit recognition of Austria's special interests and rights in Italy restored, by international agreement,
the situation which had existed in international practice in the
years preceding Bonaparte's appearance. Under the governments
established 1815, to advocate Italian unity was treasonable
and revolutionary, because it was subversive of existing states.
There were eight of these (more or less, depending on how one
defines a state). The prosperous regions of Lombardy and Venetia
became a province in the dynastic collection of the Austrian House
of Habsburg. King Victor Emmanuel I of the House of Savoy was
restored to the hybrid Kingdom of Piedmont-Sardinia, the "Italian
Prussia." His repeal of all laws passed during the French occupation, and the military-aristocratic character of his regime, augured
little sympathy for liberal causes. Petty sovereigns dependent on
Austria were restored to the duchies of Modena, Parma, Lucca,
and the Grand Duchy of Tuscany. The Papacy recovered the States
of the Church intact, from Rome and the Tiber in the southwest,
to Bologna and Ferrara (the Legations) in the Romagna to the
north and east side of the peninsula. The Bourbon king returned
to the roadless, lawless Kingdom of the Two Sicilies, to exercise a
government of despotism checked by anarchy, famed throughout

Europe for its corruption and indolence, whose politics often
seemed no more enlightened than a choice among bandit cliques.

Italian national patriotism being unlawful, peaceable folk who
believed in it were obliged to hold their tongues. The only channels
for action were underground—the Carbonari. The "Charcoal-
Burners" were especially active in Naples, but after 1815 a loose
organization, based on Freemasonic precedents and attracting
many of the sorts of people Freemasonry had attracted, developed
through much of Italy. The Carbonari had been founded in 1810
to further Italian national resistance to French rule, but after
Napoleon's fall they transferred their enmity to the Austrians and
their puppets. Apart from their advocacy of some kind of popular
sovereignty (the apparent alternative to the regimes that existed),
their political ideals were mixed and vague: what characterized the
carbonaro was that he wanted to *do* something. The society was
especially effective among bored junior army officers of the garrison
towns, and in 1820 and 1821 there were military coups with liberal
aims in Naples and in Piedmont. Rulers in both places promptly
succumbed, but were restored to power by Austrian arms; the first
revolutionary wave in Italy after 1815 produced only martyrs.
After the July Revolution of 1830 in Paris, hope for support from
the new liberal French regime prompted new risings in Italy, including the Papal States; but these too were futile, and easily
suppressed with Austrian aid.

Among those who fought and failed then for an Italian Republic
was one Andrea Orsini, who had fought in Napoleon I's armies in
the campaign against Russia. One who fell for Italy was a nephew
of the great Napoleon. That nephew's younger brother, Prince
Louis Napoleon, also fought, but escaped arrest and its consequences when the Archbishop of Spoleto, Monsignor Mastai-
Ferretti, provided him with false passports. In 1858 Mastai-Ferretti
was Pope at Rome; Louis Napoleon was Emperor of the French,
and Orsini's son was executed for an attempt on the Emperor's
life. For a young Piedmontese officer of engineers, Count Cavour,
the repressive wave of 1831 meant an end to hopes for a successful

military career; and for the young *carbonaro* Giuseppe Mazzini
it meant imprisonment, exile, and a new idea of Italian unity.

2. Mazzini and his Rivals, 1831–58

Chief credit for Italian unity is shared by Camillo di Cavour and
Giuseppe Mazzini; and yet they were the bitterest of rivals, and
their rivalry still arouses the passions of historians today—and
not only Italian historians. On many occasions Cavour would
doubtless have hanged Mazzini if he could have caught him. And
while Mazzini would probably never have ordered Cavour assassinated, still if such a thing had happened he would have seen the
hand of Providence in it. To understand Cavour and what he was
thinking at Plombières is one of the main elements of the problem
presented in the sources that follow; to interpret his actions it is
important to form an idea of the influence exercised by his great
rival. Then we shall consider alternative paths to Italian national
unity, and then the position of Napoleon III.

Mazzini, like Cavour, was a subject of the king of Piedmont-
Sardinia, but he resented the delivery of his native city of Genoa
to that kingdom in 1814–15, and never ceased to distrust its
ruling House of Savoy. Mazzini's father, again like Cavour's, had
served in the reforming Napoleonic administration. But here the
similarity ends, and the divergent paths of the two men toward
Italian unity must start from their radically different temperaments.
Mazzini, born in 1805, had first followed his father into the study
of medicine, until his horror at the dissection room turned him
to law; he took his degree at Genoa in 1826. "For a short time,"
he wrote later, "my mind was somewhat tainted by the doctrines
of the foreign materialist school; but the study of history, and the
intuitions of conscience—the only tests of truth—soon led me
back to the spiritualism of our Italian forefathers." Elsewhere he
attributes his conversion to the Italian national cause to an experience of 1821, when he and his mother, walking in Genoa, were
stopped by desperate revolutionary fugitives who begged for alms

to help them escape the police dragnet. The personality of Mazzini's doting mother, in whose company the experience occurred, is another key to his temperament. She was a Jansenist, a believer in what has been called "Catholic Puritanism," with its emphasis on piety, predestination, personal moral responsibility, and the necessity for profound feeling in emotional experience.

Historians and analysts who argue that nationalism is a kind of post-Christian religion always cite Mazzini and his ideas as evidence, with good reason—with good reason, that is, if by religion they mean a channel for moral passion and faith which supersedes calculation and material gain. During the 1820's Mazzini wrote on literary topics, supporting the young romantic school against the classicists, and he joined the Carbonari. Jailed for six months in 1831, he formulated his nationalist faith in a cell from which he could see only the sky (Mazzini was fated throughout his life to see only fragments of the Italian land and people whose prophet he sought to be). In the years of exile that followed he put forward the tenets of his faith in essays and exhortations whose extravagance of language and thought resists summary, order, or even translation. Cavour's first published writing, by contrast, was an analytical abstract of the English Poor Laws.

At the center of Mazzini's body of beliefs was faith: faith in God, indeed, but not in the God of the Christians, who in the nineteenth century had become so remote. It was rather a God who moved with history, who *was* history. In each era of this God's developing plan and changing nature, Mazzini believed, men are responsible for finding and carrying out their appointed roles. The period of the French Revolution and of Napoleon had been the climax of one such era, the era of individuality, with its emphasis on personal freedom. The new principle was "Association," an idea and a slogan which Mazzini the nationalist shared with the so-called "Utopian Socialists" of the Europe and America of his time and generation, just as he shared in the religious style of their sentiments and their utterances.

In this divine era of Association, Mazzini urged, men must move beyond their individual rights, beyond the understanding of their duties to themselves and to their own dignity, and learn to understand and cultivate their moral duties to one another. This era's God was Humanity; "God and the People" must be its slogan. And its Messiah would be the newly united Italian nation, an Italy which, true to its Messianic role, must be created by the dedication of every citizen to the divinely inspired mission of the Community.

How to bring this about was the object of a second slogan of Mazzini's: "Education and Action." The Italian people had to be made conscious of their role if it was to be fulfilled and not perverted; consciousness was a faith, and Mazzini preached it as a faith and sought its propagation as a faith. Education was exhortation; and action was to provide examples: heroes, martyrs if need be until the time came when the people were ready for their triumph.

Now, from these rather mystical and grandiose notions, increasingly concrete corollaries followed, so that they were not empty hallucinations—as Cavour, and the European conservatives who hated Mazzini, were quite aware. Of course the Italian nation could not fulfill itself while it was ruled by aliens (nor could any other nation, for that matter). But further, it could find fulfillment only in a unitary, democratic Republic. There had to be complete democracy, to begin with, because neither monarchy nor constitutional government by any self-appointed elite (for example, the individualist liberals) could arouse the commitment of all social classes to the duties of citizenship in the age of Humanity. Democracy was the association of all with all. And the same was true of Unity. Unity meant the overcoming of the regional divisions of the Italian people, just as Democracy meant overcoming their social divisions. A federal Italian state, especially one created by a single region, could only perpetuate jealousies and frustrate true association; it would end in the rule by one Italian region over the others.

It followed further that the unitary, democratic Republic could not be achieved by relying on French intervention, as in the days

of Napoleon, to liberate and unify Italy. That had been the error
of Carbonari and liberals in 1830–31. For Mazzini the point was
not so much that this was bad strategy; it was bad ideology, bad
theology—one is tempted to say heresy, although as with most
heresies the practical consequences were inseparable from the ideal.
Italy must do it herself, and must create the unitary democratic
nation-state without appeal to an interest, a class, a region, or a
government.

Mazzini's appeal was directed to a generation, in keeping with
his sense of history and history's God. Only the youth of Italy
could express the new era; only they were free of older men's at-
tachments to a class, a community, a region, or a regime; only they
could speak for and speak to the whole Italian people. And the
movement he established (from exile in 1831) bore the name of
Young Italy. Young Italian "Congregations" soon spread over
much of Italy. Theirs was the mission of exhorting and providing
examples. Popular risings had to be made even when they were
bound to be suppressed, if not indeed for that very reason, for
they helped create national sympathy and awareness. For propa-
ganda purposes Mazzini was always ready for new risings, whatever their prospects. Of course, events which made the Italian
people aware of national democratic revolution made their rulers
aware as well, and brought intensified suppression. The lesson that
revolution invited reaction was one Mazzini could accept with
complacency. But the same lesson turned others to a search for
some plan for Italian unity which could be achieved without revolutionary violence.

The most important of these was put forward in 1843 by a
former member of Young Italy, a Piedmontese priest Vincenzo
Gioberti, in a book entitled "The Civil and Moral Supremacy of
the Italians." Gioberti's proposal can be called the Neo-Guelf
alternative, for it looked to the Roman Papacy for leadership in
expelling the northern invader and uniting Italy. Centuries of
Roman history, wrote Gioberti, showed Italy's natural pre-emi-
nence in the world; now Rome must again lead in restoring it. The

obvious tactical advantage of this plan was that Italy would be united *by* the Pope and the Church, and not against them. It would be a federated Italy, rather than a fully unitary one, to allay the fears and attract the support of the several Italian regions; and the Pope's presidency of the Federation would pacify or forestall the Italian princes and the conservative powers of Europe, led by Austria.

Since that time it has become hard to conceive how any nine-teenth-century Pope could be proposed as a spokesman for Italian nationalism. But perhaps Gioberti and his adherents knew the Church politics of the 1840's better: at any rate, in 1846 the College of Cardinals, rather to its surprise, elected to be Pope the liberal Cardinal Mastai-Ferretti. For those who had read Gioberti's book—they included the new Pope Pius IX—this was an electrifying event. We have seen Mastai-Ferretti helping young Prince Louis Napoleon escape Italy in 1831; but he was widely known to be a man of liberal persuasion and boldness of action, and an enemy of the obscurantist aspects of papal rule and papal policy. His first actions as Pope showed that he sought the role of a progressive, liberating, and compassionate sovereign. There were political amnesties by the thousands, prison reforms, and the severity of the laws was relaxed. The papal government announced that there would be gaslights for the city of Rome, and that a railroad might be admitted to the Patrimony of Saint Peter. Pius IX sounded out several Italian states on the possibility of an Italian customs union, or common market, which could be considered (like the German Zollverein) a first step toward political unity.

Thus by the end of 1847 moderate Italian liberals might well believe that the new era of unity, progress, and freedom was at hand. Camillo di Cavour, who had spent the years since 1831 traveling, developing family estates, and writing for French journals, founded together with political friends a newspaper at Turin entitled *Il Risorgimento*. But old Prince Metternich in Vienna wrote to *his* political friends that a liberal Pope was a contradiction in terms, as the coming year, 1848, would prove.

And so it did prove. When the revolutionary wave of 1848 swept Europe, and Austrian weakness and preoccupation brought the forces of Italy into the field against her, papal troops marched to the north along with the rest. But there they were paralyzed by a papal encyclical declaring that a Pope could never make offensive war, least of all against Catholic Austria. Pius IX had had to decide, and the decision began his progressive alienation from liberal nationalism. By that autumn, popular radicalism and insurrection in the city of Rome had completed the alienation; the Pope even had to flee Rome and the Papal States, and seek protection in the Kingdom of Naples. That completed his political conversion: for the rest of his long pontificate (to 1878) he was the most conservative of popes, setting the stamp of his political and social views on Church policy for a century to come. The Neo-Guelf alternative was dead; and by 1851 Gioberti in a second book was pointing to the king of Piedmont-Sardinia as the only remaining hope for Italian unity.

The Piedmontese experience of 1848–49, at first glance, seemed to leave that kingdom hardly a more promising candidate for leadership of Italian unity than the Pope. When Metternich's Austria had seemed to crumble in that spring, to be sure, King Charles Albert had granted a liberal constitution to his subjects, and had invaded Austrian Lombardy as an ally of revolution and the nation. But after two military defeats by the redoubtable Marshal Radetzky he was obliged to abdicate his throne. Despite and perhaps partly because of severe Austrian pressure, though, his proud son and successor, Victor Emmanuel II, refused to repudiate the constitution. This was a matter of Piedmontese integrity, not of Italian nationalism. Yet amid the wave of Italian reaction, Piedmont stood as the only important Italian government which a man like Cavour, though a moderate liberal to the right of center, could join and come to dominate.

For Mazzini and the Republican solution, 1848 added one more glorious failure. Mazzini had always believed that Rome must ultimately be, naturally and historically, the capital of the Italian nation, once the Pope could be got out of it. After Pius IX had fled and Rome had declared itself a Republic, Mazzini hastened to Rome (he had been made its first honorary citizen) and became a member of the governing triumvirate. There he showed himself in practice a man of greater moderation and discretion than his readers might have supposed. But the Republic in which he governed could not survive the troops sent to pull it down by Prince Louis Napoleon Bonaparte, president of the French Republic. After a dramatic and heroic defense led by the partisan leader Garibaldi, the Roman Republic fell, and Mazzini returned to London exile. More and more Italians were ready to say that Mazzini and his tactics, however dramatic and morally attractive, cost altogether too much blood and trouble. In the cooler, tougher decade after 1848, much of the romantic dash of the Italian national movement had faded, though nobody could be sure whether a Mazzini or a Garibaldi might not rekindle it again.

Camillo di Cavour, during the early 1850's, was rapidly becoming one of the most promising politicians in Italy—whatever that might amount to. He intended it to amount to something. Soon after he entered the Piedmontese cabinet in 1850 (he became Prime Minister in 1852), Cavour began maneuvering skillfully to reinforce the new constitution in two ways: first, by seeking to reduce the elements of feudal and clerical privilege which remained in Piedmont; and second, by building a broad reliable majority which would consolidate the parliamentary system and the positions of those prepared to work through it. The first policy provoked the antagonism of the "Blacks," the traditionalist and clerical party, who probably would have held a parliamentary majority if the suffrage had not been so narrow as to exclude poorer and more dependent social elements. For the second, therefore, he turned to the Left Center, and made an alliance with its leader, the 1848 democrat Urbano Rattazzi.

By broadening his political base in this fashion in Piedmont, Cavour was also attracting support outside the kingdom from those who clung to hopes for a liberally united Italy. The most dramatic evidence of this came when Daniele Manin, former chief of the revolutionary 1848 Republic of Venice, publicly broke with

Mazzini in 1855 and declared that henceforth he must put his trust in Piedmont—albeit conditionally and even a little sullenly:

> The Republican party [Manin's] . . . performs an act of abnegation and sacrifice on behalf of the National Cause. Convinced that above all Italy must be made, the Republican party says to the House of Savoy: *Make Italy and we are with you.* If not, no. We say: . . . Plan to make Italy, not to aggrandize Piedmont; be Italian patriots, and not exclusively Piedmontese, and we are with you. If not, no.

In 1856 Manin became a head of the newly formed Italian National Society (pro-Piedmontese, subsidized and quietly supported by Cavour), and he died in the next year without ever having to decide what 1858 meant for the "If not, no." But for Mazzini there had never been an if, only a no. In his newspaper *Italia del Populo*, he addressed a savage attack to Cavour:

> You have corrupted our youth, by substituting a policy of artifices and lies for the serene, frank, loyal policy of him who desires to rise again. . . . Between you and us, sir, an abyss yawns. We represent Italy—you, the old, covetous, faint-hearted ambition of the House of Savoy. We desire above all National Unity; you, territorial aggrandizement. We believe in the initiative of the people of Italy—you fear it, and rely on diplomacy and upon the consent of European governments. We desire that the country, when emancipated, shall determine its own government—you deny national sovereignty and insist on monarchy. We devote ourselves body and soul to a campaign for freeing Italy—you devote yourself to persecuting us. We adore one faith—the National Faith—and one principle—the Popular Republican Principle—you bend your knee to the principle of force.

That was just a few months before Cavour journeyed to Plombières to meet the Emperor of the French.

3. The Limitations of Bonapartism, 1848–58

Force had its limitations, even for a Bonaparte; and the choices even of an Emperor are not free. Napoleon III's personality and ultimate aims were indeed remarkable—even though historians cannot agree on the true nature of either. Albert Guérard's short biography, assigned in part as one of the sources for the Plombières problem, gives one favorable account of these. Here it may be helpful to describe some other elements and personalities of the French political world in which he moved and acted.

Historians have recently debated whether the regime of Napoleon III was a precursor and a prototype of twentieth-century European fascist dictatorships. The debate may be of more than passing interest, because both Napoleon III's assailants and his defenders have argued that his political practices and aims were peculiarly adapted to the modern political age. The division has not quite come over what one thought of the modern world, but rather over what Napoleon's policies implied for the future, and how one described them. Demagogic pursuit of support from the masses, or advanced and compassionate programs of social welfare? International adventurer seeking pinchbeck popularity, or European statesman trying to build a modern, reasonable, and stable political order based on democratic and national self-determination?

An interesting feature of the debate is that a very similar one took place in Napoleon III's own time—without, of course, having directly to do with twentieth-century dictators. And yet their future appearance was implied, because at that time too, both the Emperor's detractors and his supporters believed his political methods to be characteristic of the modern age. And most interesting of all, when they thought of the modern age they were likely to have something from the past in their minds: the reign of Napoleon III's uncle, the great Napoleon I, heir to the Revolution, reformer and arbiter of Europe.

The "Napoleonic legend" therefore united memories of past glories (or tyrannies) with patterns for the present and future. Louis Napoleon relied upon it publicly as a practical political asset, but also he studied his uncle's reign with care and tried to work out its application for his own situation. It was not always easy to do so, and it created the risk of false analogy and error; whatever one thought of the modernity of Napoleon I, France in the 1850's was *not* the France of a half-century before, though perhaps similar enough to be misleading. And it was possible to misinterpret the history of the First Empire. One of the imponderables was the distribution of power among the various elements or classes in French society, and how that bore on high domestic and foreign policy.

Discussion of this must begin with the Revolution of 1848 in France, which finally gave Louis Napoleon his chance for power. When the Revolution broke out, King Louis Philippe of the House of Orleans had been in power for eighteen years, presiding over what was commonly called the Bourgeois Monarchy, partly because of the middle-class habits of the king and his entourage but also because of the important political influence enjoyed by people of wealth. Political life was constitutionally restricted to a small electorate of 200,000, led by an "establishment" elite of education, wealth, and social prominence. The rule of these *notables* in the July Monarchy proved unable to withstand rivalries among themselves, pressures for political influence from the lower bourgeoisie, and the volatile revolutionary potential of an urban working class hard-hit by the dislocations and cyclical depressions of early industrialism.

In the first shocks of February and March 1848, the regime of the *notables* seemed to have been overwhelmed, and replaced by a government dominated by the rebellious elements of the capital. But they were saved by the French peasantry, who, once enfranchised by the Republic, voted to be represented not by the republican revolutionaries of Paris but by local *notables*. Paris insurrections provoked by the return of the *notables* were suppressed by the republican government. During these crucial months, therefore, the Republic found itself alienated from the two most numerous elements of the population. It had been repudiated by the ballots of the peasantry—ballots cast against the whole Paris crowd—and now it had alienated the working class by the bloody suppression of June 1848.

The Republic's difficulties were aggravated by defects drawn into its constitution. There was a powerful presidency and a powerful legislature, with no certain means of resolving conflicts between them. Into that powerful presidency, universal suffrage (meaning mainly the peasants) in December 1848 elected Louis Napoleon Bonaparte. A few months later the electorate sent more of the old Orleanist *notables* to the legislative body. The *notables* of the legislature had tended to support Louis Napoleon for the presidency, as an alternative to republicans and socialists, and as someone they had reason to believe they could control. Disturbed and frightened by the revolutionary radicalism of the urban workers, they now set about ensuring that it would not return. One means would be to strengthen the position of the Church as a bulwark of social defense: an aim all the more attractive because of a renewed interest in religion among the French upper classes in recent years.

To reinforce the Church meant helping its supreme head regain his position, and so it was that troops of the French Republic were sent to attack Mazzini's Roman Republic and restore Pius IX in 1849, with the blessings of the Legislative Assembly and the participation of the Prince-President. Louis Napoleon liked to have a hand in Italy, and apparently he wished to exact liberal reforms from the Pope in return for his restoration, but he was in no position to enforce such views, either in France or in the Papal States.

In 1850 the *notables* of the legislature passed the Falloux Law, which in effect handed French education over to agencies of the Church, again with the apparent acquiescence of the President. At about the same time they drew up an electoral law which, by requiring long residence, disenfranchised the mobile and volatile working-class elements. They might have tried to get rid of the Republic altogether in favor of a monarchy, except that they could not agree on a candidate for the throne: whether he should be the Orleanist heir to Louis Philippe or the "Legitimist" pretender of the senior Bourbon line ousted by Louis Philippe in 1830.

In any case, the *notables* had achieved considerable success for their aims by dominating the legislature. The President had

made no constitutional resistance, and seemed to be the amenable
puppet they had meant him to be. But here they miscalculated.
Louis Napoleon had been building up his own position and mar-
shaling his own supporters, not only within the administrative
establishment but also in the country at large. He sought support
among the peasantry by touring the country, giving full billing to
his glorious name, and telling French rustics they were the back-
bone of France. And at the same time he encouraged a Bonapartist
party in the cities and towns, appealing to the shopkeeping, artisan,
and working-class people disappointed by the Republic of the
notables. This "Left Bonapartist" campaign stressed the popular
and progressive aspects of the Napoleonic tradition: it was democratic and anticlerical, and it emphasized what a strong French
executive could do for distressed parts of the population and for
the brother-oppressed nations of the world, such as Poland
and Italy.

The rivalry between Louis Napoleon and the *notables* became
a race to see which would overthrow the Republic first, and resolve
the constitutional deadlock between them in his own interests. In
such a race the executive branch, with its control of army, police,
and bureaucracy, had immense advantages, especially in the city
of Paris. Louis Napoleon executed a *coup d'état*: on the morning
of December 2, 1851, Paris awoke to find the walls covered with
posters announcing that the Legislative Assembly had been dissolved, that full universal suffrage had been restored, and that the
people would soon be asked to ratify a new constitution. The
notables were helpless, for the Paris workers could not be rallied
to defend *their* Republic, and the peasants of the countryside, by
and large, supported the name of Napoleon as they had in 1848.
There were only a few casualties, about six hundred, occurring
when troops fired on crowds of respectable people who presumably supported the *notables* or at least the Republic; even these
few, though, marred the event for Louis Napoleon, and caused
him embarrassment later on. But on the whole this day seemed
to free his authority from political limitations and restraint; the

social antagonisms had cancelled one another out, leaving him free to act. He told the Piedmontese ambassador who hastened to congratulate him: "Now that I can do what I want, I shall do something for Italy."

The new constitution of what became the Second Empire gave Emperor Napoleon III maximum authority, on the pattern of the First Empire. The Emperor was declared to be responsible only to the people of France, whose will might be expressed in plebiscites held to register approval or disapproval of his policies, as he stated them. Cabinet ministers were his agents, appointed and dismissed at his will, and often were kept ignorant of what was going on in agencies of government other than their own, let alone in the Emperor's personal circles and instruments. Unsurprisingly, such positions did not attract the best governmental talent in France but more commonly persons whose meager and peculiar qualifications commended them mainly to the Emperor. The governments of Europe long addressed their official dealings with the French Empire to Count Walewski, whose only apparent title to the office of Foreign Minister was that he was the out-of-wedlock result of a famous liaison between Napoleon I and a Polish countess.

The leading personnel of the Second Empire were indeed a motley and disorganized lot. Napoleon himself is said to have described them so: "What a curious government I have! The Empress is a Legitimist, Morny is an Orleanist, Prince Napoleon is a Republican, I am a Socialist; only Persigny is a Bonapartist, and he's crazy."

The Empress Eugénie, impulsive daughter of minor Spanish nobility, was a devout clerical and a passionate opponent of political liberalism. Her influence on the Emperor derived partly from her personality, but was enhanced by the domestic commonplace that he was unfaithful to her with such frequency that she could always get something out of him in return for forgiveness.

Morny, the Emperor's bastard half-brother, was in fact an Orleanist *notable* at heart, always seeking to attract the *notables*

to the regime by increasing the powers of the legislative branch
of government.

Prince Napoleon, the Emperor's cousin, known to his few
friends and many detractors as Plon-Plon (a childhood nick-
name), constituted the Republican opposition within the imperial
entourage. Apart from the spectacular nature of his personal morals, he constantly embarrassed the Emperor at awkward moments
by declaring publicly that the Empire should carry on a Republican
domestic and foreign policy, courting the working class at home
and making war abroad to free captive nations.

And Napoleon's old comrade Persigny was perhaps the only one
of the group besides the Emperor himself who really believed in
the Napoleonic legend, and spoke for a policy of basing the Empire
on the masses, not the *notables*.

The Second Empire from the outset risked the necessity of
making a fateful and dangerous choice: on which of the contending social groups should it base itself? On the lower-middle and
working classes, discouraged with political republicanism but
seeking political leadership which would alleviate their social
grievances? Or on the *notables,* angered by the *coup d'état* and by
Napoleonic autocracy as directed against themselves, but thankful
for a strong regime as alternative to a red republic? And always
there was the peasantry, the great majority of the population,
indispensable for plebiscitary endorsement, but too localized and
inert for positive political purposes.

Napoleon would have preferred to reconcile these social classes,
or perhaps balance them, rather than choose among them. But in
some instances he could not avoid choice, with important effects
on his policies at home and in Europe. He had to make a choice
in 1852, at the very beginning of the Empire. The occasion was
elections to the legislative body. The legislature was not, to be sure,
constitutionally intended to be a real parliament; it had no right
of initiative and little independence or public prominence. But
yet it existed; it was elected by universal suffrage and thus drew
on popular sovereignty even as the Emperor did; and its members

would become the chief intermediaries between the public and the regime.

The choice for Louis Napoleon and his entourage seemed to be this: Should they build their own strong Bonapartist party out of the Left Bonapartism of the cities, as champions of the oppressed of France and of Europe? Or should they take measures to reconcile the *notables* to the regime, instead of seeking to defeat them? Napoleon found himself choosing the latter course, whatever its incongruities with the Napoleonic legend. Morny and the Orleanist position prevailed over Prince Napoleon and Persigny. The decision was to favor the seating of *notables*, not potential candidates of Left Bonapartism, in the Legislative Assembly. This did not grant the legislature additional constitutional powers; in fact it may have caused the Emperor to seek greater independent powers for himself. But it sharpened the ambiguity of Imperial politics, reviving in a sense the constitutional dilemma of the Second Republic, with its uncertain distribution of power between the executive and the *notables* of the legislature.

The choice was probably made for the practical reasons that press upon the day-to-day actions of a political chieftain. For one thing, the regime needed the participation and support of able and eminent men if it was to govern effectively, and such men were mainly to be found among the *notables*. Beyond this question of administrative effectiveness, a regime which included such figures as Walewski and Plon-Plon urgently needed respectability, at home and abroad. More generally, Napoleon still hoped he might create around his person a consensus among the social groups in France: the peasants he knew he could rely on, the lower and working classes he could hope to secure; but if the wealthy and the educated stood aloof, no consensus could be achieved. French society was no atomized mass in which men could rise or be dismissed from eminence at a ruler's will. And finally, one can never exclude the effects of bribery, intrigue, and other forms of political hanky-panky on decisions like this.

In any case, the necessity for choice was a significant portent

for the history of the Second Empire. The decision to seek
accommodation with the *notables*, inevitable or not, laid important
limitations on the actions of the Emperor who had thought himself
so free only a little time before. It meant that so long as he was
committed to this political alliance, his own interpretation of the
Bonapartist mission would have to be limited in the end by what
the *notables* in the administrative system and the legislature would
tolerate. Though he might on occasion exceed those limits, ultimately he would have to return to them, to restore consensus by
regaining the approval of this relatively small body of influential
men.

The effects were apparent in both domestic and foreign policy;
and often the two were intimately interlocked in true nineteenth-
century style. Surely no other European crowned head of the
time, for example, could ever have written a book on *The Extinc-
tion of Pauperism*, but Napoleon III had done so (not to mention
one on *Napoleonic Ideas*). Yet measures to improve the conditions
of the working poor were few and small under his regime, most
of them coming in 1852, before the alliance with the *notables*. Yet
this need not condemn his earlier sentiments as hypocritical demagogy; and even if they were, it is clear that government action
in the social and economic interests of the working class was
firmly opposed by the eminent and secure men who believed in
laissez-faire, at least in this respect. Under such circumstances
the working classes began to drift back into Republican opposition
to the Empire, attracted to such leaders as Jules Favre.

The Emperor kept a very close check on public opinion; the
Ministry of Interior collected through local officials periodic reports
on the sentiments of all classes and regions. One of the questions
on which public opinion was examined, before *and* after Plombières, was the possibility of war in Italy to achieve a degree of
Italian unification. The urban working class was enthusiastically
pro-war, but the peasantry and especially the *notables* were reported as being unalterably opposed. Crossing the Alps could not
free the Emperor of the limitations of Bonapartism.

THE MEETING

Cavour to Victor Emmanuel

To H. M. the King   Baden-Baden, 24 July 1858
Sire

The cipher letter which I sent Y. M. from Plombières could give
Y. M. only a very incomplete idea of the long conversations I had
with the Emperor. I believe he will consequently be impatient to
receive an exact and detailed narration of them. That is what I hasten to do, having just left France, by means of this letter, which I
shall dispatch to Y. M. by M. Tosi, attaché at the legation at Berne.

As soon as I was brought to the Emperor's study, he raised the
question which was the purpose of my journey. He began by saying
that he had decided to support Sardinia with all his power in a war
against Austria, provided that the war be undertaken for a non-revolu-
tionary cause, which could be justified in the eyes of the diplomatic
circles, and still more, of the public opinion of France and of Europe.

Because the search for such a cause presented the main problem
we had to resolve if we were to reach an agreement, I felt obliged to
treat that question before any others. First I suggested that we make
use of the grievances occasioned by Austria's bad faith in not carrying
out her commercial treaty with us. To this the Emperor answered: that
a commercial question of piddling importance could not be made the
occasion for a great war which would change the map of Europe.

Then I proposed to revive the issues we had used at the Congress
of Paris as protests against the illegitimate extension of Austrian
power in Italy: that is, the treaty of 1847 between Austria and the

Camillo Cavour, *Lettere edite ed inedite,* ed. L. Chiala, II (2nd ed.), 568–82.

Dukes of Parma and Modena; the prolonged occupation of the Romagna and the Legations; the new fortifications encircling Placentia.

The Emperor did not agree to that proposition. He observed that since the grievances we put forward in 1856 had not been judged sufficient to bring French and British intervention in our favor, it would be incomprehensible how they now could justify an appeal to arms.

"Besides," he added, "inasmuch as our troops are in Rome, I can hardly demand that Austria withdraw hers from Ancona and Bologna." A reasonable objection. It was therefore necessary to give up my second proposition; I did so reluctantly, for it had a frankness and a boldness about it which went perfectly with the noble and generous character of Your Majesty and the People He governs.

My position became embarrassing, because I had no further clearly defined proposals to make. The Emperor came to my aid, and together we set ourselves to traversing all the States of Italy, seeking those grounds for war; they were hard to find. After we had journeyed through the whole peninsula without success, we arrived almost unawares at Massa and Carrara, and there we discovered what we had been so ardently seeking. After I had given the Emperor an exact description of that unhappy country, of which he already had a clear enough idea anyway, we agreed on getting a petition made from the inhabitants to Your Majesty, asking protection and even beseeching the annexation of the Duchies to Sardinia. This Your Majesty would decline, but he would support the cause of the oppressed populations, by addressing a haughty and menacing note to the Duke of Modena. The Duke, confident of Austrian support, would reply in an impertinent manner. Thereupon Your Majesty would occupy Massa, and the war would begin. As it would be the Duke of Modena who was responsible, the Emperor believes the war would be popular not only in France, but in England as well, and in the rest of Europe, because that Prince is considered, rightly or wrongly, the stalking horse [bouc émissaire] of despotism. Besides, since the Duke of Modena has not recognized any sovereign who has ruled in France since 1830, the Emperor has less to be cautious about with him than with any other Prince.

That first question being resolved, the Emperor said to me: "Before going further we must consider two grave difficulties which we shall encounter in Italy: the Pope and the King of Naples. I must deal with them gingerly: the first, so as not stir up French Catholics against me, the second so as to keep for us the sympathies of Russia, who makes it a kind of point of honor to protect King Ferdinand." I answered the Emperor that as for the Pope, it would be easy to maintain him in peaceful possession of Rome by means of the French garrison established there, while letting the provinces of Romagna revolt; that since the Pope had been unwilling to follow the advice he had been given in their regard, he could not complain if those countries took the first favorable occasion to free themselves of the detestable form of government which the Court at Rome had stubbornly refused to reform; and, as for the King of Naples, there was no need to worry about him unless he took up the cause of Austria; but his subjects should be left free to disencumber themselves of his paternal domination if they seized this chance.

This answer satisfied the Emperor, and we passed to the main question: what would be the objective of the war?

The Emperor agreed readily that it was necessary to drive the Austrians out of Italy once and for all, and to leave them without an inch of territory south of the Alps or west of the Isonzo.

But how was Italy to be organized then? After a long discussion, which I spare Your Majesty, we agreed generally to the following principles, recognizing that they were subject to modification by the course the war took. The valley of the Po, the Romagna, and the Legations would be constituted the Kingdom of Upper Italy, under the rule of the House of Savoy. Rome and its immediate surroundings would be left to the Pope. The rest of the Papal States, together with Tuscany, would form the Kingdom of Central Italy. The borders of the Kingdom of Naples would be left unchanged; and the four Italian states would form a confederation on the pattern of the German confederation, the presidency of which would be given to the Pope to console him for the loss of the major part of his estates.

This arrangement seemed to me quite acceptable. For Your Majesty, sovereign in law over the richest and most powerful part of Italy, would be sovereign in fact over the whole peninsula.

The question of what sovereigns would be installed in Florence and in Naples, in the probable event that Your Majesty's uncle and his cousin wisely chose to retire to Austria, was left open; nevertheless the Emperor did not disguise the fact that he could with pleasure see Murat return to the throne of his father;* and for my part, I suggested that the Duchess of Parma, at least for the time being, might occupy the Pitti Palace. This last idea pleased the Emperor immensely; he appeared anxious not to be accused of persecuting the Duchess of Parma, because she is a princess of the Bourbon family.

After we had settled the future state of Italy, the Emperor asked

*The French general Joachim Murat had been King of Naples under the regime of Napoleon I.

me what France would get, and whether Your Majesty would cede Savoy and the County of Nice. I answered that Your Majesty believed in the principle of nationalities and realized accordingly that Savoy ought to be reunited with France; and that consequently he was ready to make this sacrifice, even though it would be terribly painful for him to renounce the country which was the cradle of his family, and the people who had given his ancestors so many proofs of their affection and devotion. And that the question of Nice was different, because the people of Nice leaned in origin, language, and customs closer to Piedmont than to France, and that consequently their incorporation into the Empire would be contrary to that very principle for whose triumph we were taking up arms. Thereupon the Emperor stroked his moustaches several times, and contented himself with the remark that these were for him quite secondary questions which there would be time for later on.

Passing then to examine the means by which a happy outcome to the war might be assured, the Emperor observed that we should try to isolate Austria and so have nobody else to deal with; that was why he deemed it so important that the grounds for war be such as would not alarm the other continental powers, and would be popular in England. The Emperor seemed convinced that what we had adopted fulfilled this double purpose.

The Emperor counts positively on England's neutrality; he advised me to make every effort to influence public opinion in that country to compel the government, which is a slave to public opinion, not to interfere in favor of Austria. He counts too on the antipathy of the Prince of Prussia toward the Austrians to keep Prussia from standing against us.

As for Russia, he has the formal and repeated promise of Alexander not to oppose his Italian projects; unless the Emperor is deluding himself, which I am not inclined to believe after all he told me, the question would be reduced to a war between France and us on one side and Austria on the other.

Still the Emperor believes that even reduced to these proportions, the matter is still of very great importance and still presents immense difficulties. There is no blinking that Austria has enormous military resources. The wars of the Empire were proof of that. Napoleon had to beat upon her a good fifteen years in Italy and in Germany; he had to destroy a great many of her armies, take away her provinces, and subject her to devasting war indemnities. Always he found her back on the battlefield ready to recommence the struggle. And one is bound to recognize that in the last of the wars of the Empire, in the terrible battle of Leipzig, it was still the Austrian battalions which contributed most to the defeat of the French army. Therefore to force Austria to renounce Italy would take more than two or three victorious battles in the valley of the Po or the Tagliamento; it would be necessary to penetrate within the confines of the Empire and place the point of the sword at its heart, which is to say at Vienna itself, to force Austria to make peace on the terms we have resolved on.

To do this will require very considerable forces. The Emperor's estimate is at least 300,000 men, and I think he is right. With 100,000 we block the fortified places of Mincio and Adige and close the Tyrolean passes; 200,000 march on Vienna by way of Carinthia and Styria. France would furnish 200,000 men, Sardinia and the other Italian provinces 100,000. The Italian contingent may appear weak to Your Majesty; but if he reflects that we are speaking of maneuverable forces, line troops, he will realize that for 100,000 effectives one needs 150,000 under arms.

The Emperor seemed to me to have very sound ideas on how to prosecute the war and what parts the two countries must play. He recognized that France must make Spezia its great marshalling area and must devote special efforts to the right bank of the Po, until mastery of the course of that river is achieved and the Austrians are forced to retire to the fortresses.

There would be therefore two grand armies, one commanded by Your Majesty and the other by the Emperor personally.

Once agreed on the military question, we came to agreement on the financial question, which, I must inform Your Majesty, is what especially preoccupies the Emperor. Nevertheless he is ready to provide us with whatever war materials we need, and to help us negotiate a loan in Paris. As for the contributions of the Italian provinces in money and material, the Emperor believes we should make cautious use of it up to a point.

The questions which I have had the honor to recapitulate for Your Majesty as briefly as possible were the subjects of a conversation with the Emperor which lasted from eleven o'clock in the morning to three o'clock in the afternoon. At three the Emperor dismissed me and engaged me to return at four o'clock to take a drive with him in his carriage.

At the indicated hour we got into an elegant phaeton drawn by two American horses which the Emperor drives himself, followed by a single servant; for three hours he took me through the valley and forests which make the Vosges one of the most picturesque parts of France.

We had scarcely left the streets of Plombières when the Emperor broached the subject of the marriage of Prince Napoleon* and asked what the intentions of Your Majesty might be in that regard. I answered that Your Majesty had been placed in a most embarrassing position, when I had communicated to Your Majesty the overtures made me by Bixio, because of doubts regarding the importance that he, the Emperor, attached to it; and, recalling a certain conversation between Your Majesty and him in Paris in 1855 on the subject of Prince Napoleon and his prospect of marriage with the Duchess of Genoa, he didn't know just how to take it. I added that this uncertainty had increased as a consequence of Your Majesty's interview with Doctor Conneau, who when pressed by every means by Your Majesty, and by me, had disclosed not only that he had no instructions, but did not even know what the Emperor thought about the matter.

I added that Y.M., while attaching great importance to doing what he could to be agreeable, was very reluctant to give his daughter in marriage because of her youth and could not impose an unwelcome choice upon her. That as for Y.M., if the Emperor strongly desired it, Y.M. would not have irremovable objections to the marriage, but wished to leave his daughter entirely free to choose.

The Emperor replied that he was very eager for the marriage of his cousin with Princess Clotilde, that an alliance with the House of Savoy was what he wanted more than anything else, that if he had not instructed Conneau to discuss it with Y.M. it was because he believed he should not make open proposals to Y.M. without being sure in advance that they would be agreed to. As for the conversation with Y.M. which I had cited, the Emperor first had the air of not remembering it, and then after a while he said to me: I remember quite clearly having said to the King that my cousin had been wrong to ask the hand of the Duchess of Genoa, but that was because I found it most improper that he should speak to her of marriage only a few months after the death of her husband.

The Emperor returned several times to the question of the marriage. Laughingly he said that it was possible that he had several times spoken ill of his cousin to Y.M.; for often he had been angry with him; but that at bottom he loved him tenderly because he had

*The Emperor's cousin, familiarly known in European society as Plon-Plon.

some excellent qualities and that for some time he had been behaving himself in such a way as to earn the esteem and affection of France. "Napoleon," he added, "is much better than his reputation; he is argumentative, he loves to be contrary, but he has a lot of heart." This much is true: that Napoleon has intelligence Y.M. can judge for himself, and I could certify it after the many conversations I have had with him. That he has judgment is proven by his conduct since the Exposition over which he presided. Finally that his heart is good is irrefutably proven by the loyalty he has shown to his friends and his mistresses. A man without heart would not have left Paris amidst the pleasures of the carnival season to make a last visit to Rachel*, who was dying at Cannes, and even though they had been separated for four years.

In my answers to the Emperor I tried not to offend him, while yet avoiding any commitment whatsoever. At the day's end, at the moment when we separated, the Emperor said to me: I understand the King's repugnance at marrying his daughter so young; nor do I insist that the marriage be immediate; I am quite willing to wait a year or more if necessary. All I want to know is what I can count on. So try to beg the King to consult his daughter, and to let me know his intentions definitely. If he consents to the marriage, then let him set the date; I ask no guarantees beyond our mutual word, given and received. With that we parted. Grasping my hand the Emperor dismissed me, saying: have the confidence in me that I have in you.

Y.M. will see that I have faithfully followed his instructions. As the Emperor did not make the marriage of the Princess Clotilde a *sine qua non* condition of the alliance, I did not assume the slightest engagement in that regard, nor did I contract any kind of obligation.

Now I beg Y.M. to let me express to him in a frank and precise manner my opinion on a question upon which may depend the success of the most glorious enterprise, the greatest work undertaken in many years.

The Emperor did not make the marriage of Princess Clotilde with his cousin a *sine qua non* condition of the alliance, but he showed clearly that he placed much importance on it. If the marriage does not take place, if Y.M. rejects the propositions of the Emperor without plausible reason, what will happen? Will the alliance be broken? That is possible, but I do not believe it will occur. The alliance will be upheld. But the Emperor will bring to it quite a different spirit

*Plon-Plon's former long-time chief mistress, who had borne him a child.

from the one which he would have brought if, in exchange for the crown of Italy which he offers Y.M., Y.M. had granted him his daughter's hand for his nearest relative. If there is one quality which distinguishes the Emperor, it is the persistence of his friendships and his antipathies.

He never forgets a service, just as he never forgives an injury. Now, the rejection to which he has laid himself open would be a blood insult, let us not deceive ourselves. Refusal would have another inconvenience. It would place an implacable enemy in the Imperial Council. Prince Napoleon, still more Corsican than his cousin, would vow deadly hatred against us; and the position he occupies and that to which he can aspire, the affection, I should almost say the weakness the Emperor has for him—these give him numerous ways of satisfying his hatred.

Let us not deceive ourselves; in accepting the proposed alliance, Y.M. and his Nation bind themselves insolubly to the Emperor and to France.

If the consequent war is successful, the Napoleonic dynasty will be consolidated for one or two generations; if it fails, Y.M. and his family run the same grave dangers as their powerful neighbor. But what is certain is that the success of the war and the resulting glorious consequences for Y.M. and his people depend in large part on the good will of the Emperor, and his friendship for Y.M.

If, on the other hand, he nurses in his heart a genuine rancor against Y.M., the most deplorable consequences can follow. I do not hesitate to declare with the profoundest conviction that to accept the alliance and refuse the marriage would be an immense political mistake, which could bring grave misfortunes upon Y.M. and our country.

But well I know that Y.M. is a father as well as a King; and that it is as a father that Y.M. will hesitate to consent to a marriage which does not seem right, and does not seem to assure the happiness of the daughter. May Y.M. permit me to consider this question not with the impassiveness of the diplomat but with the profound affection and absolute devotion which I have dedicated to him.

I do not think that the marriage of Princess Clotilde to Prince Napoleon would be unsuitable.

He is not a King, to be sure; but he is the first Prince of the Blood of the first Empire of the world. He is separated from the throne only by a two-year-old child. Y.M. may well have to content himself with a Prince for his daughter anyway, because there are not enough available Kings and hereditary rulers in Europe. Prince Napoleon does not come from an ancient sovereign family, to be sure; but his father endowed him with the most glorious name of modern times, and through his mother, the Princess of Württemberg, he is connected with the most illustrious princely houses of Europe. The nephew of the dean of Kings,* the cousin of the Emperor of Russia, is by no means the kind of parvenu with whom it is shameful to contract an alliance.

But the main objections which can be made to this marriage lie perhaps in the personal character of the Prince and on the reputation that has been placed upon him. On that subject I permit myself to repeat with complete conviction what the Emperor said to me: that he is better than his reputation. Hurled very young into the whirlpool of revolutions, the Prince was allowed to develop some very exaggerated opinions.

That fact, about which there is nothing extraordinary, has raised against him a mob of enemies. The Prince has become quite moderate; but what does him great honor is that he remains faithful to the liberal principles of his youth while renouncing the application of them in any unreasonable or dangerous fashion, and that he has kept his old friends even when they were loaded with disgrace.

Sire, a man who on reaching the pinnacle of honor and fortune does not disavow those who were his companions in misfortune, and does not disavow the friendships he had in the ranks of the defeated —such a man does not have a bad heart. The Prince has braved the anger of his cousin to keep his old affections; he has never given in to him on this point, nor does he give in today.

The generous words he spoke at the distribution of prizes at the Poitiers Exposition are clear proof of it. The conduct of the Prince in the Crimea is regrettable. But if he was unable to stand up under the boredom and privations of a long siege, he nevertheless showed courage and coolness at the battle of the Alma.

Besides, he will be able to make good on the fields of Italy the harm he did himself on the ramparts of Sevastopol. The private conduct of the Prince has sometimes been unsteady, but it has never given occasion for serious reproach.

He was always a good son, and though he has infuriated his cousin more than once, still in serious matters he has always remained faithful and close.

*Probably Cavour means the old king of Württemberg, who was looked upon as a sort of senior king.

Despite all I have just said, I realize that Y.M. still hesitates and fears to compromise the future of his well-beloved daughter. But would she be more tranquil if her fate were tied to an old princely family? History is there to show us that Princesses risk a sad existence indeed even when their marriages take place in accordance with propriety and ancient usage. To prove this truth, I need seek no remote examples; I could place before Y.M.'s eyes what has happened these days in the bosom of his own family.

Y.M.'s uncle, King Victor Emmanuel, had four daughters, models of grace and virtue.

Eh bien! what became of their marriages? The first, and she was the luckiest, married the Duke of Modena, and associated her name with that of a Prince who is universally detested. Surely Y.M. would not consent to a comparable marriage for his daughter.

The second of her aunts married the Duke of Lucca. I need not remind anyone of the result of that marriage. The Duchess of Lucca was and is as unhappy as it is possible to be in this world. The third daughter of Victor Emmanuel, it is true, mounted the throne of the Caesars, but that was to unite herself with a husband who was impotent and an imbecile and who was obliged ignominiously to abdicate after a few years.* Finally the fourth, the charming and perfect Princess Christine, married the King of Naples. Y.M. certainly knows the gross treatment to which she was subjected and the griefs which brought her to the tomb with the reputation of a saint and a martyr. In the reign of Y.M.'s father another Princess of Savoy was married: Y.M.'s cousin Philiberte.** Is she happier than the others, and would Y.M. wish the same fate for his daughter?

The examples I have been putting before Y.M.'s eyes show that his consent to the marriage of his daughter to Prince Napoleon would have a better chance of making her happy than if, like his uncle and his father, he married her to a Prince of the House of Lorraine or of Bourbon.

But let Y.M. permit me a last reflection. If Y.M. does not consent to the marriage of his daughter to the Prince Napoleon, whom does he wish her to marry? The Almanach de Gotha† is there to prove that there are no Princes suitable for her; and that is quite natural. Religious difference prevents alliances with the families of most of the sovereigns who reign in countries with institutions like ours. Our

*Emperor Ferdinand I of Austria.
**Married to a Neapolitan prince.
†A sort of genealogical handbook of European royalty and nobility.

struggle against Austria, our sympathies for France make impossible alliances with members of families connected with the Houses of Lorraine or Bourbon; these exclusions reduce Y.M.'s choice to Portugal and a few more or less mediatized petty German principalities.

If Y.M. condescends to meditate on the considerations I have just had the honor to submit to him, I dare flatter myself that he will recognize that as a father he can consent to the marriage, and that the supreme interest of the State, the future of his family, of Piedmont, and of all Italy counsel him to agree to it.

I beg Y.M. to pardon my candor and the length of my report. In so important a question as this I did not know how to be more reserved or more brief.

The sentiments which inspire me and the motives that stir me are an excuse which Y.M. will surely accept.

Having been obliged to write this endless epistle on the corner of a table at an inn without any time to copy it, nor even to reread it, I beg Y.M. to judge it with indulgence, and forgive what disorder there may be in its ideas and what incoherence in its style. Despite the shortcomings I have just mentioned, and because this letter contains a faithful and exact description of the communications which the Emperor made to me, I beg Y.M. to be good enough to preserve it so that on my return to Turin notes extracted from it can serve in the course of the negotiations which may take place.

In the hope of being able, at the end of next week, to place at the feet of Y.M. the homage of my profound and respectful devotion, I have the honor to be Y.M.'s

Sire, very humble and very obedient servant and subject

Diary of Count Hübner, Austrian Ambassador in Paris

Friday, 30 July, 1858 . . . As for me, the conference* gives me plenty to do; the interview at Plombières follows me day and night. What sort of a deal have these two conspirators made? Nobody knows, not even Walewski.** I write to Buol:† "About two weeks ago the Marquis Villamarina,‡ with an air of secrecy and without giving

*On the disposition of the Danube principalities.
**French Foreign Minister.
†Austrian Foreign Minister.
‡Piedmontese Ambassador in Paris.

Count Joseph A. v. Hübner, *Neun Jahre der Erinnerungen eines österreichischen Botschafters in Paris*, II, 121–23.

any reason, asked for the postponement of a session of the conference. Later it was learned that he had gone secretly to Culoz near Geneva, to meet Cavour. At the same time Belgian newspapers, which were less close-mouthed than Villamarina, announced that Cavour would travel to Plombières. Before the last session on Thursday, the 22d, this was openly spoken of in Villamarina's presence. That plenipotentiary denied it categorically and swore by all he held holy that nobody had ever thought of such a thing. He said that to his mind nothing was more terrible than the wanton inventions of the press, and nothing more untrue than the rumor of a visit by the head of the Sardinian government to the Emperor of the French. But by that time Cavour had arrived in Plombières, three days before—the evening of Monday the 19th. He was received by the Emperor on Tuesday and departed on the following day. Count Walewski himself told me about this without my asking. This audience was neither sought through him nor arranged by him.

"Now, what was Cavour seeking at Plombières? That is what Count Walewski does not know, because the Emperor has told him nothing about it in their private correspondence; but he will find out soon after the return of his Master to Paris.

"I gave Count Walewski to understand that if Cavour was making a new effort to kindle the flames of discord between the powers, which certainly would be the case if the name "Italy" was spoken aloud in the conference, then I should have to hold to my instructions, which read very explicitly. These would forbid even my passive presence at a debate over Italian questions.

"Count Walewski once more gave me positive assurance that there would be no talk of Italy in the conference. Cavour's purposes, says Walewski, go beyond that. It is not words he needs, it is deeds. His position is compromised, and can scarcely be maintained any longer. He can go no further with the Left without spoiling his relations with France. It is impossible for him to accept the reconciliation offered him by the Right without a quarrel with Left, in which case he would lose his majority in the Chamber. To save himself he needs some event that he can exploit in the sense of the Italian Cause. The Cagliari affair* was good business for him. You have no idea of the intrigues, the energetic activity, the various tricks he uses to win over the Emperor and pry concessions out of him behind the backs of his ministers. Now obviously he is trying to make up another Cagliari

*An incident arising from a revolutionary expedition against the King of Naples, which sailed from Genoa and was partly manned by Piedmontese.

case. How did the Emperor respond to it? That I shall soon learn. Meanwhile I shall operate with watchful prudence. The Emperor received Cavour on Tuesday morning, and on the same evening he wrote me in his very own hand that he, in order to please *my* Emperor, had refused to make common cause with Cavour. One must recognize how hard this decision was for him in order to judge how much weight he lays on good relations with Austria.

"I need not add that I am keeping my eyes open and shall endeavor to get to the bottom of this new secret of Cavour's."

II
CAVOUR

Cavour to an English Friend

1829

. . . While all Europe travels the road of progress, this poor Italy is ever oppressed by the same old system of civil and religious despotism. Take pity on those who, though their spirits were made to nourish the generous principles of modern civilization, are forced to see their country ravished by Austrian bayonets. Say to your compatriots that we are not unworthy of liberty, and that though we have rotten branches, yet we have men worthy to enjoy the blessings of enlightenment. Forgive my passion: but with my mind overburdened with indignation and sorrow, it gives me sweet consolation to open myself up this way to someone who knows the cause of my sorrow, and who surely shares it with me. . . .

Cavour, *Lettere*, I (1st ed.), 1.

Cavour to an English Friend

1832

. . . Pressed on one side by Austrian bayonets and on the other by papal excommunication, our condition is really deplorable. All free exercise of thought, every generous sentiment is strangled either as a sacrilege or as a crime against the state; nor can we hope to win by ourselves any surcease from our terrible misfortunes. The destiny of my country, and above all that of the Romagna, is really something to

Cavour, *Lettere*, I (1st ed.), 3.

make one shudder; and the steps takens by the mediating powers* have managed only to make matters worse. The intervention of France does not seem adequate to obtain even the tiniest and most reasonable concession from the Pope; only the voice of England, speaking in firm and positive tones, could obtain for the people a government at least bearable and in harmony with the ideas and the ways of our century.

*Risings in northern and central Italy in 1831 had brought vain demands from the Powers that the Pope institute a series of civil reforms. Further risings had brought Austrian intervention and suppression, and French occupation of Ancona as a countermove to Austria.

Cavour to the Countess Anna Maria de Sellon at Geneva

Turin, 4 January 1832

. . . You must have heard of all the vexations I have had to undergo, the suspicions that have been attached to me, the measures which some have felt obliged to take against me, and finally the decisive step I felt I had to take. But it is not my own particular afflictions that trouble me most. The state of Italy, of Europe, and of my country have been the source of my heaviest grief. How many deceived hopes, how many unrealized illusions, how many misfortunes have fallen upon our beloved country! I accuse nobody; it was perhaps the force of circumstances that decided it this way, but the fact is that the July Revolution, after letting us conceive the finest of hopes, has plunged us back into a state worse than before. Ah! if France had known how to take advantage of her position, if she had drawn the sword that spring, perhaps . . . But I do not wish to linger on so painful a subject, and on a subject respecting which you may not share my opinions. Do not believe that all I have suffered, in spirit I mean, has at all diminished my love for the ideas I had. These ideas are part of my existence. I shall profess them, I shall sustain them as long as I have a breath of life. . . .

Cavour, *Lettere*, I (1st ed.), 3–4.

Cavour to Professor Augusto de la Rive at Geneva

Turin, May 1833

. . . If you would be interested in knowing a person as distinguished as she is reasonable and moderate, with the most elevated and just ideas I know respecting her country, make the acquaintance of Mme. X, who accompanies her husband. In her you will find something rare and precious in these days, the liveliest of sentiments combined with the greatest moderation of principles.

Many things have happened, dear friend, since our political arguments on our walks at Presinge. A terrible commotion, which we did not then foresee, has shaken the political world to its very foundations, and God knows when it will recover a stable posture. The general commotion has reacted on individuals, and everybody's opinions have been shaken by it, modified, and in some cases even changed. Among my friends and circle of acquaintances, there has been inconceivable change; some moderate reformers have been thrown headlong into [the party of] Movement, and now are content with nothing less than complete overturn; others, of the same hue, have recoiled in fright toward ultraism [extreme conservatism]; some people who would have been delighted by reasonable concessions now want the republic; and others who were only afraid of overprecipitous reforms have recoiled clear back to the century of Louis XIV, evoking memories of the Great King to govern the peoples of the nineteenth century.

As for me, I was undecided for a long time between these contrary directions. Reason held me to moderation; infinite longing to punish our reactionaries thrust me toward Movement; finally, after much violent agitation and oscillation, I ended by placing myself, like a pendulum, in the *juste-milieu*. So I inform you that I am an honest *juste-milieu*, wishing, waiting, working for social progress with all my power, but determined not to purchase it at the price of a general upheaval, political and social. My state of *juste-milieu* meanwhile does not stop me from hoping the soonest possible emancipation of Italy from the barbarians who oppress her, nor accordingly from foreseeing that a crisis of at least some violence is inevitable; but I want that crisis to be as restrained as the state of things allows, and besides I am *ultra persuadé* that the fanatic efforts of the men of movement will only delay it and make it riskier.

Now that I have made you my profession of faith, let me ask you if it conforms with your point of view. I flatter myself that it does,

Cavour, *Lettere*, I (1st ed.), 9–10.

and this idea sustains me in the battles I wage to left and to right. For the rest, I hope to take a junket to Geneva this fall, and after that to look you up at Presinge, where we shall formulate our political beliefs at our leisure.

Cavour to Professor Augusto de la Rive

Paris, 31 March 1835

. . . For my part I assure you that I have found nothing in the pleasures and the salons of Paris which could take the place for me of those evenings when, sitting by the stove, we comfortably devoted ourselves to the affairs of Europe, straightened out faulty systems, remade bad ministries, and arranged everything for the better. However little effort our political lucubrations required of us, I firmly believe that if they had been put into effect, they would have been just as beneficial for humanity as what has been done without our permission.

If you had not been in Paris last year, I would give you my opinion of the things and the people moving on the political scene. But the truth is that for the most part I should only be repeating conversations we have had together.

Yet one fact which seems to me new, or rather something that is happening without being clearly visible, is a transformation occurring within the extreme parties. All their skillful men and those accustomed to affairs are working to rid the opinions they represent of what is narrow and absolute. They are undertaking a labor of rapprochement. They hope thereby to attract to themselves that vast inert mass which has no political predilection, which is attached only to its material interests, and which is concerned as little for Louis-Philippe as for Henri V,* provided its repose is not disturbed; and if they cannot gain its support, they would like at least to render it neutral and detach it from the present system, which it supports as the sole guarantee of public order.

This transformation is noticeable especially among the strong men of Carlism.** The latter, who have no more hopes from a Europe which pays no attention to them, and who have finally recognized that they are a minority in the nation, and that they can accomplish noth-

*The Bourbon pretender to the throne of France.
**Right-wing monarchists.

Cavour, *Lettere*, I (1st ed.), 10–13.

ing by violence, have imagined that by making large concessions to the new ideas they will reach their goal. This is yet another thing than the Carlo-republican alliance. The latter had only violence as its purpose, and there was no nexus between the parties but mutual hatred [of moderates]. Now wise Carlists would have it believed that they hate nobody and have absolute antipathy for no party. They loudly profess moderation and the necessity of the fusion of parties. They make all possible advances to the great mass of the *juste-milieu*; to please it, they say they are ready to sacrifice all their aristocratic prejudices and constitute themselves defenders of order against extreme republicans. In a word, they think that if they can bring things to a question purely of persons, France will always prefer Henri V to Louis-Philippe.

Of all the plans the Carlists have ever proposed, this is the most reasonable, because it tends to reconcile them little by little with more sensible ideas; it has only the fault of being impracticable, first because with so undisciplined a party, as soon as the troops see their chiefs' aims they will abandon them, or rather disband themselves, one party going right over to the enemy and the others dispersing themselves under more impassioned banners. Likewise those republicans who have kept a modicum of good sense recognize their numerical weakness, and are engaged in resuming work at the grass roots and in making use of the irresistible democratic instincts of society, to circulate among the masses their doctrines of absolute equality and of social transformation. These people can in a distant future become dangerous, because they clearly have working for them the tendency of the century and the movement toward material and intellectual levelling operating on all classes of society.

We cannot avoid recognizing it; society is making great strides toward democracy; it is perhaps impossible to foresee the forms it will assume; but as for that essential fact, in my eyes at least there can be no doubt.

And you, my dear friend, are you not of my opinion? Do you believe in the possibility of the reconstruction of any kind of aristocratic power? The nobility crumbles everywhere; princes as well as peoples tend equally to destroy it. The patriciate, a particularist and restricted power, no longer has any place in actual social organization.

What is left, then, to resist the popular tide? Nothing solid, nothing powerful, nothing durable. Is this good? Is it bad? I do not know for sure; but in my view it is the inevitable future of humanity. Let us prepare for it, or at least let us prepare our descendants for it, whom it concerns more than us. . . .

Cavour to M. Naville de Chateauvieux at Geneva

London, 1843

. . . I have read little in the French newspapers since I left Paris, so that I have lost sight of French politics. But I have seen with great satisfaction the system of equal tariffs adopted for sugars. This decision will have, I hope, more importance than is attributed to it. Monopolies are interdependent. The decision to sacrifice a privileged industry deals a mortal blow to the protective system. Manufacturers of domestic sugar will become partisans of commercial liberty; and the precedent established by the Chamber of Deputies will be successfully invoked in other instances.

The great European question of this moment is the commercial question. At least that is the opinion of all the thinkers in England. Despite the reaction in favor of the protective system manifested in several states, I have no doubt that the cause of liberty is making progress among all enlightened minds. In England, it is completely victorious in the intellectual world. There is no longer anybody of the slightest importance who is not fundamentally in favor of the abolition of protective tariffs. In this respect no real difference exists between Sir Robert Peel and Lord John Russell. Both want to apply the doctrines of the economists to their country; it is only that the one wishes to get there by cunning, whereas the other would like to attain his purpose by more open and perhaps more violent means. The genuine Tories are furious. They have realized that Peel is tricking them, but they cannot shake off his control, because he has been able to disorganize them and deprive them of their natural chiefs. As the Duke of Wellington has adopted Peel's commercial policy, the Tories cannot revolt; they champ the bit and content themselves with telling dreadful stories about particular ministers. The death of the Duke of Wellington would probably bring a split in the Tory party. The troglodytes would break with Peel, who probably would seek support from the moderate Whigs, from whom he differs only by imperceptible nuances.

I have already travelled a lot on the railroads. What I have seen makes me more eager than ever to see them established on the continent. Distance no longer exists in England. The mail leaves twice a day from London in nearly every direction. The letters are sorted en route. Several carriages are needed now for letters, whereas one simple carriage was enough a few years ago. . . .

Cavour, *Lettere*, I (1st ed.), 47–49.

Cavour to M. Naville de Chateauvieux

Turin, 1844

. . . Affairs move hopelessly slowly with us, especially now that the same person holds the ministries both of Interior* and Finance. Things are alarmingly in arrears, which will not be overcome until these combined ministries have been separated again.

. . . Our government dislikes industry; I am more convinced of this every day; it sees in it an auxiliary to liberalism and feels a repugnance for it which it cannot overcome; in our country, anybody who wishes to live in peace had better devote himself only to agriculture. . . .

If beet sugar really can only be produced with the help of a kind of monopoly and by a privilege noxious to the general interest, then it would not have been appropriate for us to introduce the industry here. That would have been to render our country a false service, and embark us on an enterprise which could not succeed unless power was in inept or privately interested hands. . . .

*The ministry responsible for internal security and police.

Cavour, *Lettere*, I (1st ed.), 62.

On Railways in Italy

[A review by Cavour of *Delle strade ferrate italiane e del migliore ordinamento di esse*, a book by Count Petitti, Councillor of State to the Kingdom of Sardinia. The review appeared in the *Revue Nouvelle* in May 1846. Translation by Professor Laurence R. Veysey.]

Today no one possessed of an ordinary share of good sense contests any longer the utility, we shall even say the necessity, of railways. A few years have sufficed to bring about a complete revolution in public opinion in their favor. The doubts which they used to inspire in statesmen, the uncertainties over their financial success aroused in the minds of the boldest speculators, have given way to an unlimited confidence. The public mind has passed almost without transition from mistrust to so great an enthusiasm that there is perhaps no longer in Europe any locality so poor, nor any joint undertaking so modest, that it does not hope directly to participate, sooner or later, in the benefits of this marvellous triumph of the nineteenth century.

Cavour, *Gli scritti del Conti di Cavour*, ed. D. Zanichelli, II, 3–11, 17–21, 29–33, 39–50.

To be sure, the impatience of the public is not free from exaggeration. Under the influence of the violent change in opinion, illusive hopes have come into being about the immediate results which railways can achieve. Nevertheless, if one looks at the future as a whole in this respect, if one seeks to develop the entire series of consequences which their general adoption must necessarily bring about, one is forced to agree that the hopes they have raised may be premature as to the exact time of their realization, but that in absolute terms these hopes still fall far short of the truth.

The steam engine is a discovery which in its effect can only be compared with that of printing, or indeed to that of the American continent. These immense discoveries, although they trace back four centuries already, are far from having unrolled before our eyes the whole series of effects which they are destined to produce. It will be the same with the triumph which the world has achieved in transforming steam into a motive force unlimited in its action and applicable to so many uses. Many generations will pass before one may calculate all its implications. Nor has anyone yet tried to determine, so far, the full extent of the changes which this new form of power must create in the economies of civilized peoples.

The influence of railways will be felt all over the world. Within the countries which have arrived at a high degree of civilization, they will give a mighty thrust to industry; their economic results will be magnificent right from the beginning, and they will accelerate the progressive movement of society. But the moral effects which must follow, greater still to our eyes than their material effects, will be above all remarkable in those nations which, in the upward march of modern peoples, have remained backward. For such nations railways will be more than a means of self-enrichment; they will be a powerful weapon with the help of which they will succeed in triumphing over the retarding forces which keep them in a baneful state of industrial and political infancy. The locomotive, we have the firm conviction, has for its mission the reduction, if not the utter disappearance, of the humiliating inferiority to which numerous branches of the great Christian family are reduced. Seen in this light, it plays a role which is in a manner providential; that may be why we see it triumph so easily and so quickly over difficulties and obstacles which seemed destined to prevent its penetration into certain countries for a long time.

If what we have just said is true, if we are not under the spell of a complete illusion, no country is more justified than Italy in basing the greatest hopes on the railway's effects. The extent of the political and social consequences which must follow in that fair country will bear witness, better than anywhere else, to the greatness of the role which these new pathways of communication are called upon to play in the world's future. Thus persuaded, we believe that it will not be without interest to the readers of this review if we proceed to develop, just as we intend to do, the questions which relate to the establishment of railways in Italy.

Our task will be singularly facilitated by the work whose title is placed at the head of this article. The learned author, Count Petitti, after having powerfully contributed as a statesman to the success of railways in his country, has sought, in his role as a distinguished publicist, to make his fellow citizens share the understanding he has acquired thanks to his long labors and fruitful researches. To this end he has composed a book in which first he has assembled the most accurate and the most detailed ideas upon all the railway projects which have been carried out in Italy, upon those whose building has begun, and even upon those which are still only in the planning stage; and then he has gone on to treat, in a profound and illuminating manner, the chief problems to which the application of railways gives rise. His study is a kind of complete manual for the use of Italian readers. It is also destined to provide the greatest service in a country where the grand questions of industrial development are familiar only to a tiny number of readers.

Everyone, no matter what his country is, who approaches these questions with a high degree of interest, will do well to read this remarkable work from cover to cover. We shall confine ourselves, in this article, to extracting from it the most salient facts, so as to enable us to conceive of the whole future system of Italian railroads, and to drawing forth the necessary documentation of our opinion concerning their great moral effects.

The fully active development of railways is still extremely restricted in Italy. Locomotives operate only on some short, isolated stubs of trackage. Nevertheless, railway projects have occupied us for a long time. In 1835 certain companies were already soliciting the governments of the peninsula for franchises to operate several important lines.

But these large-scale enterprises initially inspired a mistrust among the capitalists which the financial crisis which followed the events of 1840 aggravated. The bad effect produced by the scant success of several French railways likewise contributed to this mistrust, the result being that these first tentative efforts bore only feeble accomplishments. The line from Naples to Castellamare and that from Milan to Monza were the only ones which may be attributed to that period of almost sterile attempts.

Since then, the results—each year more remarkable and better known—of the British, German, Belgian, and French railways have enormously changed the Italian attitude. There, as everywhere else, the demand has arisen for the building of these marvellous paths which make child's play of time and space alike. Yielding to popular wishes, most of the Italian rulers have declared themselves in favor of railway construction. Several governments have taken direct charge of the building of major lines, without declining, however, the aid of private industry for the secondary routes; others limit themselves to encouraging the formation of powerful private companies which are charged with constructing all the lines within their borders.

At the present time, if one excepts the Roman States and some minor principalities, all the countries of Italy have actively put their hands to the task of railway building. Work has begun on several considerable routes, and a much greater number of plans are so far advanced that one cannot doubt but that construction will immediately proceed. At the point to which things have now arrived, it is possible to determine, if not with perfect precision then at least roughly, the future outlines of the great network of railways destined in some years' time to link every point in Italy, from the foot of the Alps to the far end of the Gulf of Taranto.

So that we may grasp the whole picture, let us trace a rapid sketch of the principal lines which will comprise the network. This picture will suffice to give an idea of its immense importance.

Geographically, Italy can be divided into two large sections. To the north, the valley of the Po, which joins itself to the Roman plains and the Marches towards Ancona and Loreto. To the south, all the regions which the Apennines divide and which the Adriatic and Mediterranean Seas surround on three sides. The first section, the valley of the Po, to which industrious Liguria [the region of Genoa] is joined by political ties and commercial interests, offers an admirable field for railway development. So it is destined, in our view, to receive the greatest actual fruition. Aware of this truth, the Austrian government and the government of Piedmont, which together control the greatest part of the area, have formally manifested their intention of cooperating in every way in their power to bring into being the network which the region deserves.

Toward this goal, the government at Turin, utilizing the considerable resources which it has at its disposal, without mortgaging its future or imposing new burdens on its subjects, thanks to the wise economy of its administration, has decided that the lines combining a considerable economic interest with a political value will be built at state expense. For the building of secondary lines, it has appealed to private industry, which, we are happy to say, has not been deaf to the call.

The government lines which have been decreed, and which can be considered as in the course of construction, are three in number. Having a common point of departure in the town of Alessandria [midway between Turin and Genoa], whose strategic importance is so great, these lines are directed toward Genoa, toward Turin, and toward Lake Maggiore. A simple glance at the map of Piedmont suffices to prove that these routes could be considered as forming the great arteries of the country. In fact, they join the capital with the sea, with Switzerland, and with the rest of northern Italy.

For the attaining of this last result, one weak gap exists, however, in the approved plans. As a result of some difficulties raised by the Austrian government, it has been impossible as yet to decide how to join the Piedmontese lines with those of Lombardy. Such a gap cannot long remain. Lombardy has too real and pressing an interest in establishing rapid and easy communication with the Mediterranean and with France for the Viennese government seriously to refuse to construct—on its own account or by granting permission to industry—the short and easy line which, going from Milan to the Ticino [River], will permit the steam engine to move without interruption throughout the whole length of the valley of the Po. The plans of the Sardinian government are not limited to those we have just indicated. It has declared its intention of executing a much more grandiose and important enterprise. It wishes to join Savoy to Piedmont by a railway which, piercing the Alps close to their base, would pass close to the pass of Mont Cenis, already notable for the road which is still considered one of the marvels of the Napoleonic regime.

This admirable project has been given study, and, if insurmountable difficulties do not raise themselves (which up to the present the most competent experts do not seem to foresee), we shall not be long in seeing the construction undertaken. [This route, involving a 7-1/2 mile tunnel, which required nearly a decade to construct, was finished in 1871, about 25 years after Cavour wrote.]

The railway from Turin to Chambéry [in Savoy, as just described], crossing the highest mountains in Europe, will be the masterpiece of modern industry; it will be the finest triumph of steam-power, the crowning piece of its glory; after having tamed the most rapid rivers and the stormy waves of the ocean, it only remains for it to conquer the eternal snows and the glaciers which rise between diverse peoples like insuperable barriers. This railway will be one of the marvels of the world; it will render immortal the name of the king Charles-Albert, who will have had the courage to undertake its construction and the energy to see it completed. The incalculable benefits which must result from it will forever endear the memory of his reign, already marked by so many glorious works, not solely in the minds of his own subjects, but among all Italians.

[Ten paragraphs omitted, dealing with the possible routes of railroads on the Italian peninsula and concluding with a proposal for a line connecting Vienna with Trieste.]

Of all the railways we have discussed so far, this last is perhaps the only one whose usefulness to Italy can be contested. The argument would be that while it would offer obvious advantages from the economic point of view by facilitating the export to Germany of the abundant products of the Italian soil, it would at the same time enhance the influence of the House of Austria upon all Italy, and facilitate action by Austrian forces to hold Italy under its control. This objection is plausible, but unfounded.

If the future holds a happier fortune for Italy, if this fair land—so one may hope—is destined one day to regain its nationality, it can only be as the result of a major alteration in Europe, or as the result of one of those great upheavals, of one of those almost providential events in which the ability to move troops more or less rapidly by procuring control of the railway will exert no influence. The time of conspiracies has passed; the emancipation of peoples can come neither from a narrow plot nor from taking the enemy by surprise. It has become the necessary consequence of the progress of Christian civilization, of the growing enlightenment. The material forces which governments have at their disposal will be powerless to maintain conquered nations in bondage, when the hour of their deliverance sounds; these governments will bow before the action of moral forces which are growing daily and which sooner or later must cause in Europe, with the aid of Providence, a political upheaval, from which Poland and Italy are destined to profit more than any other country.

The railway which will place Vienna and Milan only a few hours apart cannot impede such great events.

That being so, the railway line from Vienna to Trieste is one of those whose construction is the most to be desired; because it is immediately advantageous to Italian agriculture in assuring it plentiful outlets, and because in the future, when the relations established by conquest have given way to relations of equality and friendship, this line will render immense services to the country, in facilitating the intellectual and moral contacts which we, more than anyone, wish to see established between grave and profound Germany and intelligent Italy.

The railway question has been confronted rather less on the right bank of the Po, as compared with the left bank. The small territorial extent of the principalities into which that area is divided, the weakness of their financial resources, the imperfections of their administrative systems, and finally the existence of prejudices not yet eradicated, render problematical the execution of railway projects within the southern part of the valley of the Po, beyond the area under Sardinian control. However, the uncertainty which we are forced to record applies only to the matter of time. It cannot be doubted that within the not very distant future the rich plains of Parma and Milan will be supplied with a network of railways just like the other regions of northern Italy. A company made up of the most distinguished elements of Bologna and the towns of the Romagna has already for a year been seeking authorization to build at its own expense a line from Ancona to Bologna, with the intention of extending it to Modena and Parma. The Papal government, by an excess of prudence which it is easier to explain than to justify, has thus far refused its consent to the project. Nonetheless it seems likely that the entreaties of the company and the repeated requests of the population, supported by the remonstrances of the distinguished prelate who administers the Legations, are on the point of triumphing over the resistance of the Court of Rome. One hopes to see appear shortly a decree from the Papal sovereign, granting a concession for the line from Ancona to Bologna to the company we have mentioned.

We appeal with all our heart for this happy change in Roman policy; we do this not solely because of the importance of the line in question, but above all because the execution of great public works in the Romagna should provide immediate relief to the lower classes of that country who have been so cruelly troubled for some time, and it should give the patriotism and activity of the upper and middle classes a nourishment which will make it easier for them to pursue the policy of patient waiting which alone is suited to the present situation in Italy.

CAVOUR ~om Ancona to Bologna will inevitably lead to the build-
~ from Bologna to the Sardinian States by way of Modena
.rma. The company which will own the first line will have such
.nterest in seeing the second constructed that it will submit to all
.e conditions which the controlling governments may wish to impose, and those governments will not long resist the ardent and
legitimate desires of their subjects, aided by the efforts of a powerful
company.

Thus one may hope that in the near future railway construction
will take place with equal ardor on both banks of the Po. Without
being considered a utopian, one can predict that within ten years the
magnificent basin which that river forms will be traversed along its
entire length by two great lines which, having Turin as their point of
common departure, will both lead to the Adriatic as their terminus—
the one to Venice, after having traversed the fertile plains of Piedmont and Lombardy, the other to Ancona, after having linked the
Sardinian States, the Duchies of Parma and Modena, the Legations
and the Marches.

To these two principal lines will be joined a host of secondary
lines which will circulate populations and wealth in all directions.
Finally, when this network is linked to the German lines through
Trieste and to the French and Swiss lines by the connection through
the Alps (that admirable proposal of King Charles-Albert), the north
of Italy will be in a position to regain the high degree of prosperity
and power to which her geographical position, the richness of her
soil, and her natural resources of every kind give her the right. That
will be, we like to think, the finest triumph of the railways.

[Seventeen paragraphs omitted.]

Tuscany . . . is the region of Italy where railway building is the
most advanced. The adjoining region, the Papal State, is in exactly
the opposite position. There nothing has been done; and, with the
exception of the line from Bologna to Ancona, so energetically solicited by the Romagna, there is no thought of doing anything.

Such a fact is sad; however, one should not exaggerate the importance of the unfortunate antipathy which railways inspire in the
Roman government. Facts always triumph over erroneous opinions.
The results of a single major line's operation will suffice, we are convinced, to modify the opinions of a goodly number of the Roman
prelates. Six months after the line from Leghorn to Florence is

opened to the public, most of the Sacred College will change its minds; one may even hope that the case for the railways will be at Rome sooner than this. We have beheld such rapid transformations of this sort, we have seen so many prejudices and antipathies which seemed invincible disappear so easily, that it seems probable to us that the Papal government will not much longer be the only one in Europe to prevent its people from also enjoying one of the greatest benefits of Providence.

When the present sentiments of the Roman court are modified, Rome will soon become the center of a vast network of railways which will tie that august city with the two seas, Mediterranean and Adriatic, and also with Tuscany and the Kingdom of Naples. This system—whose execution, it is true, offers material difficulties, but not beyond the reach of modern industrial efforts—assures Rome a magnificent position. The center of Italy, and in a sense of all the countries surrounding the Mediterranean, her power of attraction, already considerable, will receive an enormous boost. Situated on the route from East to West, the peoples of every land will crowd within her walls to pay their respects to the ancient mistress of the world, the modern metropolis of Christianity, which, despite innumerable vicissitudes, is still the richest of cities in precious memories and magnificent hopes.

Thank heaven, after we cross the Roman frontier [to the south] we are no longer reduced to hypotheses and conjectures. In the Kingdom of Naples one finds some railroads already built, some in the course of construction, and a great number of wisely elaborated projects whose realization will not take long.

Naples was one of the first States of Italy to witness the inauguration of a railway line. Already two years ago locomotives were running from Naples to Castellamare and shortly afterward from Naples to Capua. These railways as yet have only small economic importance; their principal merit consists in the entertainment they provide for the Neapolitan populace and its numerous visitors. They are, above all, an admirable means of travelling past enchanting vistas; but they will not be long in playing a more important role, because they are destined to become the center of the principal routes of the kingdom. Their extension has been approved. The Capua line will be extended to the Roman frontier and thus will become an important portion of the line destined to link the two greatest cities of Italy, Rome and Naples. The southern line, from Nocera, should run eastward and reach the Adriatic at a point not yet determined. This second project, less advanced than the first, is nonetheless being studied, and its execution will not long be waiting.

The Neapolitan railways will not stop when they have reached the Adriatic; it is probable that, turning southward, they will cross the rich provinces washed by that sea; and that extended to the bottom of the peninsula they will form the farthest line of communication between the European continent and the eastern world.

It is scarcely possible to foresee the exact time when the Neapolitan network will be brought to completion; it will likely be outstripped by the network in the valley of the Po. Nevertheless, the advantages which the railway is bound to offer to private enterprise in as populous a country as the Kingdom of Naples, and the well-known inclination of the king, permit us to hope that the south as well as the north of Italy will be well supplied with these new pathways, whose marvellous effects are destined powerfully to influence the fate of the beautiful Italian peninsula.

After the review we have just made of what is happening throughout Italy, we are ready to take measure of the great development which railways will achieve in this country. Within a few years the Po basin will be traversed in every direction by a vast system of rail routes, which will link all major points in the area, and extending toward France by way of Savoy and toward Germany by way of Trieste, will put Italy in constant communication with the European continent. This system will be joined by one or two routes to the Tuscan network, destined, as we have seen, to be greatly extended. Finally, in the Kingdom of Naples a complete system radiating from the capital will enable steam engines to move from one sea to the other, and extending to Taranto or Otranto, will extend its hand toward the Orient.

Judging the future only by what has been done so far, one is forced to agree that the picture we are tracing is blurred by the gap which the Roman States present. But this annoying blemish will also disappear. The Papal government will bow, like so many others, to factual evidence and to the incessant demands of its subjects. Then the railway lines will extend without interruption from the Alps to Sicily, making disappear the obstacles and the distances which separate the inhabitants of Italy and which prevent them from forming a single and great nation.

Now that the general railway system which Italy may expect has

been described, it remains to seek out what effects they will probably
produce, and to justify the hopes of more than one kind which we
should like to bring our compatriots to share.

[Here follow ten paragraphs describing the material economic benefits
which railroads would bring to Italian industry and agriculture.]

In short . . . Italy will be called to a new and high commercial
destiny. Its position at the center of the Mediterranean, where, like an
immense projection, it seems destined to join Europe to Africa, will
incontestably make it, when the steam engine traverses it throughout
its whole length, the shortest and most convenient route from the
East to the West. From the moment when one can embark at Taranto
or at Brindisi, the present maritime distance between England, France
and Germany, on the one hand, and Africa or Asia on the other,
will be halved. There is then no doubt that the great Italian lines will
serve to transport most of the travellers and some of the more highly
valued merchandise which move between these vast regions. Italy will
furnish the most rapid means to proceed from England to the Indies
and to China; this will be yet another abundant source of new profits.
After all the preceding, it seems to us clearly demonstrated that the
railways open up to Italy a magnificent economic perspective, and
that they ought to furnish the means to recover the brilliant commercial position which she occupied during the whole Middle Ages.

But, however great may be the material benefits which railways are
destined to spread throughout Italy, we do not hesitate to say that
these will remain well below the moral effects which they are bound
to produce.

Some brief considerations will suffice to justify this assertion in the
eyes of all whose opinions about our fatherland do not rest on erroneous foundations.

The misfortunes of Italy date from long ago. We do not seek to
point out their numerous sources in our history. Such a labor would
be misplaced here and would moreover be beyond our powers. But
we believe we can state with certainty that the primary cause should
be attributed to the political influence which foreigners have exercised
among us for centuries, and that the principal obstacles which prevent
us from freeing ourselves from that baleful influence are in the first
place the internal divisions, the rivalries, I will almost say the
antipathies, which animate the different parts of the great Italian
family against one another and, secondly, the mistrust which exists
between the national rulers and the most energetic part of the popula-

tion. This group is plainly the one whose often immoderate desire for progress, whose more vivid feeling of nationality, and whose more ardent love of country make it the indispensable aid, if not the principal instrument, in all attempts at emancipation.

If the influence of the railways diminishes these obstacles, and perhaps even makes them disappear, it naturally follows that this is one of the things that will do most to advance the spirit of Italian nationality. A system of communications which will provoke an unceasing movement of persons in all directions, and which will forcibly place in contact peoples hitherto foreigners to each other, ought powerfully to contribute to the destruction of petty municipal passions, born of ignorance and prejudice, which already are undermined by the efforts of all the enlightened men of Italy. This induction is so evident that no one would dream of contesting it.

This first moral consequence of the establishment of railways in the Italian peninsula is so large in our eyes that it suffices to justify the enthusiasm which railways excite among all the true friends of Italy.

The second moral effect which we expect, although it may be less easy to grasp in its full impact at first approach, has still more importance.

The organization which Italy received at the time of the Congress of Vienna was as arbitrary as it was defective. Supported by no principle, no more heedful of violated legitimacy in respect to Genoa and Venice than of national interests or the popular will; taking into account neither geographic circumstances nor general interests nor the particular interests which twenty years of revolution had created, this august assembly acted solely by virtue of the rights of the strongest, raising a political structure deprived of any moral foundation.

Such an act could only produce bitter fruit. Thus, in spite of the paternal conduct of several of our national princes, the malcontentment provoked by the new state of things grew rapidly during the years which followed the Restoration, and storm-clouds formed, ready soon to burst forth. The ardent spirits, the fomenters of innovation, utilizing the bellicose passions whose development had been furthered under the Empire, and finding support in the generous feelings frustrated by the decrees of the Congress of Vienna, succeeded in bringing about the sad protest movements of 1820 and 1821.

These revolutionary efforts, however easily they were suppressed (because the upper classes were divided and the masses played only a weak part), nevertheless had deplorable consequences for Italy. Without rendering tyrannical the governments of the country, these disastrous attempts aroused in them a strong mistrust against all ideas of nationality, and halted the development of progressive tendencies which were natural to them and of which one could already see visible signs. A weakened, discouraged, and profoundly divided Italy could for a long time thereafter not think of making any effort to better its lot.

The passage of time began to efface the somber traces of the events of 1821, when the July Revolution [of 1830] arrived to stir the European social structure to its foundations. The repercussions of that great popular movement were considerable in Italy. The thunder of the victory achieved by the people over a blameworthy but regularly constituted government excited democratic passions to the highest degree, if not among the masses, at least among the enterprising spirits who aspired to sway them. The chance for a war of principles enveloping all Europe came to awaken all the hopes of those who dreamed of the complete emancipation of the peninsula with the help of a social revolution. The movements which were organized after 1830, with the exception of one located in a province where administrative conditions were peculiar, were easily suppressed even before they had openly broken out. It had to be so; for these movements, founded solely on republican ideas and demagogic passions, could not have wide appeal. In Italy a democratic revolution has no chance of success. To convince oneself of this, it is enough to analyze the elements which compose the faction favorable to political change. This party meets no great sympathy from the masses, who, except for some rare urban groups, are in general too attached to the old institutions of the country. Active power resides almost exclusively in the middle class and in one part of the upper class. Now, both of these have some very conservative interests to defend. In Italy property, thank heaven, is not the exclusive privilege of any class. Even where there exist the faded remains of a feudal nobility, the latter shares the landed property with the third estate.

Among the classes so strongly interested in maintaining social order, the subversive doctrines of Young Italy have taken little hold. Thus, with the exception of youthful spirits, among whom experience has not yet modified the doctrines imbibed in the exciting atmosphere of the schools, one may affirm that there exist in Italy only a very small number of persons seriously disposed to put into practice the fiery principles of a sect embittered by misfortune. If the social order were truly menaced, if the great principles on which it reposes were in real danger, one would see, we are persuaded, a good number of the most determined and violent partisans of the most extreme republicans, turn up at once in the ranks of the conservative party.

The revolutionary agitations which followed from the events of 1830 had consequences as baleful as the military insurrections of 1820 and 1821. The governments, passionately attacked, pondered only how to defend themselves; putting aside all idea of progress and of Italian emancipation, they displayed an exclusive preoccupation with averting the dangers which menaced them and which were heightened in their eyes by the perfidious exaggerations of the reactionary party. Without wishing to justify all the repressive measures of which they made use in those sad circumstances, we believe that one could not justly reproach the motives which these measures revealed. Because, for governments as well as for individuals, there exists a supreme right of self-conservation, to which the most rigorous moralist cannot set limits without letting himself to fall into gross contradictions or ending up with absurd conclusions, contrary ot the simplest notions of good sense.

Thank heaven, the stormy passions which the July Revolution aroused are calmed down and their traces nearly effaced. Things in Italy having returned to their natural course, the shaken confidence among the national princes has little by little been reestablished; already the peoples feel the salutary effects of this happy change, and everything shows that we are moving toward a better future.

This future, which we call for with all our prayers, is the triumph of national independence, that highest good which Italy can only attain by the combined efforts of all her children, the thing without which she can hope for no real or lasting improvement of her political condition, nor walk with confident step forward along the road to progress. What we have just advanced in joining our feeble voice to the eloquent one of our friend Signore Balbo, is not an idle dream, the result of unreflecting feeling or of exalted imagination; it is a truth which to us seems susceptible of rigorous demonstration.

The history of all ages proves that no people can attain a high degree of intelligence and morality unless the feeling of its nationality is strongly developed. This remarkable fact is a necessary consequence of the laws which govern human nature. The fact is that the intellectual life of the masses moves within a very limited range of ideas. Among those which they can acquire, the noblest and the most elevated are certainly, after religious ideas, the ideas of fatherland and of nationality. If, now, the political circumstances of the country prevent these ideas from manifesting themselves or give them a baneful direction, the masses will remain plunged in a state of deplorable inferiority. But this is not all: among a people who cannot be proud of their nationality, feelings of personal dignity will exist only in exceptional cases, among a few privileged individuals. The numerous classes who occupy the humblest positions in the social sphere have need of feeling themselves important from the national point of view, in order to acquire awareness of their own dignity. Now, this awareness, we do not hesitate to say, even at the risk of shocking some too rigid publicist, constitutes for peoples, as well as for individuals, an essential element in morality.

So then, if we so ardently desire the emancipation of Italy, if we declare that before this great question all the questions which can divide us must retreat and all private interests must keep still, it is not solely to see our fatherland made glorious and powerful, but above all so that she may raise herself on the ladder of intelligence and of moral development to the level of the most civilized nations.

Unless there is a European upheaval whose disastrous consequences are such as to make the hardiest recoil, but which, thanks to heaven, becomes less probable every day, it seems evident to us that the precious triumph of our nationality can only be realized on the condition that the effort combines all the aroused forces of the country, that is to say by the national princes freely supported by all parties. The history of the last thirty years, as well as the analysis of the elements which compose Italian society, demonstrate clearly how small a scope military or democratic revolutions can have among us. Leaving aside, then, these impotent, useless methods, the sincere friends of the country should recognize that they can only cooperate for the true good of their fatherland by grouping themselves around those thrones which have deep roots in the national soil and by promoting, without impatience, the progressive inclinations which the Italian governments manifest. This mode of conduct, conforming to the wise counsel of a man whose patriotism and enlightenment are beyond doubt, Signore Balbo, in his remarkable book *On the Hopes of Italy*, will restore the union which it is so necessary to see established among the different members of the Italian family, so as to put the country in a position to profit from the favorable political circumstances which the future must bring by freeing itself from all foreign domination.

This union which we preach with so much ardor is not so difficult to obtain as one could suppose, if he judged the society from its external appearances, or let himself remain preoccupied by the memory of our sad divisions. The sentiment of nationality has become general, each year it augments itself, and already it is strong enough to hold all the parties of Italy together despite their sharp differences. It is no longer the exclusive possession of a sect or of men professing wild doctrines. Thus are we persuaded that the eloquent appeal which Signore Balbo has lately addressed to all Italians will have thrilled more than one highly-decorated breast from among the high dignitaries of State, and that it will have aroused more than one echo among those who, faithful to the traditions of their ancestors, make the principle of legitimacy the basis of their political beliefs.

All the classes of the society can, in some measure, cooperate in this important work. All those who have some education and some influence in Italy have, toward this goal, a partial mission to fulfill, following the distinguished writers who, like Signore Balbo and the Count Petitti, consecrate their efforts to instruct and to enlighten their fellow citizens, even down to the humble individuals who, in the narrow circle where they move, can raise the intelligence and the moral character of those who surround them.

All these individual efforts, it is true, will remain sterile without the accord of the national governments. But we shall not lack that accord. The mistrusts which 1830 had aroused, long kept alive by a faction weak in numbers but powerful in intrigue, are almost entirely dissipated. Our sovereigns, reassured, follow their natural tendencies, and each day we see them give new proofs of their paternal and progressive dispositions.

It will suffice us to cite in this regard what is happening in Piedmont. The development given to primary instruction, the establishment of several [academic] chairs dedicated to the teaching of moral and political science, the encouragement accorded to the spirit of association in the arts as well as in industry, and several other measures, without speaking of the railways, sufficiently attest that the illustrious monarch who reigns so brilliantly over that kingdom has decided to maintain that glorious policy which, in the past, has made his family the leading Italian dynasty, and which must in the future elevate it to still higher destinies.

But, more than by all other administrative reforms, as much perhaps as by large political concessions, the realization of the plans for railways will contribute to the consolidation of that state of mutual confidence between the government and the people on which our coming hopes are based. The governments, in endowing the nations whose destinies are confided to them with these powerful instruments of progress, give high testimony to the benevolent intentions which animate them and to the security which they feel. On their side, the people, made gratefully aware by such a great benefit, will come to hold complete faith in their sovereigns; docile but full of ardor, they will let themselves be guided by them in the acquisition of national independence.

If the preceding reasonings have some foundation, no one will be able to dispute that we are correct in placing the moral effects of railways in Italy above their material effects, and in celebrating their introduction among us as the presage of a better future. This is why, borrowing the vigorous language of Signore Balbo, we love to point to them as one of the principal hopes of our fatherland.

Cavour to Professor William de la Rive at Geneva

1847

... You will not be slow to recognize that the truth equally contradicts the excesses of the innovators and the prejudices of the immobile conservatives. This poor *juste-milieu* is, I know, not at all to the taste of young people; but experience and reason eventually become stronger than passion and imagination; and the man of good faith ends up persuaded that though he should not give himself up to the current which bears society toward unknown regions, still it is by no means reasonable to try to force it back up to its source. There is in morals and politics a law of gravity which is just as absolute, just as irresistible as the one that makes rivers and torrents descend from the mountains to the sea. . . . But I do not wish to go further over the political terrain, for if I continued I should end up appearing a demagogue in your eyes, which would pain me a great deal, without rehabilitating myself in the eyes of X and his disciples, who consider me an arch-reactionary. . . .

Cavour, *Lettere*, I (1st ed.), 110–11.

Cavour to Professor William de la Rive

1847

. . . I shall not speak to you of politics, though we are in a state of great agitation here. The reforms of the Pope raised all spirits, and the brutal acts of Austria have redoubled the sentiment of hatred we feel for the foreigners. This agitation is to my mind all to the good; it calls to life the Italian nation and strengthens the ties that bind national governments to peoples. So far everything goes well; if our princes can be at the same time prudent and adroit, firm and conciliatory, then the work of our political regeneration will be accomplished without internal ruptures.

. . . Better not to think about Savoy. Better to stay in Switzerland or go to France. As she is, she is not very agreeable. If she changes it will be to become French, and then you might as well go to France right away. . . .

Cavour, *Lettere*, I (1st ed.), 116–17.

Cavour to the Marquis L. Costa de Beauregard at Champigny

My dear Leon   Leri, October 1847
I have waited several days before answering your kind letter of 30 September so as to be able to write you in Touraine, where you must be at this moment. Despite the delay, I hope you will not doubt the sincerity of my appreciation of what you said to me about my position. The interest you show gives me a right and a kind of a duty to explain to you the motives of my conduct, which seems to surprise you. That is why I am going to talk openly about it with you.

You find it strange that I live in the country and make no efforts to get into the government. According to you I should bestir myself to get a position and play a role on the political scene. Speaking with a friend like you, I should not pretend a false modesty and say I think myself incapable of serving the king and my country. I may be wrong, but I acknowledge that I hold no such opinion, that on the contrary I delude myself to the point of believing that I have as much capacity and knowledge as most of the people who occupy the highest echelons of politics. If I stand aside, it is for another reason. It is

Cavour, *Lettere*, I (1st ed.), 112–16.

because I am convinced that between me and power there are obstacles which I could not surmount without the sacrifice of my personal integrity; and even then it is probable that the sacrifices I should be prepared to make would be in vain.

This position is vexing, but I do not know how to change it. Perhaps you will judge it as I do, after I give you in a few words some details of my history. Made a page [at court] when very young, I was the very marked object of favor of the Prince of Carignan.* I responded very badly to this high preference; seized by the ardor of youth and by the exaltation of sentiments which at bottom I do not disavow to this day, I broke with the court, thanks to some imprudent words uttered on leaving the Academy. The Prince treated me with excessive severity; he denounced me to Charles Felix,** who, to my great astonishment, behaved very tolerantly toward me. Far from the court, I gave free rein to my opinions, which, I admit, were very exaggerated. I spent five years in the Engineers, from sixteen to twenty-one, hiding my way of thinking from nobody, but still without committing the smallest act or undertaking the slightest engagement contrary to the oath I had taken. When the Prince mounted the throne, one of his first acts was an act of severity against me. He sent me to the fortress at Bard, at a time when there was neither any work to do nor workmen to be supervised. I submitted to this exile, but at the end of eight months I obtained from my father permission to leave the army and return to private life.

Since then I have always been occupied with serious matters. Age and study have much modified my opinions, but still without changing them. At bottom I am as liberal as I was at eighteen, in the sense that I always desire that which can bring about the greatest good for humanity and the development of civilization. I am persuaded, just as I was when I left school, that the world is swept up into an inevitable march toward a new goal. That to try to stop the course of events is to rouse the tempest, with no chance of bringing the vessel back to port. But I am now persuaded that the only real progress is progress that is slow and wisely directed. I am convinced that order is necessary for the development of society and that of all the guarantees of order, a legitimate power with deep roots in the history of the country is the best. Thus overall I do not think myself more liberal than a great many of those who occupy the avenues to power.

Some highly placed men have judged it so, and on several occasions

*Later King Charles Albert (1831–1849).
**King of Sardinia (1821–1831).

they have sought to attach me to the government. But they have always met an insuperable obstacle in the sovereign will. Count Pralormo, who as you know was tenacious in his ideas, made repeated attempts, but without success.

What happened several years ago has recurred for a stronger reason now. I was young then and could not comfortably accept a subordinate position. I could not, or if you prefer, I would not, even now. Eight years ago I was popular enough. I no longer am. In the Agrarian Society I fought energetically against a party of extreme liberalism. The government supported that party; this harmed me, and I lost simultaneously my position in the Association and the favor of the liberals. I have done nothing to get it back, so that if the king were to give me a position, he would annoy more people than he would please. Therefore there is no reason why he should think of me, and should anybody submit my name to him, he would have no reason to suppress the repugnance which it inspires in him.

There, my dear Leon, is a candid explanation; it will make my conduct seem less strange to you. I have devoted myself to agriculture. I practise it on a scale grand enough for it to be of genuine interest. So far I have had considerable success. I have left the ordinary paths and tried improvements of a new kind. I have found them quite successful. I am not remote from the country's business and I try to be useful to it, at least perhaps in one particular. I have managed to found a discount bank at Turin, which will bring, I hope, great benefit to agricultural trade and production as well as to manufacturing. I have created a vast fertilizer and chemicals factory which has, I think, no rival in Italy. Finally I flatter myself that I have contributed more than anyone else to the erection of the magnificent rice mill which is about to commence activity at the Park.

If I am telling you what I do, it is not to vaunt myself, but only to prove to you that I am not at all a lazy man who with the pretext of tilling the fields spends his life in sweet repose. It is not virtuous of me to work, for idleness is a burden to me, and I should have asked nothing better than to be able to consecrate all my time and all my means to state service in a public position. If I remain in private life it is because I cannot leave it with dignity, nor in such a way that I can be genuinely useful to the country.

There, my dear Leon, is a very long justification; but I think that at Champigny you have time to read the ramblings of your friends. I shall close with two remarks on the events of the day. You surely know of the ministeral changes that have taken place. So far the new ministers have done nothing which could indicate the line they expect to follow. Public opinion grows tired of waiting, and becomes more demanding every day. They cannot resign themselves to stay behind Rome and Tuscany, after the demonstrations which have occurred at Casal, and in other circumstances. In fact, it is impossible to continue for very long to make liberalism on the far side of the Ticino and to try to repress any movement on this side of the river. Foreign policy is contiguous with domestic policy; too sharp a contrast between them cannot long survive. All men of sense, whatever their shades of opinion, know this. The king himself, I am sure, is convinced of this; neither do I doubt that he is working for concessions. But what will they be? and how will they be granted? that is what I could not tell you. There is talk of a press law, of the abolition of exceptional jurisdictions, and I don't know what else. Giovanetti, once your colleague on the Council of State, makes grand elaborate projects with Castagnetto.

The public, to keep patience, amuses itself by crying *Long live Pius IX** and being chased away afterwards by the cavalry. I do not think that a serious movement is probable, nor even possible; but the excitement is immense and the means of suppression could only be temporarily effective. The malady which belabors this country is grave; by violence one could put an end to the state of crisis, but only to fall into a chronic state in which the slightest shock from outside or any internal commotion could become fatal.

I have deposited 540 francs with Cotta, as you charged me to do. Adieu, friendly regards. . . .

*The new Pope was expected to lead liberal reform in the Papal States and in Italy.

Cavour to Professor Augusto de la Rive

Turin, 12 Nov. 1847

. . . I should very much like to talk with you about the serious political events that are taking place and that are about to take place in Europe and particularly in Italy. I have spent a great deal of effort organizing a moderate liberal party capable if necessary of keeping the extremists within bounds, though there are few in Piedmont anyway. We are going to put out a journal* edited by Balbo, Santa Rosa, and a few other friends. . . . I shall try to make foreign policy more

*Il Risorgimento.

Cavour, *Lettere*, I (1st ed.), 117–18.

moderate. As for domestic policy, I am sure it will not be difficult for me to follow a judicious line, because the party of order is for the moment the most numerous. What gives it the most strength is that the Catholic clergy has put itself at the head of Movement. Now the clergy, however liberal and anti-Austrian, is nonetheless very moderate in political fact. . . .

The Influence of Reforms on the Economic Condition of Italy

The new public spirit spreading so rapidly in every part of Italy cannot fail to have a very great influence on material conditions. The political rebirth of a nation can never be separated from its economic rebirth. When a people governed by a benevolent Prince progresses in the ways of civility it must of necessity progress in wealth and material power. The conditions for the two kinds of progress are identical. Civic virtue, provident laws which safeguard all rights equally, and good political ordinances, indispensable for the improvement of the moral conditions of a nation, are also the principal causes of its economic progress.

Where there is no public life, where national sentiment is languid, there will never be vigorous industry. A nation kept in intellectual infancy, whose every political action is prohibited, whose every innovation is an object of suspicion and is blindly obstructed, cannot attain a high degree of wealth and power, even though its laws be good and its administration benevolent.

The history of the past three centuries, and also the present state of the European nations, offer many incontestable proofs of this great truth.

In every country where political progress did not come from the collapse of the feudal regime, either industry did not arise or it languished undeveloped; and not infrequently it declined. In those whose political circumstances improved, in which the nation was called to participate in the work of governing, industry grew steadily, in some places so gigantically that it filled the world with its marvels. Compare the cases of Spain and of England. At the beginning of the last century Spain, though in decline for about a hundred years, seemed still second in riches and in power. Though the English population was more energetic, the Spanish was larger and richer; and the

From *Il Risorgimento*, 15 December 1847.

colonies she had established in the four corners of the world were
more numerous and blooming. Both, after the Treaty of Utrecht,
enjoyed uninterrupted internal peace; and though they were disturbed
by foreign wars, the treatment they received in them was about the
same. Though the Seven Years' War was a glorious success for England, sustained by the fiery might of Lord Chatham, the War of
American Independence turned out disastrously for her. And yet by
the end of the eighteenth century the relative economic conditions
of the two countries had been utterly changed. The British Empire,
where public life was broadly established, where the political system
had steadily progressed, found that its industry, wealth, and strength
had so increased that it was able almost alone to resist the fury of
the French Revolution and the overwhelming power of Napoleon.
Spain on the other hand, even though its empire had not yet been
diminished in size, despite the energetic character of its inhabitants,
despite the natural riches of its own soil and those copiously furnished
it by its colonies, had nevertheless fallen so low, through the fault of
a government sharply opposed to anything new, that it could no longer
exercise the slightest influence on the affairs of Europe.

Further arguments for our proposition could be brought in from
the histories of other civil societies; but restricting ourselves to Italy,
we note that among the various states that compose it Piedmont has
almost always been outstanding for its economic progress, which it
owes chiefly to the wise and mild government of its rulers, who knew
enough to introduce into the State changes appropriate to the spirit
of the times; it owes it to having had in the eighteenth century and
in the nineteenth two reformist rulers; it is because the great king
Charles III prepared the path of reform for the magnanimous Charles
Albert.

The economic condition of a people is best improved when the progressive movement operates in an orderly fashion. Yet for industry to
develop and prosper there must be such a degree of liberty that we
do not hesitate to affirm that progress will be more general and more
rapid in a State which is actually inquiet, but solidly endowed with
liberty, than in a more tranquil State which lives under a system of
compression and regression. Thus Spain, despite the civil wars, political confusion, and administrative disorder which have harassed her
for almost twenty years, has made much more economic progress
during this period than during the quiet and peaceful reigns of the
successors of Philip II and of the Bourbon kings. From this we see
that violent change is a condition less harmful to Spanish industry

than the calm of obscurantism. It grew amidst civil tempests, but lay prostrate under the tranquil dominion of a despotism averse to any change.

Fully convinced of this truth, we frankly declare that the political rebirth of Italy, celebrated with fraternal enthusiasm in the Romagna, in Tuscany, and in Piedmont, is the unmistakable sign of a new era for the industry and commerce of our country.

We have complete faith in the future of Italian industry, not so much from the beneficial reforms instituted by our princes, not so much from the principles of the tariff league, nor from domestic and foreign conditions of Italy which will impel rapid improvements; but mainly because we confidently expect to see an awakening among our compatriots, animated by a generous and harmonious spirit, called to new political life; we expect to see aroused in them that vigor, that industriousness, that energy which made their fathers famous, powerful, and rich in the Middle Ages, when the manufactures of Florence and Lombardy and the fleets of Genoa and Venice had no rivals in Europe. Yes, we have faith in Italian vigor, energy, and industriousness; they are more apt to bring commercial and industrial progress than over-protection and unjust privilege.

This journal will endeavor with all its power to induce and to propagate this kind of economic rebirth. It will seek out facts which can be useful to commerce and production both in agriculture and manufacture. It will endeavor to spread good economic doctrines, combatting the false ones which are the offspring of ancient prejudices, or masks for special interests. It will endeavor to bring out all questions which bear directly or indirectly on the production and distribution of wealth.

The journal will not hesitate to declare itself openly in favor of freedom of exchange; but it will seek to move prudently along the path of Liberty, so that the transition may take place gradually and without grave disturbances. Yet it will support the transition as effectively as it can, so that all internal Italian tariffs may be removed and the economic unity of the peninsula established; it will advise on the other hand a steady but moderate process of reform in the tolls imposed on foreign products.

Anticipating that little by little our markets must be opened to foreign competition, it will be this journal's task to seek out the most suitable means of meeting and overcoming it. Thus it will endeavor to promote institutions of credit, professional schools, and industrial honors: means which if wisely used will aid the rapid development of the various branches of industry especially suited to Italian conditions, which may within a short time raise her to a place among the first economic powers of the world.

But the increase of national production will not be the only economic target the journal will aim at; it will pay as much or more attention to the factors which affect the betterment of that part of society which contributes most directly to the creation of public wealth: the worker class. For this reason all those who heartily undertake the publication of this journal unanimously declare that no increase in wealth would do good or be really useful to the country if those people who make up part of it, the greatest part, did not participate in the benefits—the workers. The industrial edifice which is arising everywhere has attained and will continue to attain such a height as to risk collapse and terrible catastrophes if its foundation is not reinforced, if one does not bind more closely to the other parts of the edifice the main base on which it rests, the working class—by rendering it more moral and more religious, by giving it a broader education and a more comfortable livelihood.

Though we are ready to combat anything which might destroy social order, we declare that we believe it our strict social duty to dedicate part of the wealth which will accumulate with the progress of time to the amelioration of the material and moral conditions of the lower classes.

England, that country of great teachings, ignored this sacred duty too long. While its great commercial centers and its immense industrial centers were growing to be giants; while Liverpool and Manchester were being transformed in little more than seventy years from humble market towns to colossal cities; while in the counties of Lancaster and York and elsewhere capital built up to the millions, nothing was done by the government and little by private persons to meet the intellectual and moral needs of the new populations which commerce and industry were concentrating in those parts of the kingdom. The effects of this culpable neglect, disastrous though it was, went long unnoticed. But when there were plain signs of rising public disorder, and threatening actions by the Chartists associations, parliament and public were forced to seek out the causes and to clean up the conditions of the workers in the great commercial and industrial centers.

A terrible spectacle came out of these investigations. England discovered with horror that while at the peak of the social edifice there glittered an enlightened, energetic, and prosperous class, yet in the lower regions the majority lay deprived of light, of moral understanding, bereft of any religious sentiment, and some in so abject a condition as not even to know the name of God, or that of the divine Redeemer!

The government and the public, distressed by such social disorder, girded itself to remedy it with that marvellous energy that distinguishes the mighty Anglo-Saxon race. Will these efforts be enough to cleanse the whole horrible sore? Let us hope so.

But let the example of England stand ever before our eyes. Let Italy learn from it, now that she stands preparing to travel the paths of industry; let her learn to hold the conditions of the popular classes in high respect, and to work eagerly and incessantly for their amelioration.

To escape the evils which harass Great Britain, let us take care to develop those benevolent instincts which honor our past history and our present, yet subjecting them to the scientific laws which must be observed if effective and really fruitful direct measures for the alleviation of human misery are to be achieved. Let us act in such a way that all our countrymen, rich and poor, the poor more than the rich, participate in the benefits of civic progress; and we shall have solved in peaceful and Christian fashion the great social problem which others pretend to solve by dreadful convulsions and frightful destruction.

J.A.R. MARRIOTT ON THE WARS OF ITALIAN INDEPENDENCE
The Year of Revolution (1848–9)

Venice and Rome

January 1848 was a bad moment to choose for dropping matches; there was much inflammable material lying about not only in the Two Sicilies, not only in every part of Italy, but throughout a great part of continental Europe. So widespread, indeed, was the resulting conflagration that the year 1848 is known pre-eminently as "the year of Revolution."

Particularly was this true of the many countries subject directly or indirectly to the rule of the Hapsburgs. No statesman of the nineteenth century has been the object of more bitter criticism than Prince Metternich. That he showed scant sympathy with the increasingly

From J. A. R. Marriott, *Makers of Modern Italy* (London, Oxford University Press, 1931), pp. 69–82, footnotes omitted. Reprinted by permission of the publishers.

fashionable doctrine of "Nationality" is true. Is he, therefore, to be blamed for "lack of foresight," for failure to discern the forces destined to re-draw the map of Europe? May it not be that he appreciated the strength of those forces more clearly than most of his contemporaries; that he realized that the existence of the Hapsburg Empire was a negation of these forces, and that unless their operation could be neutralized, if not defeated, the doom of the House he served was certain? The triumph of the principle of "self-determination" in 1918 involved the disintegration of the conglomerate Empire which it was Metternich's care to maintain. "The Emperor does not intend to lose his Italian possessions." Such was the emphatic assertion of Metternich when, at the beginning of 1848, the hour of fate seemed to have struck. Metternich himself fell; but the Empire which for more than thirty years he had served so well emerged intact from the troubles of the year of Revolution. To the events of that year in Italy we now turn.

At the close of the year 1847 Italy was on the tiptoe of expectation. It had not long to wait. On the 5th of January a demonstration occurred in the streets of Messina, and the windows of the royal palace were broken; on the 12th, the birthday of King Ferdinand, a serious insurrection broke out in Palermo, under the veteran patriot Ruggiero Settimo, Prince of Fitalia. The insurrectionists demanded the "English Constitution of 1812." The King's reply was the dispatch of 5,000 troops; but in face of tumults in Naples itself, and the refusal of the Pope to allow Austrian troops a passage through his dominions, the King deemed it prudent to promise concessions. A new ministry of a liberal complexion was appointed, and on 10 February a Constitution, closely modelled on the French Constitution of 1830, was promulgated.

The North did not lag behind the South. The relaxation of the Press censorship in Piedmont in 1847 had given a great stimulus to journalistic activity, and in the *Risorgimento*, men like d'Azeglio, Balbo,. and Cavour vehemently urged Charles Albert to establish parliamentary government in the sub-alpine kingdom. The King hung back; but Cavour in particular insisted that nothing less than a Constitution could save the Crown. On 4 March the King gave way and a Constitution was promulgated which formed, later on, the basis of responsible government in the Kingdom of Italy. Elsewhere thrones were tottering. In France the July monarchy had collapsed in February, and the Republic had once more been proclaimed. By 17 March news began to reach Italy of the still more significant revolution in Vienna. Metternich had been forced to resign on the 13th, and on the 14th was already on his way as a refugee to England.

Before the end of March, Pope Pius IX in Rome and Duke Leopold in Tuscany had followed the lead of Piedmont, and conceded parliamentary Constitutions to their respective subjects. The Roman Constitution was predominantly clerical: the College of Cardinals was to form the Senate, and even in the Lower House nominees of the Pope were to be associated with the elect of the people. Still, a Parliament, however constituted, meant an immense advance upon a pure Theocracy.

Earlier in the year there had been renewed symptoms of unrest in Milan and Venice. The "Tobacco Riots" in Milan (January), though half-burlesque in character, were indicative of the rising temper in Lombardy.* Daniele Manin, a Venetian jurist of Jewish origin, was arrested by the Austrian authorities in Venice (18 January), and on 22 February martial law was proclaimed throughout Lombardy. But with the fall of Metternich Austrian government in Italy collapsed. Count O'Donnell, the Austrian Vice-Governor of Lombardy, announced large concessions on 18 March; his proclamations were pasted over with the words "Too late"; revolution had already broken out, and for five days (the *Cinque Giorni* of Milan) a fierce conflict raged in the streets of the city. The casualties were variously estimated at from 500 to 5,000; but the fighting ceased only when the Austrians evacuated the city. Marshal Radetsky, the veteran Commander-in-Chief of the Austrian forces in Italy, was compelled to retreat on the Quadrilateral. The whole of Lombardy was lost to Austria.

On 17 March the citizens of Venice rose and released all the political prisoners, among whom were their heroes Daniele Manin and Niccolo Tommaseo. Manin at once took control of the situation, on the 23rd he proclaimed the Republic and was himself elected President. Not a drop of blood was shed in Venice; the Austrians bowed to the inevitable, evacuated the city, and by the end of March their flag flew only over the great fortresses of Mantua, Verona, Legnano, and Peschiera. Radetsky had made the Quadrilateral virtually impregnable, and the value of that great strategical position, guarding the route from Vienna and Innsbruck by the Brenner Pass into north Italy, was amply demonstrated in the days immediately ahead.

On the day when the Republic was proclaimed in Venice Charles Albert of Piedmont declared war on Austria. His subjects, notably in

---

*In order to deal a blow at the Austrian revenue and to demonstrate their own willingness to make sacrifices on the altar of patriotism the Milanese agreed to boycott the use of tobacco, and for the first two days of January 1848 none but Austrian soldiers and unpatriotic citizens were seen smoking in the streets of Milan. Collisions occurred between smokers and non-smokers, and Radetsky used the opportunity to repress disorder by violence.

Genoa, had for weeks past been clamouring to be led against the
white-coats. Cavour in the *Risorgimento* had been urging his sovereign
to take the plunge. "The supreme hour of the dynasty has struck;
there are circumstances where audacity is prudence; where temerity
is wiser than calculation." A similar crisis arose in the history of Italy
in 1853, and Cavour, as we shall see, gave identical advice. But we
anticipate.

Duke Leopold of Tuscany promptly followed the lead of Piedmont
and published a stirring proclamation to his troops as they left Florence
for the north:

> Soldiers! the holy cause of Italy's independence is now to be
> decided on the Lombard plain. The citizens of Milan have al-
> ready bought with their blood their liberty. Already the
> Sardinian army, led by its great-hearted king, moves into the
> field. Sons of Italy, heirs of Tuscan glory, shall not remain
> in slothful ease at such a moment. Fly then to the succour
> of our Lombard brothers.

The Tuscans needed no bidding; they flew to join the troops of
Piedmont.

Even King Ferdinand and Pope Pius IX were forced to simulate
sympathy with the general enthusiasm, and Neapolitan and Roman
troops were dispatched to the north. As far as the sovereigns were
concerned, it was, however, a mere empty demonstration. The Pope
subsequently declared that he had never any intention of fighting
Austria and that the troops were not to cross the frontiers of the
Papal States. King Ferdinand, despite his fervid protestations of adherence to the cause of Italian liberty and nationality, recalled his
troops as soon as the domestic situation made it safe for him to do so.

For the moment, however, the tide of Italian enthusiasm seemed
likely to carry everything before it.

The spirit of those days was exactly captured by a gifted English
poetess:

> Italia Una! Now the war-cry rang
> From Alp to Etna: and her dreams were done,
> And she herself had wakened into life,
> And stood full armed and free; and all her sons
> Knew they were happy to have looked on her,
> And felt it beautiful to die for her.

Those were great moments in the history of the Italian *Risorgimento*;
but the brutal fact remained, the Austrian power was essentially un-

broken. Not even the enthusiasm of Garibaldi, not the ardour of Mazzini who hurried back from exile to enrol himself as a volunteer in the Garibaldian legion, could avail against the military skill of Radetsky.

Moreover, the unity of Italy was as yet entirely superficial. Military cohesion in the war zone was loose; political unity was hardly skin-deep. The Pope, Pius IX, was the first of the rulers to draw back. On 29 April he addressed to his Cardinals an allocution in which he disavowed all participation in the war against Austria, declared that the Papal troops had been sent north only to defend the frontiers of the States of the Church, and definitely repudiated the Neo-Guelph idea of an Italian federation under his presidency.

This declaration was a shattering blow to the hopes of Italian Catholics; for the moment it gravely discouraged the movement towards Italian unity, and even towards Italian independence. In the long run, as we shall see, it served both causes well by compelling concentration upon the hegemony of the House of Savoy. Encouraged by the attitude of the Papacy, King Ferdinand, who at the end of March had been deposed by his Sicilian subjects, effected a *Coup d'état* in Naples (15 May), and recalled the army which, under the command of General Pepe, was on the march for Lombardy. Pepe refused to obey, but his army melted away, and when he joined Charles Albert in Venetia he brought him less than fifteen hundred men.

Nor were things going too well in the north. The Piedmontese army had crossed the Ticino on 24 March, but their reception in Milan was by no means cordial. In Milan and other Lombard cities separatist and republican feeling was still strong. Venice had definitely proclaimed the Republic. To drive out the Austrians was one thing; to accept the Piedmontese monarchy was another. "You drive out an Emperor only to make submission to a King." Such was the taunt of the Milanese republicans to their pro-Piedmontese compatriots. In April proposals for peace reached Charles Albert from Vienna: the Emperor was prepared to give up Lombardy, but not Venetia. Lord Palmerston advised Piedmont to accept the compromise. Charles Albert, however, refused to desert Venice and on 26 April crossed the Mincio. Yet in Venice, as in Milan, the spirit of civic independence was still strong, and when at last (3 July) the Venetian Parliament decided upon fusion with Piedmont, Manin resigned. Milan, Parma, Piacenza, and Modena had, by plebiscite, decided on fusion in the early summer. The union of north Italy under the hegemony of Sardinia seemed to be assured.

Yet the position of Charles Albert was, alike in a military and a diplomatic sense, precarious. Prussia and Russia had withdrawn their ministers from Turin; the French Republic had mobilized an army of observation on the frontiers of Savoy, and had hinted that if Piedmont annexed northern and central Italy, France ought to receive compensation in Savoy. Palmerston, however, though urging moderation on Charles Albert, would not have permitted spoliation at the hands of France. But the Austrian power in Italy, based on the impregnable Quadrilateral, was unbroken.

Charles Albert had won a few skirmishes, but he proved himself as undecided in the field as in the council chamber; Radetsky was allowed to retake Vicenza (10 June); other Venetian towns soon shared the fate of Vicenza, and on 25 July Charles Albert suffered a serious defeat at Custozza. That battle decided the campaign; Charles Albert retreated on Milan, but found it impossible to hold the city, which Radetsky entered on 6 August. Three days later an armistice, providing for the evacuation of Lombardo-Venetia by the Italian troops, was signed at Vigevano.

The Milanese, goaded to frenzy by the surrender of their city, turned upon Charles Albert. The unhappy king barely escaped from Milan with his life; even in Turin and Genoa his position was gravely imperilled; in fine, the Sardinian leadership of the hegemony was, for the time being, at an end.

The extreme republicans did not conceal their satisfaction. "The war of the Princes is over," said Mazzini; "now for the war of the peoples." "Good news! The Piedmontese have been beaten. Now we shall be our own masters; we will fight a people's war; we will chase the Austrians out of Italy, and set up a federal republic." Such was the comment of Cattaneo, the leader of the Milanese republicans, and it reflected the views of not a few republicans in other cities. Few were those who could think in terms of Italy. Most Italians still cherished the old ideal of the City-State, independent and preferably republican.

But could the isolated cities achieve or maintain independence? The brilliant generalship of Radetsky, still vigorous in his eightieth year, had not only saved Lombardo-Venetia for Austria; it had gone far to re-establish the Hapsburg Empire. Throughout that Empire the reactions of the Italian victories were felt far and wide; but the story of Hapsburg recovery is outside the scope of this narrative.

In Italy itself the failure of the Sardinian leadership encouraged the Mazzinians and republicans; notably in Venice and Rome. In Rome the relations between the Pope and his subjects became increasingly strained during the summer of 1848, until in mid-September Pius IX called to his councils Pellegrino Rossi, who, though Italian by birth, had been French ambassador in Rome, and was known as a man of strong character and enlightened views. Rossi, though mistrusted alike by clericals and republicans, laboured assiduously to bring order into the chaotic administration of Rome, till on 15 November he was foully assassinated. His murder dispelled all hope of a reformed or reforming Papacy. The Pope fled in terror to Gaëta, where he placed himself under the protection of King Ferdinand of Naples. Rome, left without government of any kind, was for the moment a prey to anarchy.

Presently, however, a Constituent Assembly met and on 9 February proclaimed the overthrow of the Temporal Power and the establishment of the Republic, not only for Rome but for the whole of Italy. The immediate government of the city was at the same time entrusted to three triumvirs, of whom Mazzini was one. Mazzini, assured that the day of his dreams had dawned, hurried south to do his part in organizing the government. But in the desperate plight of the Papacy the new President of the French Republic saw his chance. Louis Philippe had alienated the army and the Church. By one stroke Louis Napoleon hoped to win the affection of both those important interests. A French expedition was accordingly dispatched to Rome, with orders to effect the restoration of the Pope. On 25 April, General Oudinot landed with 8,000 men at Civita Vecchia, and on the 30th attempted to capture Rome by surprise. But on their side the defenders had been reinforced by the arrival of Garibaldi, who, on the outbreak of the Revolution, had hurried back from exile in South America to place his person and his sword at the service of his country. His offer was coldly received by Charles Albert (June 1848), and accordingly Garibaldi went on to Milan, where he was enthusiastically welcomed. From all parts of Italy volunteers flocked to the standard of the now famous chieftain, and in a very short time he found himself at the head of 30,000 men. With this band, notwithstanding the armistice of Vigevano, Garibaldi carried on a desultory but harassing campaign.

This guerrilla warfare, though it did not materially improve the political or even the military situation, succeeded in doing two things: it stimulated the enthusiasm of the populations from which the volunteers were drawn, and it concentrated that enthusiasm upon the gallant adventurer who commanded them. Before the opening of the campaign of 1849 Charles Albert offered Garibaldi a regular command; but almost simultaneously news came from Rome which caused Garibaldi

—to whom, as to Mazzini, Rome represented the embodiment of patriotic aspiration—to fly with a band of 1,500 followers to her aid. He was immediately entrusted with the defence of the frontier which was menaced by Ferdinand of Naples.

Garibaldi and his legion covered themselves with glory in two battles at Palestrina and Velletri (May 1849), where they inflicted crushing defeats on Bomba's Neapolitans. But the heroic struggle was drawing to a close. "The situation," wrote Garibaldi, "grows more difficult every day." An Austrian army was advancing through the Legations and General Oudinot, largely reinforced from France, was preparing to assault the city. After a heavy bombardment his troops stormed the breaches, and on 3 July the French entered the Holy City.

Just before the entry of the French, Garibaldi, accompanied by his heroic wife and some 4,000 followers, escaped from the city and took to the country, resolved, as he said, "to try our fate again rather than submit to the degradation of laying down our arms before the priest-ridden soldiers of Bonaparte." Dogged first by the French and then by the Austrians, Garibaldi and his band crossed the Apennines, and then, after a month of hairbreadth escapes (which the wise reader will follow in Mr. Trevelyan's brilliant narrative) embarked at Casena-tico (1 August), meaning to make their way to Venice, which was still maintaining its superb struggle against the Austrians. But in the Adriatic they were confronted by an Austrian squadron which com-pelled them to put back and land near Ravenna. "I leave it to be imagined," wrote Garibaldi, "what was my position at that unhappy moment: my poor wife dying, the enemy pursuing us inshore, and the prospect of landing on a coast where more enemies probably awaited us." Many of the boats were taken, but Garibaldi with Anita and a few followers managed to reach the shore. Still the pursuers came on; many of his friends, including Ugo Bassi, were captured and shot; Garibaldi himself escaped, but not until he had seen his beloved Anita expire in his arms. For four years he was a wanderer; but in 1854 he settled down in his island home in Caprera, until he was again called forth from retirement by the events of 1859.

Meanwhile, the Roman Republic collapsed and the Pope was re-stored to his temporal power; but Venice still held out. On 12 March, Charles Albert of Piedmont had denounced the armistice, and had again taken the field with a mixed force of 80,000 men, though the command was entrusted to a Polish general, Chrzanowski. Within a fortnight, however, the Piedmontese suffered a crushing defeat at the hands of Radetsky at Novara (23 March). On the evening of that fatal day the old King resigned his sceptre to his son, famous to all time as the creator of Italian unity—Victor Emmanuel. Charles Albert went immediately into exile and in July died at Oporto. The young King's first task, no easy one, was to negotiate a truce with the Austrian conqueror. He showed his characteristic courage in his negotiations with Radetsky. The latter offered generous terms, but on condition that the Parliamentary Constitution of Piedmont were abolished. Victor Emmanuel was adamant in his refusal.

> Marshal [he said] sooner than subscribe to such conditions I would lose a hundred Crowns. What my father has sworn I will maintain. If you want war to the death, be it so. I will call my people once more to arms. If I fail, it shall be without shame. My house knows the road of exile but not of dishonour.

Radetsky insisted on an indemnity, on the evacuation of all districts occupied by the Italian army outside Piedmont, on the occupation of certain places in Piedmont until the peace was concluded, and on the withdrawal of the Italian fleet from the Adriatic. These harsh terms were perforce accepted; but the Piedmontese Constitution was intact; the son had kept his father's pledge inviolate, and all Italy could look, and came to look, to *il re galantuomo,* to the man who kept his word, as the destined liberator of his country, the champion of Italian unification.

Novara was followed by restorations; restorations by reaction. Bomba re-established autocracy in Naples, and Sicily was compelled again to submit to his rule; Leopold was reinstated in Tuscany. Venice still held out. By the end of May, however, the devoted city was blockaded by land and sea; in July the bombardment began and continued for three weeks; within the city cholera was raging, the horrors of famine were added to those of plague, and at last on 23 August the capitulation was signed, and the siege, which had lasted 146 days, was at an end. Radetsky made a triumphal entry into the city on the 30th, and the Patriarch celebrated the restoration of Austrian rule by a *Te Deum* in St. Mark's.

Radetsky had promised an indemnity to all who had taken part in the defence of the city, but had excepted Manin, and thirty-nine others. The "forty" left Venice on board a French steamer, and Manin settled in Paris, where he earned bread for himself, his son, and a sick daughter, by giving lessons in Italian. His wife had died at Marseilles, and in 1854 his daughter, after years of suffering,

passed away. Three years later death brought release to Manin himself
(22 September 1857). But the years of his exile had not been spent
in vain. He made many friendships among the best Frenchmen of the
day. "He helped to keep alive in France the flame of her Italian
sympathies. He helped to lay the foundations for Plombières." For he
had come to believe with Cavour that French help was indispensable
to the liberation of Italy; he had renounced his republican creed, and
was content to merge the City-States, even the city he had saved, in a
united Italy under the House of Savoy. Shortly before his death
he published the following manifesto:

> Faithful to my flag—independence and unification—I reject
> everything opposed to it. If regenerated Italy must have a
> King, there must be only one, and that one the King of Pied-
> mont. The Republican party, so bitterly calumniated, now
> performs another act of abrogation, and makes a sacrifice to the
> national cause. . . . It says to the House of Savoy: *Make Italy
> and I am with you. If not—no.*

Meanwhile, in the Italy Manin had left for ever, the triumph of
Austria and the absolutism for which Austria stood was to all out-
ward seeming complete. The year of Revolution, at one time bright
with hope for Italy, had come and gone and had left Italy, to all appearance, as helpless and hopeless as ever. "The Pope," wrote Mazzini, "clutches the soul of the Italian nation; Austria the body whenever it shows signs of life; and on every member of that body is en-
throned an absolute prince, viceroy in turn under one or other of
those powers."

Well might Mazzini and the republican zealots despair of the situation. Yet the Italy of 1850 was not the Italy of 1815, nor even of
1847. She had awakened from the death-sleep of centuries. The insurrections of 1820, 1831, and 1848, abortive as they appeared, had
at least proved that the Italians were conscious of their degradation,
that they had begun to dare to hope. Most of them had begun to
hope for freedom; some of them to dream of unity; and gradually
they had begun to realize, however provincial their patriotism, that
the one was impracticable without the other, that liberty could only
be achieved through unity. But neither of liberty nor of unity could
there be any hope until the army which encouraged disunion and
maintained autocracy was driven from Italian soil. More than one
lesson had been taught by the events of the last few years. It was
vain to look for political salvation to a reformed and reforming

Papacy. The Neo-Guelph ideal was shattered. Republicanism nurtured on civic patriotism was unequal to the task of national emancipation. A unitary Republic was as impracticable as Papal Federalism. Mazzini's ideal, like Gioberti's, was shattered. Mazzini had done a great work for Italy; but it was as teacher of Ethics rather than of Politics. To him Democracy meant not the rule of an uneducated proletariate, still less of a lawless mob; but as he himself defined it, "the progress of all through all under the leading of the best and wisest." To him the sole origin of every right lay in a duty fulfilled.

If [he says in the preface to his *Duties of Man*] you would emancipate yourselves from the arbitrary rule and tyranny of man you must begin by rightly adoring God. And in the world's great battle between the two great principles of Good and Evil you must openly enrol yourselves beneath the banner of the first and ceaselessly combat the second. . . . It was because I saw these two lies—Machiavellism and Materialism —too often clothe themselves before your eyes with the seductive fascinations of hopes which only the worship of God and Truth can realize that I thought to warn you by this book. I love you too well either to flatter your passions or to caress the golden dreams by which others seek to win your favour. My voice may sound too harsh and I may too severely insist on proclaiming the necessity of virtue and sacrifice; but I know, and you too, untainted by false doctrines and unspoiled by wealth, will soon know also, that the sole origin of every right is in a duty fulfilled.

Life [he said elsewhere] is a mission; duty, therefore, its highest law. . . . Each of us is bound to purify his own soul as a temple; to free it from egotism; to set before himself, with a religious sense of the importance of the study, the problem of his own life; to search out what is the most striking need of the men by whom he is surrounded, and then to interrogate his own faculties and capacity and resolutely and unceasingly apply them to the satisfaction of the need. . . . Young brothers, when once you have conceived and determined your mission within your soul let naught arrest your steps. Fulfil it with all your strength; fulfil it whether blessed by love or visited by hate; whether strengthened by association with others or in the sad solitude that almost always surrounds the martyrs of thought. The path is clear before you: you are cowards, unfaithful to your own future, if in spite of sorrows and delusions you do not pursue it to the end.

Not a few of the younger men of Italy had learnt the lesson taught by Mazzini; they had studied the problem of their lives; their choice was taken; their mission was determined; their path was clear, they had vowed to pursue it to the end. But to pursue it, paradoxical as it may sound, they had to renounce the ideal of the master who had first inspired them with the fire of patriotism. In politics, as in ethics, it is often so: life is made possible only by death. For modern Italy to live it was necessary that Mazzini's immediate ideal should die.

Thus in the general disillusionment of federalists and republicans, by the exhaustion of alternatives, the hopes of all patriotic Italians began to be concentrated on the House of Savoy. Yet they, too, had suffered disillusionment in 1848–9. *L'Italia farà da sè*. Such was the hope and expectation of Charles Albert. It proved vain. Italy, unaided, could not work out her own salvation. Diplomacy must come to the assistance of idealism. The prophet must yield place to the statesman. Where Mazzini had failed, Cavour shall succeed. But he will not succeed without the steadfast support of his own king, nor without the mercenary assistance of Napoleon III.

Cavour to Baron Enrico Vicario di Sant'Agabio at Vercelli

Most Honored Sir,   Turin, April 1848
I am sending you by express five hundred copies of the circular which, following your advice, I am directing to the voters of Vercelli.

Be so good as to distribute them in the city to all those who will directly or indirectly participate in the coming election.

I should be obliged to you if fifty copies were consigned to Signore Mambretti, who is working very hard in my support.

It seems to me that the lawyer Stara could run with solid hope of winning the Santhia constituency. Candidacy for this was offered me by someone I regard as very influential, Count Feliciano Gattinara. This candidacy would have the support of people who certainly exercise power in that area.

The lawyer Stara surely has lots of connections there, so that by joining his strength to mine, one could be almost certain of making his candidacy successful.

I shall be coming to you next week, but before leaving I shall let

Cavour, *Lettere*, I (1st ed.), 125–29.

you know, so that you can tell me what further steps I have to take to commend myself to the voters among your fellow-citizens.

You speak to me of Casanova. I tell you here that if he had been in Vercelli, I should never have aspired to be deputy of that city, this honor necessarily devolving on him.

His absence and the certainty that he did not at present aspire to be elected deputy induced me to present myself to the people of Vercelli, in the hope of taking the place of my friend, whom no one loves or esteems more than I do, nor could anyone more wish to see him seated in the Parliament.

Believe me, with distinguished sentiments,

(P.S.) Perhaps you will find my circular too brief. But haste and my aversion for resounding promises and sonorous clichés induced me to be sparing of words. I hope that the voters, in view of the verbosity of my articles, will excuse me.

[The circular, which was printed in the *Risorgimento* of 13 April 1848, ran as follows:]

To the voters of the district of Vercelli:

The Electoral Committee formed from among you having urged all those who feel a lively desire to serve their country in the high office of Member of Parliament to come forward, I make bold to ask your votes for the coming election, even though I am conscious of how scant and how weak my claims to merit being chosen to represent your ancient and illustrious city can be.

Yet I am comforted by the profound conviction that the principles that permeate the manifesto of your Public Committee are those of my entire life; they are the principles for which I have sacrificed an honorable career begun at a young age under most favorable auspices; they are the principles I have always openly shown in my writings and my words, in times when it was held prudent to conceal liberal ideas; they are the principles I have sought to propagate and to unfold in the field of journalism, from the moment when the press was set free. Yes, I believe I can declare from the most secret part of my conscience that, like the members of the Committee, I have always sought with tenacious purpose an *Italy united and free*, and sought for our country full possession of a genuine constitutional system, in which the throne rests upon the firm and broad base of popular liberty.

I was in the past and am still a sincere and devoted friend of constitutional monarchy, because I consider that it alone, in the present conditions of European and in particular of Italian society, is capable of reconciling liberty with order; the stability necessary for economic development with the moral and political ameliorations which the just and growing demands of the people require, because the constitutional monarchy is the only system of government in which the progressive movement which bears Christian civilization to higher destinies can be sustained within the limits assigned by reason.

Thus the Constitution will be our political symbol; but the Constitution considered not only as the consecration of the many great and fertile principles of liberty, but also as the most effective and suitable means of introducing into the political and economic order all the reforms and all the improvements demanded by tested experience or incontestable scientific reason, and all those which the future is yet to reveal to the enquiring spirit of modern peoples.

This statement contains my whole confession of political faith. I think I have been true to it in all the discussions carried on in the journal directed by me, the journal in whose creation many of you participated.

In these discussions I have openly published, without fear of offending either the holders of power or the shifting expressions of more ardent public opinion, what my particular judgment was on the major political arguments which the country's attention has focused on for the past four months. I take liberty to point to these as a more detailed program of the conduct I intend to pursue if I am elected deputy.

But political questions are not the only ones which a deputy determined to fulfill his mandate must watch. He must also guard the economic and administrative interests of the State.

Vercelli province, source of rich income for the public treasury, merits the special attention of the government. My frequent visits to your province and long practice and serious study of your chief industry, agriculture, give me leave to hope I can fight not unworthily in the Parliament for the cause of the material and moral progress of our province.

It will be your deputy's duty to work as hard as he can for the spread of primary schooling, still so limited, and for the improvement of secondary schooling, which is so inadequate for the needs of society; it will be his duty to procure the improvement of internal communications, which remain for the most part in a shamefully abandoned state. It will be his duty simply to try every means of reconciling the interests of the owners of the main canals of Vercelli province with the interests of agriculture and of the public, so that the irrigation of our country ceases to be abandoned to private cupidity and carried out in a way so penurious as to conflict regularly with the welfare of agriculture, with the canons of propriety, and sometimes even with the prescriptions of morality.

It is with these professions of faith, with these open and brief declarations that I have felt obliged to answer the invitation of your Committee. If by chance they are such as will commend me to your voters, I am sure actions will respond to words. Then if your choice falls on someone else, more worthy than I, I shall still be glad to have spoken these words, if they earn me the esteem and the sympathy of any among you.

Cavour to Countess Anastasia de Circourt at Vevay

Turin, 29 April 1849

The dramatist to whom you entrusted your answer forgot to relay it to me, so that for a year I have been deprived of the pleasure of having news of you.

During that period, sad and momentous events have taken place. Piedmont, after noble efforts, has succumbed under Austrian blows, less because of the power of our enemies than because of the incomparable incompetence of the ultra-democratic party, which had seized power. It disorganized everything, and was unable to utilize a fraction of the immense resources of power the country possessed.

Betrayed by King Charles Albert, and inadequately supported by the great majority of the country that shared its opinions, the moderate party was obliged to cede power to demagogues without talent and without energy who stupidly believed that a nation could reconquer its independence and its liberty with phrases and proclamations.

The army was disgusted, the better officers being ignored; and the democrats launched young recruits hardly able to handle guns against Radetsky's seasoned troops. Instead of giving command of the army to young generals who had the army's confidence, they nominated as general a Pole known only for administrative work, who looked ridiculous and who had a name (Chrzanowski) which our soldiers could never learn to pronounce.

We were defeated when we had everything we needed for victory.

Cavour, *Lettere*, I (1st ed.), 146–48.

Prodigious sacrifices of men and money, lasting for a year, resulted in nothing but to place us in a worse position than we were in before the Milanese revolution.

Excessive vanity may mislead me; but I am profoundly convinced that if they had listened to my advice, if power had been in my hands, I would without effort of imagination have saved the country, and would have had the Italian flag floating at this moment on the Styrian Alps. But my friends joined with my enemies to keep me out of power. I spent my time bemoaning mistakes it would have been easy to avoid.

Now it is impossible to predict what will happen. What is certain is that we only have a choice between disasters. I see that you prophesy nothing better for France. I like to believe that your visions of the future are exaggerated and that your country will avoid the terrible misfortunes which menace it. Whatever wrongs France has done us, I cannot help my interest in her fate, as if it were our own. Besides, whatever the men who govern may do, the fate of Italy depends on that of France. If you manage to establish that which is free and strong, you will be obliged to extend your hand to us. If you are caught up in a revolutionary upheaval, or if you fall temporarily into the snares of reaction, Italy will remain shackled or will be ravaged by the flames of revolution.

I am still editing the *Risorgimento*. I have ordered that it be sent to M. B. I shall receive with pleasure the *Impartial de Rouen*. Our letters are not opened here; besides, the general director of the mails is a good friend of mine. So do write freely to me, and give me some sidelights from the drama unrolling in Paris. Your letters will be a treasure for me.

Adieu, my dear [*ma bonne amie*]. It is sweet to be able to call you that.

Cavour to Professor Giovanni Giuseppe Garnier at Nice

Turin, 20 October 1850

It is a real pleasure that in response to your letter to me of the 14th of this month, I can express the lively interest which H. M. and I in particular take in the educational establishment which genuine patriots have founded at Nice, which you are to direct.

Cavour, *Lettere*, I (1st ed.), 167–69.

Professional education is one of the primary needs of modern times, and one for which there is unfortunately the least provision in our country. An excess of classical education is a cause of the spiritual imbalance which produces the most troublesome consequences. Instead of elevating the mass of men and making them skilled *producers*, ready to pursue the numerous careers which agriculture, industry, and commerce offer to the middle and upper classes—so far efforts have been devoted only to the creation of men of letters or of the robe: doctors and rhetoricians.

I do not hesitate to say that in my opinion this imbalance between the needs of society and the educational system we have inherited from our fathers is one of the principal causes of the moral disorder which afflicts a number of the nations that are leaders in the march of civilization.

I see with pleasure that it is your intention to give important place in your curriculum to political economy. The name you bear gives you a kind of special obligation in this regard. The brother of the learned professor of the school of bridges and roads at Paris cannot but be a fervent apostle of sane economic doctrines, doctrines I consider the sole moral antidote to the poisons of socialism. Yes, Monsieur, I agree with the great French economists, with M. Bastiat, with M. Blanqui, with M. your brother, that there is only one way to halt the progress of anti-social doctrines, and that way is liberty. Let us preach political liberty, liberty of education, and above all industrial and commercial liberty, and we shall be doing more against socialist dreams than laws and persecutions can.

Because I take such a lively interest in the attempt you are making, I should be much obliged if you would be so kind as to keep me abreast of the progress of your establishment, and let me know what the government can do, without departing from its sphere of functions, to help advance its expectations for a high degree of success.

Receive, Sir, assurance of my high regards.

Cavour to Count G. Ponza di San Martino at Turin

Dear Friend,   Paris, 4 September 1852
Your letter of the 24th has only now reached me. I don't know whether it came into the hands of some other Cavour; but it is certain that it did not come by the fastest route.

Cavour, *Lettere*, I (1st ed.), 282–84.

We have been in Paris for a week, which I have spent seeing every kind of person. From the foreign minister clear to the lower clerks. Only tomorrow I see Louis Napoleon. From what I have seen so far I think I can deduce that the French government wants us liberal, so that we won't fall under Austrian domination; but it would still like us flexible in our international relations. For whatever the government's sentiments may be, its conduct will be guided by its interests; and we shall be supported, or we shall be sacrificed, at the moment when it profits L. N. to combat Austria, or to make her his friend. Our greater or lesser liberalism can have no effect on the government. On the Roman question I have heard only reasonable talk. Clerical excesses are beginning to give the government pause. It assuredly wishes clerical support, but it knows that France is willing to tolerate anything before clerical domination.

I agree with all you say on our affairs. We do not have to be hostile toward Azeglio;[1] in fact we have to give him loyal support; but we cannot sacrifice our reputation to him, and come back under his domination like stray lambs. I don't think on the other hand that Azeglio has ever thought of making us conciliatory proposals. His speeches sound just the opposite. I learned certain things in London which made me certain of the real sentiments of the good Massimo, at least where I am concerned. Hudson must know of this now, otherwise I do not think he could continue to give you the advice you tell me about.

When I return we shall get together, we'll go find La Marmora and have a frank talk with him. It is time for this game of Azeglio's to come to an end. If he wants to stay in power let him say so, and he will find us loyal allies. But if he wants to stay in power no longer let him go, and stop making government almost impossible by this continuing presence of his. I have personal complaints against d'Azeglio, who has not done right by me and has gravely offended me; but I hold no grudge against him. I only think that after his conduct toward me, he himself would stop respecting me if I consented to take power, as long as foreign policy continues to be directed as it has been in the past.

Good-bye, write to me, for I shall be in Paris for the whole month of September and believe me your friend.

1. D'Azeglio was at this time Prime Minister of Piedmont, but his position was threatened by the growing influence of Cavour, who was Finance Minister. In November d'Azeglio fell and was replaced by Cavour.

III

EUROPE AND THE ITALIAN QUESTION

J.A.R. MARRIOTT ON THE CRIMEAN WAR
The Crimean War

Origins of the Crimean War

What Aristotle said of revolutions is true also of wars. The occasions may be trivial, the causes are always important. Emphatically was this the case with the Crimean War. It may be that the faggots were laid by the squabbles of the Greek and Latin monks in the Holy Land. Louis Napoleon may have applied the match to highly inflammable materials. The personalities of the Tsar Nicholas, of his ambassador Menschikoff, of Lord Stratford de Redcliffe, even, in another sense, of Lord Aberdeen, may have contributed to the outbreak. But to regard such things as the essential causes of the war implies a singularly superficial apprehension of the majestic and deliberate operation of historic forces. Kinglake wanted a villain for the central figure of his brilliant romance, and found him in the Emperor Napoleon. Much may be forgiven to a supreme artist, and something, as was hinted, to the disappointed suitor.* But scientific history is compelled to look further and deeper.

That Louis Napoleon was the immediate firebrand is indisputable. In 1850 he took up with great zeal the cause of the Roman Catholics in the Near East. In 1852 M. de Lavalette, the French ambassador at Constantinople, was instructed to insist upon the claims of the Latin

---

*Alexander Kinglake, author of an eight-volume history of the Crimean War, is said to have been a suitor for the favors of a mistress of Napoleon III.

From J. A. R. Marriott, *The Eastern Question: An Historical Study* (Oxford, 2nd ed., 1918), pp. 251–84 with deletions; footnotes omitted. Reprinted by permission of the Clarendon Press, Oxford.

monks to the guardianship of the Holy Places in Palestine. "Stated in bare terms," writes Kinglake, "the question was whether for the purpose of passing through the building into their Grotto, the Latin monks should have the key of the chief door of the Church of Bethlehem, and also one of the keys of each of the two doors of the sacred manger, and whether they should be at liberty to place in the sanctuary of the Nativity a silver star adorned with the arms of France." So stated, the question at issue seems puerile to the verge of criminal levity. But behind a question superficially trivial was the tradition of three hundred years of French diplomacy in the Levant. The privileged position bestowed upon France and its clients by Suleiman the Magnificent had, as we have seen, been specifically renewed and guaranteed by the more formal *Capitulations* of May 28, 1740. Since 1740 the Latin monks had neglected their duties as custodians of the Holy Places, the Greeks had stepped into their shoes, with the tacit assent of France who had lost interest in the matter.

Louis Napoleon saw his chance. He was now on the brink of achieving his lifelong ambition. After two humiliating, but not futile, fiascoes the "man of destiny" had come forward, at the precise psychological moment in 1848, and, declaring his name to be "the symbol of order, nationality, and glory," had announced his candidature for the Presidency of the Second Republic established on the collapse of the July Monarchy. In the contest which ensued, Lamartine, the hero of February, received less than 18,000 votes; Cavaignac, who in the terrible "days of June" had saved the State, received less than a million and a half; the unknown man, who bore the name of Napoleon, received 5,434,226. But Louis Napoleon had still to make good. He obtained a confirmation and prolongation of his Presidency by the *coup d'état* of December, 1851, and after a second *coup d'état* in December, 1852, he transformed the Presidency into an hereditary empire. He relied for support fundamentally upon the peasants of France, but more immediately on the two highly organized forces in France, the Church and the Army. The Bourgeois Monarchy had failed to touch the imagination of France. "La France s'ennuie," as Lamartine had sagaciously observed. Her prestige abroad had suffered severely from the conduct of foreign affairs under Louis-Philippe, particularly in that quarter as to which France was most sensitive— the Levant. Lord Palmerston had elbowed France out of the Concert in 1840, and had admitted her on sufferance in 1841.

Such a position was wholly inconsistent with the Napoleonic interpretation of "la gloire." That interpretation the new emperor was determined to revive. The traditions of French diplomacy dictated the direction. Nor was a personal motive lacking. With studied contempt Nicholas had refused to accord the successful conspirator the courtesy which prevailed between crowned heads: he had addressed him not as "frère" but as "bon ami." The Greek monks at Bethlehem and Jerusalem were to pay for the affront put by the Tsar upon the protector of the Latins.

But if the prestige of France had suffered at the hands of Lord Palmerston, not less had that of Russia. Ever since the days of Peter the Great, Russia had set before herself two supreme objects: a virtual protectorate over the Christian subjects of the Sultan; and the domination of the Bosphorus and the Dardanelles. These objects had been practically attained when the Sultan, in 1833, signed the Treaty of Unkiar-Skelessi. That treaty Lord Palmerston had torn up.

For Great Britain, though tardy in realizing the significance of the Near Eastern Question to herself, was now deeply impressed with a sense of the danger to be apprehended whether from a French protectorate over Egypt or from a Russian protectorate over Turkey. To repudiate the exclusive pretensions of both Russia and France was, therefore, the key-note of English foreign policy throughout three-quarters of the nineteenth century.

Not that England asserted any exclusive claims on her own behalf. On the contrary, the principle to which she firmly adhered was that the problem of the Near East could be solved only by the Powers in Concert. That concert she has honestly endeavoured to maintain, and in maintaining it she has, to a large extent unconsciously, given room and opportunity for the growth of a new and vitalizing principle, the principle of nationality.

In this diagnosis of the situation the modern reader will detect, or imagine that he has detected, a palpable omission. What, he will ask, was the attitude of the German Powers, Austria and Prussia, and of Italy? Austria was deeply interested, but preoccupied. The Habsburg dominions, German, Magyar, Bohemian, and Italian, had barely emerged from the crisis of 1848–9: the crisis which had displaced Metternich, and threatened with disruption the empire which he had so long governed. Only the intervention of the Tsar Nicholas had preserved Hungary to the Habsburgs, and though gratitude, as events were soon to prove, is not the most conspicuous attribute of the Austrian House, the policy of the young emperor was at the moment in complete accord with that of his preserver. Prussia had played no independent part in Eastern affairs since Metternich's accession to power. Italy had not yet come into being. But, as we shall see, the man destined to create it was no sooner in power than he firmly asserted that the Italy of the future had a vital interest in the solution of the Near Eastern Problem. For the moment, however, the game was in the hands of the Tsar Nicholas, Napoleon, and Great Britain.

The demands made, on behalf of the Latin monks, by Napoleon were supported by the other Roman Catholic powers: Austria, Spain, Sardinia, Portugal, Belgium, and Naples; and after some delay they were, in substance, conceded by the Sultan. The concession roused bitter resentment in the mind of the Tsar Nicholas, who demanded, from the Porte, its immediate rescission. Thus the Porte found itself, not for the first time, between the upper and the nether millstone; and, in order to escape from that embarrassing situation, the Sultan played an old diplomatic trick. His decision on the points at issue was embodied in a letter to the French chargé d'affaires, and in a Firman addressed to the Greek patriarch at Jerusalem. The language of the two documents was not identical: the letter laid stress upon the substantial concessions to France; the Firman dwelt upon the claims denied. In the upshot France was satisfied, Russia was not.

Accordingly, in March, 1853, the Tsar dispatched to Constantinople Prince Menschikoff, a rough and overbearing soldier, who was charged not only to obtain full satisfaction in regard to the Holy Places, but to demand from the Sultan a virtual acknowledgement, embodied in a formal treaty, of the Tsar's protectorate over all the Orthodox subjects of the Porte. On the question of the Holy Places the Tsar had a strong case; his claim to a protectorate over the Greek Church in Turkey was, on the contrary, an extravagant extension of the vague and indefinite engagements contained in the Treaty of Kainardji, and in subsequent conventions concluded between Russia and the Ottoman Empire.

This demand appeared to the British Government to be wholly inadmissable.

"No sovereign," wrote Lord Clarendon, "having a proper regard for his own dignity and independence, could admit proposals so undefined as those of Prince Menschikoff, and by treaty confer upon another and more powerful sovereign a right of protection over a large portion of his own subjects. However well disguised it may be, yet the fact is that under the vague language of the proposed Sened a perpetual right to interfere in the internal affairs of Turkey would be conferred upon Russia, for governed as the Greek subjects of the Porte are by their ecclesiastical authorities, and looking as these latter would in all things do for protection to Russia, it follows that 14,000,000 of Greeks would henceforth regard the emperor as their supreme protector, and their allegiance to the Sultan would be little more than nominal, while his own independence would dwindle into vassalage."

Inadmissable in substance, the Russian demand was urged upon the Sultan by Prince Menschikoff with insufferable insolence. But by this time Menschikoff himself had to reckon with an antagonist in whose skilful hands the blustering Russian was a mere child. On April 5 Lord Stratford de Redcliffe returned to Constantinople, and the whole diplomatic situation quickly underwent a complete transformation.

The Tsar Nicholas had always, as we have seen, been anxious to maintain a cordial understanding with England in regard to the Eastern Question, and early in the spring of 1853 he had a series of interviews with Sir Hamilton Seymour, then British ambassador at St. Petersburg. During these interviews he discussed, in the most friendly manner, the relations of their respective countries in the Near East. Recalling his personal friendship with the head of the new ministry, Lord Aberdeen, he insisted that the interests of England and Russia were "upon almost all questions the same," and expressed his confidence that the two countries would continue to be on "terms of close amity." "Turkey," he continued, "is in a critical state . . . the country itself seems to be falling to pieces . . . we have on our hands a sick man—a very sick man: it will be, I tell you frankly, a great misfortune if, one of these days, he should slip away from us before all necessary arrangements were made." In the Tsar's view it was therefore "very important that England and Russia should come to a perfectly good understanding on these affairs, and that neither should take any decisive step of which the other is not apprised." The Tsar further asserted that he had entirely abandoned "the plans and dreams" of the Empress Catherine, but frankly admitted that he had obligations in regard to the Christian subjects of the Porte which treaties and national sentiment alike compelled him to fulfil. In his view, however, the governing fact of the situation was that the Turk was in a state of hopeless decrepitude. "He may suddenly die upon our hands: we cannot resuscitate what is dead; if the Turkish Empire falls, it falls to rise no more; and I put it to you, therefore, whether it is not better to provide beforehand for a contingency than to incur the chaos, confusion, and certainty of a European war, all of which must attend the catastrophe, if it should occur unexpectedly and before some

ulterior system has been sketched." England and Russia must settle
the matter. But neither England nor any other Great Power must
have Constantinople. Nor would Russia take it permanently; temporarily she might have to occupy it *en dépositaire* but not *en
propriétaire*. For the rest, the principalities might continue to be an
independent State under Russian protection; Serbia and Bulgaria might
receive a similar form of government. To counterbalance these indirect
advantages to Russia, England might annex Egypt and Crete. On one
further point the Tsar was particularly insistent: "I never will permit,"
he said, "an attempt at the reconstruction of a Byzantine Empire, or
such an extension of Greece as would render her a powerful State:
still less will I permit the breaking up of Turkey into little Republican
asylums for the Kossuths and Mazzinis and other revolutionists of
Europe; rather than submit to any of these arrangements I would go
to war, and as long as I have a man or a musket left would carry it on."

The English ministers, who had been captivated by the personality
of the Tsar in 1844, were aghast at the coolness and candour of the
specific proposals which were submitted to them in 1853 through the
ordinary diplomatic channels. They refused to admit that the dissolution of the sick man was imminent; they repudiated with some heat
the idea of a possible partition of his inheritance; they pointed out,
with unanswerable force, that "an agreement in such a case tends very
surely to hasten the contingency for which it is intended to provide;
they urged the Tsar to act with forebearance towards the Porte; they
objected to an agreement concluded behind the back of Austria and
France; and, finally, they declined, courteously but very firmly, to
entertain the proposals of the Tsar."

Those proposals were in form almost brutally candid, but there is
no reason to doubt that they were put forward with a genuine desire
to find a solution for a hitherto insoluble problem. Nor was the Tsar's
diagnosis of the case substantially inaccurate. It is tempting to specu-
late as to what would have happened had the Tsar's advances been
accepted by the English Government; but the temptation must be
resisted. That they were refused was due largely to the mistrust inspired among ministers by the Treaty of Unkiar-Skelessi, much more
to the popular detestation of Russia aroused by her treatment of the
Poles, and most of all to the part played by the Tsar in the suppression
of the Hungarian insurrection in 1849. Conversely, the Sultan was high
in popular favour owing to the asylum he had chivalrously afforded
to Louis Kossuth and other Hungarian refugees.

Still, none of these reasons, though potent in their appeal to popular

passions, can in the dry light of historical retrospect be regarded
as an adequate justification of a great European war.

Into that war, however, the Powers were now rapidly "drifting."
The expression was Lord Aberdeen's, and to him and to several of
his colleagues it was undeniably appropriate. To one Englishman it
was not. Lord Stratford at Constantinople knew precisely where he
was going, and where he intended to go. He was persuaded that there
could be no real settlement in the Near East until the pretensions of
Russia had been publicly repudiated and until the Tsar had sustained
an unmistakable defeat either in diplomacy or in war. If without war
so much the better, but by war if necessary.

Lord Stratford's first task was to persuade Menschikoff to separate
the question of the Holy Places from that of a general Russian protectorate over the Greek Christians. This important object was attained
with consummate adroitness, and Stratford then induced the Porte
to give satisfaction to Russia on the former point. Before the end
of April the dispute as to the Holy Places was settled. But the concession made by the Porte effected no improvement in the diplomatic
situation. On the contrary, as the Porte became more conciliatory,
Menschikoff became more menacing. But he was now on weaker
ground, on to which he had been lured by Lord Stratford's astuteness.
The latter advised the Porte to refuse the protectorate claimed by
Russia, and on May 22, 1853, Menschikoff and the staff of the Russian
Embassy quitted Constantinople. A week later the Porte addressed to
the Powers a Note announcing that "the question of the Holy Places
had terminated in a manner satisfactory to all parties; that nevertheless the Prince Menschikoff, not satisfied with that, had demanded
from the Porte a treaty to guarantee the rights and privileges of all
kinds accorded by the Sultan to his Greek subjects." "However
great," it continued, "may be the desire of the Porte to preserve the
most amicable relations with Russia, she can never engage herself by
such a guarantee towards a foreign Government, either concluding
with it a treaty or signing a simple official Note, without compromising
gravely her independence and the most fundamental rights of the
Sultan over his own subjects." Despite all this the Porte, though
bound to take measures of self-defence, did not abandon hopes of
peace.

The hopes became fainter day by day. A large Russian army under
Prince Gortschakoff had been mobilized in Bessarabia during the
spring; on July 21 it crossed the Pruth and occupied the principalities.
Russia thereupon announced to the Powers that the occupation was

not intended as an act of war, but as a "material guarantee" for the concession of her just demands. But while condescending to offer this explanation, the Tsar was not greatly concerned as to the attitude of the Western Powers. He was confident that, if war really threatened, Austria and Prussia would send an army to the Rhine and keep France quiet. His confidence was misplaced. Austria, forgetful of the debt she had recently incurred to the Tsar, was more jealous of Russia than of France, and more ready, therefore, to mobilize upon the Danube than upon the Rhine. Moreover, on the news of the impending occupation of the principalities, the combined fleets of England and France had been sent into Besika Bay, and Palmerston believed that the only chance of now convincing Russia that we were in earnest and thus averting war would be to order them up to the Bosphorus and, if necessary, into the Black Sea. But Aberdeen still hung back, and the Sultan was advised, "in order to exhaust all the resources of Patience," not to resist the Russian invasion by force.

The Vienna Note, July 31

Meanwhile, Austria, though unwilling to fight, was anxious to avert the all but inevitable war. Accordingly, the representatives of England, France, Austria, and Prussia met at Vienna in July and agreed upon a "Note" which it was hoped might satisfy both Russia and Turkey. The Note simply reaffirmed the adherence of the Porte to "the letter and spirit of the Treaties of Kainardji and Adrianople relative to the protection of the Christian religion." The Note was accepted by Russia, though not, as subsequently appeared, in the sense intended by the mediators. Turkey, like Russia, perceiving its ambiguities, insisted on amending it. For the words above quoted the Porte proposed to read: "To the stipulations of the Treaty of Kainardji, confirmed by that of Adrianople, relative to the protection *by the Sublime Porte* of the Christian religion." To a superficial view the amendment may appear a strangely inadequate reason for provoking a European war. But the addition of the words "by the Sublime Porte" had revealed, in succinct epitome, the whole question at issue between Russia and Turkey. Did the Treaty of Kainardji give to Russia a general protectorate over the Orthodox subjects of the Sultan? Since Russia claimed that it did, the Vienna Note was sufficient for her purpose. The diplomatists at Vienna were simple enough to imagine that they had discovered a formula which might, by studied ambiguity, postpone or even avert war. Lord Stratford, however, was quick to perceive the ambiguity, and by the addition of four words, seemingly unimportant, brought Russia out into the open. These words implicitly repudiated the Russian claim to a general protectorate over the Greek Christians. The latter were to be protected not by the Tsar but by the Sultan. Russia promptly refused to accept the amendment; Lord Stratford encouraged the Sultan to insist upon it. "No man," wrote the editor of the *Edinburgh Review*, "ever took upon himself a larger amount of responsibility than Lord Stratford when he virtually overruled the decision of the four Powers, including his own Government, and acquiesced in—not to say caused—the rejection of the Vienna Note by the Porte after it had been accepted by Russia. The interpretation afterwards put upon that Note by Count Nesselrode showed that he was right; but, nevertheless, that was the point on which the question of peace and war turned. . . . Russia had formed the design to extort from Turkey, in one form or another, a right of protection over the Christians. She never abandoned that design. She thought she could enforce it. The Western Powers interposed, and the strife began."

Russo-Turkish War

On October 5 the Porte demanded from Russia the evacuation of the principalities within fifteen days, and on October 23 Turkey declared war. The British fleet had already been ordered up to the Bosphorus—an order of which Russia had some cause to complain as an infraction of the Treaty of 1841. Nevertheless, Russia and the Western Powers still remained at peace, and the Tsar declared that, despite the Turkish declaration of war, he would not take the offensive in the principalities. The Turks, however, attacked vigorously on the Danube, and on November 30 the Russian Black Sea fleet retaliated by the entire destruction of a Turkish squadron in the Bay of Sinope.

The "massacre of Sinope" aroused immense indignation in England and France, and must be regarded as the immediate prelude to the European War. "I have been," wrote Sir James Graham, "one of the most strenuous advocates of peace with Russia until the last moment; but the Sinope attack and recent events have changed entirely the aspect of affairs. I am afraid that a rupture with Russia is inevitable."

The Cabinet decided that in consequence of the "massacre" of Sinope the allied fleets must enter the Black Sea. On January 4, 1854, this momentous order was executed, and it was announced that the English and French admirals had instructions to "invite" all Russian ships in the Black Sea to withdraw into harbour. Even yet the Western Powers were not at war, and on February 22 Austria, always anxious about the presence of Russian troops in the principalities, but not too straightforward in her diplomacy, intimated that if the Western Powers would present an ultimatum, demanding the evacuation of Moldavia and Wallachia before a given date, she would support them. England and France promptly acted on this suggestion, and on February 27 Lord Clarendon informed Count Nesselrode that Great Britain, having exhausted all the efforts of negotiation, was compelled to call upon Russia "to restrict within purely diplomatic limits the discussion in which she has for some time been engaged with the Sublime Porte," and by return messenger to "agree to the complete evacuation of the Provinces of Moldavia and Wallachia by the 30th of April."

Russia refused this ultimatum on March 19, and on the 27th and 28th the Western Powers declared war. It was then made manifest that Austria's promised support was only diplomatic; Prussia—to the great indignation of Queen Victoria—followed Austria's lead; the concert on which so much depended was broken, and England and France were left alone to sustain an exceptionally arduous struggle.

Can the Crimean War be justified before the tribunal of impartial history? Retrospective criticism has tended to the view that the war, if not a crime, was at least a blunder, and that it ought to have been and might have been avoided. Sir Robert Morier, writing in 1870, perhaps expressed the current opinion when he described it as "the only perfectly useless modern war that has been waged." Lord Salisbury, some twenty years later, enshrined in classical phrase the opinion that "England put her money on the wrong horse." The Duke of Argyll, on the contrary, writing at the close of the century, confessed himself though one of the Cabinet responsible for the war "to this day wholly unrepentant." More recently Lord Cromer has reaffirmed his conviction that "had it not been for the Crimean War and the policy subsequently pursued by Lord Beaconsfield the independence of the Balkan States would never have been achieved, and the Russians would now be in possession of Constantinople." Kinglake has popularized the idea that England was an innocent tool in the hands of an unscrupulous adventurer, anxious to establish a throne unrighteously attained, by a brilliant war causelessly provoked. But to suggest that either Stratford or Aberdeen was the dupe of Napoleon's ambition is grotesquely inaccurate.

Popular passions had, as we have seen, been aroused by recent events against the Russian Tsar. More reflective opinion inclined to the view that the time had come for a sustained effort to repel the secular ambition of his people. The bias of Russian policy during the last century and a half was unmistakable. From the Treaty of Azov to that of Unkiar-Skelessi the advance had been stealthy but continuous. Was the dissolution of the sick man to be hastened now to satisfy the impatient avarice of the heir presumptive? Was the Tsar to be allowed to convert the Black Sea into a Russian lake, and to establish an exclusive and dangerous domination in the eastern waters of the Mediterranean? Was Europe in general, and England in particular, prepared to permit Russia to force upon the Porte a "diplomatic engagement which would have made her the sole protector of the Christian subjects of the Porte, and therefore the sole arbiter of the fate of Turkey"? Rightly or wrongly England came, slowly but steadily, to the conviction that the matter was one of vital concern to Europe at large and to herself in particular; that the Tsar was determined to assert his claims by force, and that only by force could they be repelled. Of this conviction the Crimean War was the logical and inevitable result.

The Crimean War (1854–6)

To the conduct of that war we must now turn. Early in 1854 a British fleet was sent to the Baltic, under the command of Sir Charles Napier, but though it captured Bomarsund the results of the expedition were disappointingly meagre, and contributed little to the ultimate issue of the war. On April 5 a British force under Lord Raglan, who had served both in the field and at the Horse Guards under the Duke of Wellington, landed at Gallipoli. It was preceded by a French army under Marshal Saint-Arnaud, the fellow conspirator of Napoleon III in the first *coup d'état*.

The Russians had already crossed the Danube (March 23) and had besieged Silistria. The prolonged defence of this weakly fortified town was due largely to two English volunteers, Captain Butler and Lieutenant Nasmyth, and in order to support it the allied army moved up from Gallipoli to Varna. There on May 19 a conference was held between Raglan, Saint-Arnaud, and Omar Pasha. On June 23, however, the Russians raised the siege of Silistria, and in July they commenced the evacuation of the principalities. Their withdrawal was due partly to the arrival of the allies on the Black Sea littoral; partly, perhaps, to the hope of luring them on to a second Moscow expedition; but most of all to the pressure of Austria, who, with the support of Prussia, had called upon the Tsar to evacuate the principalities. As soon as that had been effected the principalities were occupied, under an arrangement with the Porte, by an Austrian army. That occupation, though perhaps dictated in the first instance by jealousy of Russia, proved in the long run of incomparable advantage to her.

By the end of the first week in August there was no longer a Russian soldier to the west of the Pruth; the ostensible and immediate object of the European intervention might seem, therefore, to have been attained. But the allies had already reached the momentous decision (June) to "strike at the very heart of Russian power in the East—and that heart is at Sebastopol." . . .

On September 14, 1854, the allied army, more than 50,000 strong, disembarked in the Bay of Eupatoria to the north of Sebastopol. On the 19th the march towards Sebastopol began. On the 20th Menschikoff, in command of 40,000 troops, tried to stop the advance of the allies on the Alma—a stream about fifteen miles north of Sebastopol. After three hours of severe fighting the Russians were routed. The allies, though victorious, suffered heavily. But Raglan, despite the lack of transport and the ravages of cholera, wanted to make an immediate assault upon Sebastopol. Had his advice been taken Sebastopol would almost infallibly have fallen. But Saint-Arnaud, in the grip of a mortal disease, vetoed the suggestion, and it was decided to march round the head of the harbour and approach Sebastopol from the south. . . .

The hesitation of the allies gave the defenders of Sebastopol a chance which they seized with consummate adroitness and skill. They cleared the Russian ships of guns and men: sank some of the largest ships at the entrance to the harbour—thus rendering the allied fleets comparatively useless—and mounted the guns on shore. . . .

Reinforced from home, Menschikoff, at the head of 30,000 men, re-entered Sebastopol, while a large detachment under General Liprandi delivered from outside an attack on the position of the allies, hoping to catch them between two fires and drive them out of Balaclava.

The familiar story of the battle of Balaclava may not be retold; enough to say that the enemy, though repulsed in their attack upon Balaclava, retained their position on the heights above, and the besiegers were now, in fact, besieged, and ten days later were made to realize the fact. . . .

On November 14 a terrible disaster befell the allies. A fierce hurricane, accompanied with storms of rain and snow, sprang up, swept down the tents on shore, and destroyed much of the shipping in the roads. *The Prince*, a new steamer of 2,700 tons, was driven on the rocks and thirty other ships foundered in the gale. Stores to the value of £2,000,000 were lost, and the men were deprived of all that might have rendered tolerable the cruel Crimean winter.

The gale was the real beginning of the sufferings which have made the "Crimean Winter" a byword in the history of military administration. For many weary months the condition of the British force before Sebastopol was deplorable. After the great fight of Inkerman (November 5) there were no operations on a large scale in the field until the middle of February. Nevertheless, the intermission of fighting brought no cessation of toil or suffering to the unhappy soldiers.

While the soldiers were thus toiling and suffering in the trenches, the diplomatists were busy at Vienna. Austria, whose policy during this phase of the Eastern Question was consistently subtle, had set negotiations on foot towards the end of 1854, and on December 28 the allied Powers, in conjunction with Austria, presented to the Russian Plenipotentiary a Memorandum embodying the "Four Points." They were as follows:

1. The exclusive protectorate exercised by Russia over Moldavia, Wallachia, and Serbia was to cease, and the privileges accorded by the Sultan to the principalities were henceforward to be guaranteed collectively by the five Powers;
2. The navigation of the Danube was to be free;
3. The preponderance of Russia in the Black Sea was to be terminated; and
4. Russia was to renounce all pretensions to a protectorate over the Christian subjects of the Porte; and the five Powers were to co-operate in obtaining from the Sultan the confirmation and observance of the religious privileges of all the various Christian communities without infringing his dignity or the independence of his Crown.

The Conference formally opened on March 15, 1855, but before that date arrived two events had occurred, each, in its way, of profound significance. The first was the intervention of Sardinia; the second the death of the Tsar Nicholas.

On January 26, 1855, Count Cavour appended his signature to a Convention with Great Britain and France, promising the adherence of Sardinia to the alliance. Of good omen for the Western Powers, this step was incomparably the most momentous in the diplomatic history of modern Italy. On the face of it the resolution to take part in the war was at once cynical and foolhardy. What part or lot had the little sub-Alpine kingdom in the quarrel between Russia and the Western Powers? To Cavour the mere question seemed to imply "a surrender of our hopes of the future." Accordingly, despite bitter opposition at home, 18,000 Italians were by the end of April on their way to the Crimea, under the command of General Alfonso La Marmora. "You have the future of the country in your haversacks." Such was Cavour's parting injunction to the troops. The response came from a soldier in the trenches, "Out of this mud Italy will be made." It was.

The adhesion of Sardinia came as a timely encouragement to the allies. To all those who were longing and working for peace, the death of the Tsar Nicholas seemed of still happier augury. Nicholas was unquestionably the prime author of the war; he had sustained it with unflagging energy, and he was bitterly disappointed at his failure to bring it to a rapid and brilliant termination. What Russian arms failed to accomplish at the Alma, at Balaclava, and at Inkerman, "Generals January and February" might be trusted to achieve. But, as *Punch* felicitously pointed out, "General February turned traitor." The Tsar was attacked by influenza, to which on March 2, 1855, he succumbed. The news of his death evoked profound emotion throughout Europe, more particularly at Vienna, where the Conference was in progress.

The accession of the new Tsar, Alexander II, did not, however, render the Russian Plenipotentiaries more pliable. The real crux lay in the proposed limitation of Russian naval preponderance in the Black Sea. To that point Palmerston in particular attached the greatest importance, and on it the negotiations, at the end of April, broke down.

Notwithstanding the failure of the diplomatists at Vienna, the war was nearing its end. Still, there was a great deal of hard fighting round Sebastopol during the spring and summer of 1855. . . .

Slowly but surely the allied armies pushed forward their lines towards the Russian fortifications. Once more the covering army, under the command of Prince Michael Gortschakoff, made a desperate and gallant effort to raise the siege. On the night of August 15–16 the Russians descended from the Mackenzie Heights upon the Tchernaya river, where the Sardinian contingent, under General La Marmora, got their first real chance. Nor did they miss it. Fighting with the utmost gallantry they contributed in no small degree to the decisive repulse of the Russian army. Thus were Cavour's calculations precisely fulfilled. In the waters of the Tchernaya the stain of Novara was wiped out for ever; out of the mud of the Crimean trenches was modern Italy built up. Henceforward Cavour could speak with his enemies in the gate. The victory of the allies at the Tchernaya shattered the last hopes of the besieged from the army in the field. . . .

On November 28 General Fenwick Williams was compelled to surrender the fortress of Kars. He had been sent to reorganize the Turkish forces in Armenia, and with a small Turkish garrison had been holding Kars for nearly six months against overwhelming odds. It was an heroic defence, and it won for Fenwick Williams undying fame. A Turkish force had been dispatched too tardily to the relief of Kars, and before it arrived the little garrison was starved out. General Mouravieff's success at Kars was a slight set-off against the surrender of Sebastopol, and predisposed the mind of the Tsar Alexander to peace.

Treaty of Paris, March 30, 1856

The Emperor Napoleon was even more anxious for it. He had got all he could out of the war; the French army had gained fresh lustre from its concluding passages; the English army had not. Napoleon's restless mind was already busy with the future disposition of Europe. He was looking towards Russia and towards Italy; for England he had no further use. Cavour too had got all he wanted. The main obstacle to peace was Lord Palmerston. He was gravely mistrustful of France, and still more so of Austria. And he had reason. The part played by Austria was crafty, selfish, and even treacherous. Her interest was concentrated upon the Principalities. She had induced England and France to pick the chestnuts out of the fire for her there. Russia having been induced to withdraw from the Principalities, not by the threats of Austria, but by the action of England and France, Austria had promptly occupied them, and had thus enabled Russia to concentrate her efforts upon the Crimea. Finally, as soon as there was a chance of peace, Austria spared no effort to detach Napoleon from the English alliance. In this she nearly succeeded; but on January 16, 1856, the Tsar (at the instance of his brother-in-law the King of Prussia) accepted as a basis of negotiation the "Four Points," including a stipulation for the neutralization of the Black Sea; on February 1 a protocol embodying these terms was concluded by the representatives of the five Powers at Vienna, and the definitive Peace was signed at Paris on March 30, 1856. The main terms were as follows:

1. The Sublime Porte was formally admitted, on the invitation of the six Powers (including the King of Sardinia), to "participate in the public law and concert of Europe," and the Powers engaged severally to respect, and collectively to guarantee "the independence and the territorial integrity of the Ottoman Empire."

2. The Sultan, "in his constant solicitude for the welfare of his subjects," announced to the Powers his intention to ameliorate their condition "without distinction of creed or race"; but the Powers, while recognizing "the high value of this communication," expressly repudiated the "right to interfere, either collectively or separately," in the internal affairs of Turkey.

3. The Black Sea was neutralized, its waters and ports were to be open to the mercantile marine of every nation, but permanently "interdicted to the flag of war"; and there were to be no arsenals, either Russian or Turkish, on its coasts.

4. Kars was to be restored to the Turks, and the Crimea to Russia.

5. The navigation of the Danube was to be open on equal terms to the ships of all nations, under the control of an international commission.

6. Southern Bessarabia was to be ceded by Russia to Moldavia. The Principalities of Moldavia and Wallachia were to remain under the suzerainty of the Porte; Russia renounced her exclusive protectorate over them, and the contracting Powers collectively guaranteed their privileges. They were to enjoy "an independent and national administration with full liberty of worship, legislation, and commerce," and were to have "a national armed force." In each province a national Convention was to be held "to decide the definitive organization of the Principalities."

7. The liberties of Serbia were to be similarly guaranteed.

. . .

Of the other results of the war the most obvious was the new lease of life secured to the Ottoman Empire. The Sultan was to have his chance, free from all interference, friendly or otherwise, from his powerful neighbour, to put his house in order. He could enter upon his task with renewed self-respect, for was he not at last admitted to the most polite society of Europe? And his subjects should realize the spontaneity of his beneficence; if he chose to persecute, it was his affair: the Powers had expressly repudiated the right of interference; equally, if he chose to extend civil or religious liberty, the extension was the outcome of his own loving-kindness towards his people. Such was the formal position secured to the Ottoman Empire by the Treaty of Paris. Yet the Sultan, if he were wise, could not fail to observe that the guarantee of independence and integrity vouchsafed to him by the Powers imposed upon them a corresponding obligation. Morally, if not legally, they were bound to see to it that the Porte behaved in accordance with the unwritten rules of polite society. In repudiating the exclusive protectorship of Russia they assumed a responsibility for the good government of the Christian subjects of the Porte which the Sultan could ignore only at his peril. On this point much will, unfortunately, have to be said later on.

To Russia the Treaty of Paris involved, for the time being, a bitter disappointment, if not a profound humiliation. For a century and a half she had pursued with singular consistency three main objects: to establish her naval and commercial supremacy on the waters and coasts of the Black Sea; to secure a free outlet to the Mediterranean; and to obtain from the Porte an acknowledgement of her position as champion of the liberties, political and ecclesiastical, of the Christian subjects of the Sultan. At times there had floated before the eyes of Russian rulers, notably those of the Tsarina Catherine, dreams even more ambitious. The Treaty of Paris not only dissipated completely all ideas of partition, but involved a disastrous set-back to those more sober and prosaic aims which had inspired Russian policy from the days of Peter the Great to those of Alexander II.

The Black Sea Question

The neutralization of the Black Sea was of special concern to England, as the leading Naval Power of the world. To the growth of the naval power of Russia, England, as we have seen, had become, in recent years, increasingly sensitive. The prolonged siege of Sebastopol had naturally made a profound impression upon the public mind. To allow Russia, in the complete security afforded by the closing of the straits, to build up a great naval force, and to convert the shores of the Black Sea into a great arsenal, seemed sheer madness to the Power which had large interests in the Near East and was paramount in the Far East.

Regarded from the Russian point of view the neutralization of the Black Sea was an insolent and intolerable interference in the domestic concerns of the Russian Empire, an attempt, inspired by petty jealousy, to arrest her natural and inevitable development. It was, therefore, absolutely certain that Russia would seize the first favourable opportunity to get rid of the shackles imposed upon her by the Treaty of Paris.

The opportunity came with the outbreak, in 1870, of the Franco-German War. Bismarck owed Russia a very heavy debt; the time had come to discharge it. . . .

In October, 1870, Prince Gortschakoff addressed to the Powers a circular denouncing on behalf of Russia the Black Sea clauses of the

Treaty of Paris (1856), and declaring that the Tsar proposed to resume his "sovereign rights" in the Black Sea. The step, if not actually suggested, was certainly approved beforehand by Bismarck. In justification of the action of Russia Gortschakoff cynically referred to the "infringements to which most European transactions have been latterly exposed, and in the face of which it would be difficult to maintain that the written law . . . retains the moral validity which it may have possessed at other times." In plain English the Tsar saw no reason why he should observe treaties when other people broke them.

The Russian circular evoked strong opposition both in England and in Austria. Lord Granville expressed the "deep regret" of his Government at "an arbitrary repudiation of a solemn engagement," and declared that England "could not possibly give her sanction." Count Beust, the Austrian minister, expressed himself as "painfully affected" by the behaviour of the Tsar, and found it "impossible to conceal his extreme astonishment thereat."

But Gortschakoff went on his way unheeding. Bismarck was behind him, and Bismarck was confident that though England might bark she would not bite.

He had reason for his confidence. Plainly there were but two courses open to Great Britain: either to acquiesce in the bold and cynical action of the Tsar, or, without allies, to fight him. To declare war upon Russia, at this juncture, would be to provoke the Armageddon which England was using all her endeavours to avert. . . .

That English prestige suffered severely from the emasculation of that treaty can hardly be denied. To the Black Sea clauses she had attached great importance; from a selfish point of view she had little else to show for a heavy expenditure in men and money.

France had not much more. But though France gained little by the Crimean War, Napoleon gained much. In 1853 his position in Europe was far from assured; the Crimean War established it; and until the advent of Bismarck his influence upon the Continent was almost overwhelming. The war gained him, paradoxically, the friendship of Russia: the peace lost him the confidence of England.

The greatest gainer by the war, excepting the Porte, was Italy. Cavour's prudent calculations were precisely fulfilled. He took his place, despite the angry protest of Austria, at the Council Board in Paris, as the representative not merely of Sardinia but of Italy. In the name of Italy he denounced the misgovernment of the two Sicilies; for Italy he conciliated the sympathy of Great Britain and the active assistance of Napoleon. The intervention of Sardinia in the Crimean War gave to her a place in the Concert of Europe, and gave to her the right as well as the opportunity to champion the cause of Italian liberation. At the Congress of Paris Cavour and the Emperor Napoleon came to an understanding; it was sealed two years later by the pact of Plombières; it bore fruit in the war of 1859.

Cavour to the Countess Anastasia de Circourt at Paris

Turin, 1855

. . . Events have led Piedmont to take a clear and decided position in Italy. This position is not without dangers, I know, and I feel all the weight of the responsibility that presses upon me, but it has been imposed on us by honor and duty. Since Providence has willed that Piedmont, alone in Italy, should be free and independent, Piedmont must make use of her liberty and her independence to plead the cause of this unhappy peninsula before Europe. We shall not draw back from this perilous task: the King and the country are determined to carry it through to the end. Your friends, the doctrinaires and the liberals who weep for the loss of liberty in France, having helped smother it in Italy, will perhaps find our policy absurd and romantic. I am resigned to their criticism, certain that generous hearts like yours will sympathize with our efforts to bring back to life a nation buried for centuries in a terrible tomb. If I fail, you will not refuse me sanctuary among the eminent vanquished who have clustered around you. . . . Receive this outpouring as the confession that my whole life is consecrated for a single work, the emancipation of my country.

Cavour, *Lettere*, II (2nd ed.), 320–21.

Cavour to General Alfonso La Marmora, Commanding the Sardinian Expeditionary Force at Kadikoi (Crimea)

Turin, 31 May 1855

. . . The newspapers will have informed you of the successive political phases. The western powers, without renouncing the Austrian alliance, are beginning to despair of ever getting Austria to take an active part in the struggle against Russia. They are planning on getting

Cavour, *Lettere*, II (2nd ed.), 332–33.

together as much force as possible, to act without Germany. England has decided to form a Swiss legion, and has asked our permission to set up depots at Evian and at Domodossola. We agreed, advising them to substitute Novara for the latter town. Hudson* has taken the matter very much to heart. He would like the legion to admit Italians. He wrote to London about it, and when he got a luke-warm answer he decided to go settle it with Lord Palmerston face to face in London. We shall see with pleasure the formation of a corps which will probably deliver us of the most turbulent part of the émigrés. Our Italian legion is being formed not far from Ticino [in Switzerland] as well, which should give Austria something to think about.

I took the occasion afforded by the publication of the documents relative to the Vienna Conferences to address an energetic note to our allies on our position in the negotiations. This note has produced a good effect in Paris and in London, where it was decided formally to recognize our right to participate in immediate or subsequent conferences. Cibrario is going to draft the note containing the recognition as his maiden effort [as Sardinian Foreign Minister].

I have received your letter of the 15th and thank you for it. I shall not speak of military operations; I abstain from any thought in that regard. You know that I have the most unlimited confidence in you, and that I know you will make the very best you can out of the difficult position you are in.

You can count on us to neglect nothing in furnishing you with all you need: you have in your knapsacks the future of the country: we do not forget it.

Adieu, my regards to Petitti. Rattazzi will tell you a thousand things. Your affectionate

*British ambassador to Piedmont.

Cavour to La Marmora

Turin, 30 July 1855

I attach to this letter a few lines in cipher.

C.C.

My dear friend,

We are happy to hear that the cholera has left the camp. Fevers are troublesome, certainly, but they can never have the terrible consequences of the terrible Asiatic plague. I hope you will soon have

Cavour, *Lettere*, II (2nd ed.), 344–46.

Petitti by your side, and that you will be able to get all your staff organized for the day of action which, I think, we shall not be waiting for much longer.

I have no important news from home to send you. Since the departure of the King of Portugal and the Duke of Brabant, King V. E. is at Pollenzo. The sojourn in the country has done him a lot of good physically and for his morale. We have been in contact with Pollenzo, and have met a reception there which shows no sign of resentment against the law on convents and the crisis it caused.

Rattazzi is at Pesio Mansion, my other colleagues are at their posts. We meet often and always there is talk of you; our prayers and our thoughts follow you on the glorious but difficult fields to which your devotion has called you.

At home we have difficulties enough, but I do not think they are very serious. The cholera has threatened us for a long time; so far it hasn't caught up with us; but two days ago it put in an appearance at Genoa, more menacing because of the memories it evokes than because of its present intensity.

The extremist parties are active. Mazzini believes that the cataclysm he dreams of is about to arrive, and so he is stirring up his cronies to get ready. There have been some arrests and seizures of weapons, but this is nothing extraordinary.

The Blacks [conservatives] are fussing a lot; they are much more powerful and much more adroit than the Reds: there's more reason to be afraid of them. They work behind the scenes and they are gaining ground. If the war goes badly, it is probable they will manage to overthrow the ministry and take its place.

These two parties are trying to exploit the tax question, with the primary purpose of destroying me. But with the exception of Genoa, they have hardly succeeded in making any embarrassment. Nevertheless, we must not deceive ourselves; these continued attacks, which have an actual basis, finally penetrate the toughest hides. And so I am beginning to sense my end approaching. In that prophecy, I invoke in my ardent prayers the day when you will return, to place in your hands my Presidential portfolio.

You would do me a great favor if you could inform me if one Cena, soldier in the engineer battalion, native of Leri, is still alive.

Adieu, all my affection. Your devoted

(In cipher)

Azeglio writes me confidentially that [British Foreign Secretary] Lord Clarendon has given him to understand that the allied generals complain of being constantly hindered in their projects by the Sardinian general, and of not having received effective cooperation from him.

While I am convinced that these complaints are unjust, still I feel obliged to urge you to avoid any cause or pretext for disagreement. If our troops could only take part in any action whatsoever, the situation would improve.

Cavour to General Alfonso La Marmora, Commander, Expeditionary Corps, at Kadikoi (Crimea)

Dearest Friend,   Turin, 14 August 1855
I have received the two letters you wrote me at the end of July. . . .

No one is more aware than I of the gravity of the difficulties you have to struggle with, and you can be sure that nothing will be left undone on my side which might help you overcome them. But you must recognize on your part that the political difficulties are no less serious than the military. The alliance has reduced them a great deal. Without it they would be insuperable. That must be for us and also for you a compensation for the cruel sacrifices we are undergoing.

The inaction of our Corps is certainly lamentable, but so far it has been necessary. I allow myself to believe that before the campaign ends you will find a way to lead our soldiers into combat, where they will prove themselves well, I am quite certain of that. Should this not happen, the consequence in the country and perhaps in Europe would be an unfavorable and unjust impression. But I shall not persist in this argument, for you are as aware of it as I.

To send new troops to the Crimea, to confront the positions taken up by Austria, is a most serious matter. I do not believe in the announced increases of that power's forces in Italy. But certainly there have not been the reductions here that have taken place in other parts of the empire. There seems to be a plan to establish several training camps, one in the neighborhood of Somma, on our border. The cholera which raged and still is raging in Lombardy, and still worse in Venetia, has so far prevented putting this into effect.

But once the levy is set up, we shall be in a position to replace soldiers dead or incapacitated by illness with new soldiers. But that will not be possible to do before there has been some feat of arms.

Cavour, *Lettere*, II (2nd ed.), 129–31.

It appears that the conversation which motivated my dispatch in cipher was not very serious, since Hudson, who arrived here some days ago from London, takes quite another line with me and with my colleagues. He even expressed in the name of his government the most complete satisfaction. You can therefore consider unsaid what was contained in that dispatch.

Colonel Percy arrived here a few days ago. I found him to be as I had imagined him, and gave him the grandest reception I could. Domenica came to Santena with Hudson. He speaks of our troops and their leader with enthusiasm.

You will have seen in the papers that the Pope has hurled his thunderbolts at me. This action produced no great sensation in the country, not even in the spirit of *Him* who, one might have feared, would be most susceptible to these ecclesiastical censures.

The cholera is mild enough on the continent. But epidemics in Sardinia, especially at Sassari. If there had not been an intendant like Conte in that town, I don't know how things might have gone. The troops were wonderful. Some officers fell victim to their zeal. Among these Major Rebaudengo is especially to be lamented, who was famed as the most distinguished officer in the Sardinian light cavalry. Greetings to Petitti. Make sure he doesn't overwork, and stays in good health. Greetings from our colleagues. Rattazzi is well, untroubled by the internal difficulties. Pepe is dead.* No troops were sent to his funeral for reasons of prudence, which seemed to me excessive.

Write to me; sincerely; etc.

*General Gugliemo Pepe, whose long revolutionary career had begun in Naples in 1820, had been living in Piedmont.

Cavour to Count Walewski* at Paris

Monsieur le Comte,   Turin, 21 January 1856

H. M. the Emperor, in his high and benevolent solicitude for Italy, was good enough to invite me, the last time I saw him, to present to him in a quite confidential fashion my opinion on what he could do in that country's interest. In response to that honorable proof of his confidence, I tried to sketch a true picture of the present state of

*Foreign Minister of France.

Cavour, *Lettere*, II (2nd ed.), 382–89.

Italy, indicating the ways in which its sad lot might be improved, whatever eventualities the great contest between East and West may present.

This over-long and yet unfinished paper was undertaken before the last *démarche* attempted by Austria could be brought to a definite result, so the conclusions to which it must lead are subject to the uncertainty which rules in political affairs. It cannot be otherwise, for if the generous sentiments of the Emperor for Italy cannot change, his action in Italy's favor can be modified, in accordance with the relations existing between France and the other great European powers, especially Austria.

At the moment when I was about to complete the task, the telegraphed news of Russian acceptance of the terms agreed upon by the western powers and of the immediate opening of conferences to make peace on the proposed bases ended the uncertainty and fixed in a clear and precise manner the point of view from which the Italian question must be envisaged. Accordingly, I ought to modify or recast my long paper and arrive at more practical conclusions. I would not hesitate to do so if it were an official document; but since this completely confidential memorandum has been requested of me as a man rather than as a minister, I prefer to leave it as it is; because, considering the different turns politics can take, it appears my duty to give a rather complete and rather exact idea of the state of Italy and of the permanent direction France may consequently wish to give its policy in the common interest of the two countries.

Still, as in politics it is wise to avoid vagueness and to make as precise as possible the steps to be taken at a given moment, I make bold to hope that the Emperor will not take it ill if I submit in advance, through Your Excellency, a succinct and precise résumé of what H. M. can do for Italy, once the preliminaries are signed and the conferences have begun.

That is what I am taking the liberty to do in addressing this letter to Y. E. and begging that you place it before the eyes of your August Sovereign. I propose to bring the complete memorandum before him later.

Austria has played an important part in the latest developments; Austria has to be considered, by a diplomatic fiction, to have rendered a signal service to Europe; accordingly, it is necessary to begin with the proposition that we cannot demand of her, at least for the moment, any territorial sacrifice in Italy. It is on that basis, a sad one for us but one which to be practical we must recognize, that I shall suggest the benefits which my country can hope for from the vigorous and benevolent action of the Emperor.

In the first place, by renouncing any claims on Austria for a modification of the Treaty of Vienna in conformity with the true interests of Europe, the Emperor has achieved a strong influence over her which, it seems to us, could assure that she do justice to Piedmont, and that she establish a less oppressive and more tolerable rule over her Italian subjects.

In view of the pledges which Sardinia gave to the cause of order by sending her soldiers to fight in the Crimea, Austria no longer has even the shadow of a pretext for violating the principles of equity in her regard, and violating the formal engagements which were given a new sanction in the treaty concluded between the two powers in 1851, by keeping impounded the goods of persons who have become Sardinian citizens after they had been absolved of the ties that bound them to their old homelands.

She no longer has a pretext to refuse to join together the railroads of the two countries, as stipulated by a formal convention, nor to impede by all sorts of police measures the commercial and personal relations between Sardinians and Lombards.

The end of the military rule which for eight years has oppressed the population of the kingdom of Lombardy-Venetia would be a real service for them without exposing Austria, at least for the moment, to any real danger. Concessions made by that power at the moment when she signs an advantageous peace cannot be interpreted as acts of weakness. And while they will not reconcile Italians to the Vienna government, they will have the effect of reducing feelings of irritation, and of making the state of things in Lombardy less precarious during the period of peace or of truce which we are about to go through. What the Emperor can obtain from Austria by friendly advice he can impose on the King of Naples.

Now that the preoccupations of the war no longer make any vigorous diplomatic action dangerous, he can demand that that prince cease to make the monarchic principle odious by a conduct which is as absurd as it is brutal. By forcing him to open the dungeons where so many illustrious and innocent victims have groaned so long, by pressing him not to give over the administration of the country to police agents as vicious as they are corrupt, France will be doing him an actual service, which cannot give even Austria cause for complaint or uneasiness.

It would be a strange illusion to hope that the beautiful kingdom of Naples could ever enjoy the benefits of good government under the scepter of the Bourbons—but at least the Emperor can procure for them a mitigation of the evil by forcing King Ferdinand to pay a little more respect to the laws of justice and humanity.

The state of things in the provinces which Austria possesses in Italy, as well as those of the Kingdom of Naples, conforms to the stipulations of the Treaty of Vienna, which for the moment the western powers, at least England, do not want to touch; accordingly, one is forced to agree that France's action in their regard is restrained within narrow and restricted limits. This is not true of an important part of Italy, I mean to say the Papal States and especially the provinces between the Apennines, the Adriatic, and the Po.

These provinces are in name still under the domination of the Sovereign Pontiff, in fact they belong to Austria, in a way contrary to the letter and the spirit of the Treaty of Vienna, which designated the left bank of the Po as the outer limit of the territorial aggrandizement accorded her.

Austrian predominance in the Legations and in the Romagna, at first temporary, has become permanent; there is no reason to suppose that it will end in the near or the distant future unless Europe takes decisive steps in that direction.

That being so, for a Congress to meet without that question being raised would almost officially sanction a state of things as unfortunate for Italy as it is dangerous for the western powers.

I consider it therefore a vital interest of France and England, and a glorious task worthy of those sovereigns to whom Europe owes the humbling of Russia, to put an end to Austrian occupation of the most beautiful provinces of central Italy.

That proposition is hardly debatable, but what if I am asked how to carry it out? I am too candid to presume to advise the Emperor to force Austria to withdraw her troops from the Legations and the Romagna, should the administrative and political condition of those countries remain as it is. It is clear that if the priestly government is maintained, the departure of the Austrians will be the signal for the most serious disorder, for the most complete anarchy.

Now, neither France nor we want either disorder or anarchy of any kind, in Italy above all.

Military occupation of the Legations and the Romagna is a necessary consequence of the regime to which those provinces are subjected; and if the one is to be ended, the other must be radically reformed.

If one reflects at all on the European state of mind, there is nothing surprising about that fact. What modern peoples accept the least, what they detest the most, is the mixing of priests in politics and administration.

This sentiment is as strong in France as in Italy. The fate of Charles X is proof of it. Everywhere people prefer the rule of the saber to that of the cassock.

And they are right, because the sacerdotal regime, seen close up, shows every kind of disadvantage without a single advantage.

Let there be no illusions about it: to leave papal government on its own in regions impregnated by the ideas which France planted there is to condemn it to immediate and certain destruction.

Austria can of course govern them in the name of the Pope with her troops, but I defy her, should she occupy them a hundred years, to succeed in molding men's minds to the point of making the sacerdotal regime acceptable to them.

In the light of that truth—and Austria herself could not seriously contradict it—one is obliged to recognize the necessity of reforming the state of affairs in the Legations and the Romagna. The one effective and lasting remedy would be to place them under a temporal prince. And since one would not want to aggravate the fragmentation of Italy, they ought to be given either to the Duke of Modena or the Grand Duke of Tuscany. This union, certainly not anti-Austrian, would give cause for a territorial reorganization in which Piedmont could find just compensation for the sacrifices she has made.

Without being full of enthusiasm for the governments of Tuscany or Modena, especially the latter, I must say that they would be in every way preferable to papal government.

Florence and Modena are more or less well-governed; Bologna and Ancona are not at all. These unfortunate countries suffer all the evils of foreign domination, of despotism and arbitrary rule, and at the very same time popular anarchy. The substitution of a temporal prince, even of the House of Austria, for the papal government would not assure complete emancipation for those countries, but it would be of great benefit to them all the same, which would make the Emperor's name blessed on this side of the Alps.

If this arrangement, which seems to me acceptable even from the Austrian point of view, should meet insurmountable difficulties, one would have to look for a solution allowing at least provisional attainment of the goal which France must set herself, the retreat of Austrian troops to the left bank of the Po.

Such a solution would consist of the absolute secularization of the government of the Romagna and the Legations, under the suzerainty of the Sovereign Pontiff. For that it would be necessary to organize a grand administrative center at Bologna, at Ravenna, or some other town on the Adriatic coast, and organize the provinces in a way analogous to what is planned for the Danube Principalities. The provinces would continue to form part of the Roman States, they would remain under the suzerainty of the Holy See; they would contribute financially within certain limits to the maintenance of the Roman Court, but they would be administratively independent. By that arrangement, while the future would not be provided for in any definite way, at least one would have got as much good as bad for the present.

In summary, I conclude that in the present circumstances, quite accepting the necessity of humoring Austria, the Emperor can render immense services to the Italy for which he has already done so much:

1. By urging Austria to do justice to Piedmont and keep the engagements contracted with her;
2. By obtaining from her a mitigation of the iron rule which presses on Lombardy and Venetia;
3. By forcing the King of Naples not to scandalize civilized Europe by conduct contrary to all principles of justice and equity;
4. Finally, by reestablishing the equilibrium in Italy as it was established by the Treaty of Vienna, by making possible the retreat of Austrian troops from the Legations and the Romagna, either by placing these provinces under a secular prince or by procuring for them the benefits of an independent administration by laymen.

Renewing my prayer to place this before the eyes of the Emperor, I take liberty again to ask Y. E. to solicit his indulgence for a paper prepared in haste under the impact of the news which the telegraph has brought us from St. Petersburg, and to assure H. M. that whatever judgment his eminent mind may make of the opinions I have taken the liberty of submitting to him, I shall always preserve a profound and unalterable gratitude for a proof of confidence which so honors me, and which testifies to the generous interest which he accords our poor Italy.

I have the honor to be, etc.,

Cavour to La Marmora at London

My dear Friend,   Turin, 21 January 1856

The peace [La paix] is deplorable for us. I am desolated by it, but, not being able to prevent it, I shall have to accept it and try to save whatever I can from the wretched position in which this sly old granny of an Austria has placed us.

In England, where the war was popular, we can let our disappointment be visible and show our opinion of Austria unreservedly; in France there is need for more caution so as not to offend the Emperor, who regards this peace as a triumph for his policy.

The conferences could begin any moment, so I thought it urgent to formulate the requests which the Emperor invited me to address to him. Azeglio* finished his memorandum, it is a magnificent work, but of inordinate length and besides has the inconvenience of not reaching any clear and precise conclusions. If I had sent it straight to Walewski he probably would not have read it; or at least he would have paid no attention to it. Consequently, I felt obliged to formulate my ideas in a several-page letter to Walewski, asking him to put it before the eyes of the Emperor. I am sending copies to Villamarina and to Azeglio with instructions to communicate it to you. You will see that our demands are modest, but in view of the position Austria has attained we have to appear in France above all very modest and very disinterested.

If we nevertheless succeed in getting our allies to acknowledge the necessity of forcing Austria to withdraw her troops from the Romagna we shall have made a great step, for we shall have got accepted the principle of the destruction of the temporal power of the Pope. From what I was able to determine during my stay in England, this idea would delight the ministry, especially Lord Palmerston. He spoke to me of giving the Legations to Tuscany. I rebuffed that question then, as I would rebuff it still if the war were continuing; but at the moment we shall have to take it as a sheet-anchor. If the Papal states were to be partitioned between Tuscany and Modena, we should have to receive compensations. I myself would be satisfied with the Duchies of Placentia and of Massa and Carrara. You can go right ahead and talk about these propositions, which would far better come from you than from a professional diplomat. You will say in England that if nothing at all is done for Sardinia, the Italian constitutional party is

*Now Sardinian Ambassador in London.

Cavour, *Lettere*, II (2nd ed.), 289–91.

lost. That people will say it let itself be duped by the cabinet at London, and that it must give place first to reaction and then to revolution.

We want to prolong your stay until the question is decided. If peace is confirmed, your presence will be less important in the Crimea, and it can be very important at Paris, where Villamarina is utterly incapable of handling big political questions.

For a while I had the idea of asking you to represent us at the conferences; but we have already promised D'Azeglio, and besides, as long as you haven't sheathed the sword, you can't hold forth an olive branch in your hand. But if peace is confirmed, you too will have to resign yourself to making a little diplomacy.

The news of Russia's acceptance has caused general pain. All shades of the liberal party have been affected by it; and the *codini** themselves are not overjoyed. The King had a moment of bad humor, then he resigned himself. Our friends the émigrés, Torelli and Oldfredi, are especially desolated; the end of the sequestrations will not console them.

Adieu, write me. Your aff.

*pig-tails, reactionaries.

Cavour to Cibrario*

Paris, 19 March 1856

As the conferences are approaching their close, I have thought it time to get our allies to take up Italian affairs. For this purpose I have worked out a plan for the evacuation of the Roman States, which I have submitted to Lord Clarendon and the Emperor. The confinement of the Empress kept the Emperor from working on it for some days.

Nevertheless at my urging and with the strong solicitations of Lord Clarendon, the Emperor consented to hold today a sort of conference attended by Lord Clarendon, Count Walewski, and me. The conference lasted two hours and a half. I do not have the time to tell you all the details. I shall restrict myself to indicating the results.

The Emperor manifested the liveliest and most sincere desire to do something for Italy. He was quite aware of the immense inconveniences

*Cibrario was Piedmontese Foreign Minister. But Cavour, as Prime Minister and Plenipotentiary to the Congress of Paris, was in full control of Piedmont's foreign policy.

Valsecchi, ed. *L'unificazione italiana*, pp. 198–99.

which would result from the silence of the Congress on the affairs of the Peninsula. He recognized the sorry condition of the provinces governed by the Pope. In short he assented to my entire presentation. When we finally came to look for ways to take action, Count Walewski raised all sorts of difficulties. He pointed out all the things Count Buol* would do to avoid or distract this discussion. Lack of authority, absence of instructions, etc. The Emperor, a practical man, was very astonished by the objections of his Minister. He was ready to propose the revision of all the treaties of 1815.

After a discussion which lasted no less than two hours, in which I took the most active rôle, thanks to the support of Lord Clarendon, the Emperor ended up by giving a precise order to Walewski to place before the Congress two questions, that of Greece and that of the Roman States. That is a first result achieved. It is not great, but nevertheless it cost me a great deal.

The Emperor then accepted the request I made him to propose to the Congress that it invite the Italian Sovereigns to grant amnesty to their subjects.

*Austrian Foreign Minister.

Note on the Romagna

[Submitted by Cavour to Walewski and Clarendon]

27 March 1856

At a moment when the glorious efforts of the Western Powers are securing for Europe the benefits of peace, the deplorable condition of the Provinces subjected to the Government of the Holy See, and above all the Legations, demands the very special attention of H. M. the Emperor of the French and the government of His Britannic Majesty.

The Legations have been occupied by Austrian troops since 1840. The state of siege and martial law have been in force there since that time without interruption. The Pontifical Government exists only in name, because above its Legates there is an Austrian general holding the title and exercising the functions of civil and military Governor. There is no indication that this state of affairs can come to an end, since the Pontifical Government, such as it is, is convinced of its inability to preserve public order, as in the first days of its restoration,

Valsecchi, ed. *L'unificazione italiana*, pp. 199–205.

and Austria asks for nothing better than to make its occupation permanent.

There are the facts, as they are: a deplorable situation, and one which grows steadily worse, in a country which is nobly endowed and contains strong conservative elements; the inability of the legitimate sovereign to govern it; a permanent danger of disorder and anarchy in the center of Italy; the extension of Austrian domination in the Peninsula, far beyond what was accorded her by the treaties of 1815.

Before the French Revolution the Legations were under the high suzerainty of the Pope; but they enjoyed privileges and freedoms which made them, at least for internal administration, practically independent. Even so, the clerical domination there was so unpopular that the French armies were received with enthusiasm in 1796.

Detached from the Holy See by the Treaty of Tolentino, these provinces were made parts first of the Republic, then of the Kingdom of Italy, until 1814. The organizational genius of Napoleon changed them like magic. French laws, institutions, and administration in a few years developed well-being and civilization there. Even in the provinces all traditions and sympathies go back to that period. The Government of Napoleon is the only one which has survived in the memories not only of the enlightened classes, but also of the towns and countryside. They are memories of impartial justice, strong administration, in short, a state of prosperity, wealth, and military grandeur.

At the Congress of Vienna there was long hesitation before the Legations were put back under the Government of the Pope. The men who deliberated there, preoccupied though they were with reestablishing the old order of things everywhere, still felt that in this way they would be leaving a hot-bed of disorder in the middle of Italy. The difficulty of choosing a sovereign to whom these provinces could be given, and the rivalries that broke out over their possession, tipped the balance in favor of the Pope; and Cardinal Consalvi got this unexpected grant, but only after the battle of Waterloo.

The Pontifical Government, upon its restoration, paid no attention whatever to the progress of ideas and the profound changes which the French regime had introduced into this part of its Estates. From then on a struggle between Government and people was inevitable.

The Legations have been prey to an agitation which has been more or less hidden, but which at every opportunity breaks out in revolutions. Three times Austria has intervened with her armies to reestablish the authority of the Pope, which is constantly disowned by his subjects.

France responded to the second Austrian intervention with the occupation of Ancona, and to the third with the capture of Rome. Every time France has found herself faced with such circumstances, she has been aware of the necessity of putting an end to a state of things which is a scandal for Europe and an immense obstacle to the pacification of Italy. The "Memorandum" of 1831* noted the deplorable condition of the country, and the necessity and the urgency of administrative reforms.

Diplomatic correspondence from Gaeta and Portici bears the imprint of the same sentiment. The reforms which Pius IX himself had initiated in 1846 were the fruit of his long stay in Imola, where he had been able to judge with his own eyes the effects of the deplorable regime imposed upon those provinces. Unfortunately the counsels of the Powers and the good will of the Pope broke against the obstacles which the clerical organization places in the way of any kind of innovation.

If there is one fact that emerges clearly from the history of these last years, it is the difficulty, or rather, the impossibility of a complete reform of the Pontifical Government in a way responsive to the demands of the times and the reasonable desires of the people.

Emperor Napoleon III, with that clear and firm vision that characterizes him, perfectly and precisely indicated the solution to the problem in his letter to Colonel Ney: *"Secularization, Napoleonic Code."* But it is evident that the Court of Rome will struggle to the last ditch and with all its resources against the carrying out of these two projects. There is a belief that it could yield the appearance of accepting civil and even political reforms, being still able to render them illusory in practice. But it knows only too well that the introduction of Secularization and the Napoleonic Code at Rome itself, where the foundations of its temporal power rest, would sap it at the base, and make it crumble by removing its main supports: *clerical privileges* and the *canon law.*

Still, while there can be no hope of introducing true reforms at the very center, where the gears of the temporal authority are so enmeshed with those of the spiritual power that it is hard to see how to separate them completely without breaking them: could one not still obtain them in a place which accepts the clerical yoke with the least resignation, where a permanent hot-bed of troubles and anarchies, furnishing the pretext for permanent occupation by the Austrians,

*A reference to an 1831 request from the European Powers that the Pope institute administrative reforms within his territories.

creates diplomatic complications and troubles the European equilibrium?

We believe this is possible, but only by separating that part of the State from Rome, at least administratively. Thus there could be formed out of the Legations an Apostolic Principality under the high suzerainty of the Pope, but ruled by its own laws, having its own courts, finances, and army. We believe that by attaching this new organism as closely as possible to the traditions of the Napoleonic regime, a very considerable moral effect would immediately be obtained, and a great step toward calming the population would have been made.

Without flattering ourselves that a contrivance of this kind could last forever, we are nonetheless of the opinion that it could for a long time suffice for the purpose for which it is proposed: to pacify these provinces and satisfy the legitimate needs of the people. By that very means it would secure the temporal Government of the Holy See, without the necessity of permanent foreign occupation. It would have the further advantage of giving the allied Powers a great and beneficent influence in the heart of Italy.

We shall summarily indicate the substantive points of the plan, along with the means of carrying it out.

1) The provinces of the Roman State situated between the Po, the Adriatic, and the Apennines (from the province of Ancona to the province of Ferrara), while remaining under the high suzerainty of the Pope, would be completely secularized and organized in administrative, judicial, military, and financial respects in a manner quite separate and independent from the rest of the State.

Meanwhile diplomatic and religious affairs would remain the exclusive domain of the Court of Rome.

2) The territorial and administrative organization of this Apostolic Principality would be made in conformity to that which existed under the reign of Napoleon I until 1814. The Napoleonic Code would be promulgated there, except for necessary modifications in the sections which bear on the relations between Church and State.

3) A lay pontifical surrogate would govern these provinces, with ministers and a Council of State. The position of the Surrogate named by the Pope would be guaranteed for the duration of his term, which would have to be at least ten years. The Ministers, Councillors of State, and all functionaries without exception would be named by the Pontifical Surrogate. Their legislative and executive power could never be extended to religious matters, nor to mixed matters, which would

be defined in advance, nor finally to anything which had to do with international political relations.

4) These provinces would contribute in just proportion to the maintenance of the Court of Rome, and to the service of the present public debt.

5) An indigenous force would immediately be organized by means of military conscription.

6) Besides the communal and provincial Councils, there would be a general council to examine and approve the budget.

Now when one considers the means of execution, it is seen that they present fewer difficulties than one would be inclined to think at first glance.

In the first place, the idea of administrative separation of the Legations is not new at Rome. It has been put forward several times in diplomacy, and even preached by several members of the Sacred College, though within more restricted limits than would be necessary to make it a serious and durable work.

The irrevocable will of the Powers and their resolve to bring an end without delay to foreign occupation would be the two motives which would bring the Court of Rome to accept this plan, which at bottom respects its temporal power and leaves the present organization intact at the center and in the greater part of its Estates.

But once the principle is admitted, the execution of the project must be confided to a high Commissioner named by the Powers. It is quite clear that if that task were left to the Pontifical Government, it would find in its traditional system ways of never completing the job and of completely subverting the spirit of the new institutions. Now, there is no hiding the fact that if the foreign occupation were to end, without the reforms being honestly carried out, and without the establishment of a public power, there would be every reason to fear the prompt renewal of troubles and political agitations, soon followed by the return of the Austrian armies. Such a development would be so much the more regrettable in that the effect would appear to condemn in advance any effort at amelioration.

Therefore it is only under the conditions above enunciated that we contemplate the cessation of the foreign occupation, which could take place as follows:

The Pontifical government now has two Swiss regiments and two indigenous regiments, totalling about eight thousand men. This force is sufficient for the maintenance of order in Rome and in the provinces which are not included in the proposed administrative separation.

The new indigenous force, to be organized by means of conscription in the secularized Provinces, would assure tranquillity there.

The French could leave Rome, and the Austrians the Legations. Meanwhile the French troops, on their way home by land, would in passage have to stay temporarily in the detached provinces. They would remain there for a time which would be fixed in advance and which would be strictly necessary for the formation of the new indigenous force, which would be organized with their help.

Congress of Paris

Protocol No. XXII—Session 8 April, 1856
Present: The Plenipotentiaries of Austria, France, Great Britain, Prussia, Russia, Sardinia, and Turkey.

COUNT WALEWSKI said that it would be desirable for the plenipotentiaries, before separating, to exchange ideas on different subjects which demand solution, which it would be useful to consider so as to avoid new complications. Although the Congress was assembled especially to settle the Eastern Question, it could, according to the Chief Plenipotentiary of France, be reproached for not having profited by the circumstance that brings together Representatives of the principal European Powers by elucidating certain questions, posing certain principles, expressing intentions, and in sum making certain declarations with the constant and single goal of assuring, for the future, the world's repose, while dissipating the clouds already visible on the political horizon before they become menacing. . . .

[After a brief résumé of the situation of Greece, Walewski passes to the situation of Italy.]

The Chief Plenipotentiary of France then recalled that the Pontifical Estates were also in an abnormal situation; that the necessity of not letting the country be delivered over to anarchy had determined France, as well as Austria, to respond to the request of the Holy See by occupying Rome with her troops, whilst Austrian Troops occupied the Legations.

He declared that France had had a double motive in deferring without hesitation to the request of the Holy See: as a Catholic Power

Valsecchi, ed. *L'unificazione italiana*, pp. 206–17.

and as a European Power. The title of eldest Son of the Church, in which the French Sovereign glories, imposes on the Emperor the duty of lending aid and support to the sovereign Pontiff; and the tranquillity of the Roman States and that of all Italy immediately touches the maintenance of the European social order, which it is a matter not only of France's special interest to maintain by all the means in its power. But on the other hand, there is no denying that there is something abnormal in the situation of a Power which to maintain itself needs the support of foreign troops.

Count Walewski did not hesitate to declare, and he hoped that Count Buol would associate himself with this declaration, that not only is France ready to retire its troops, but that it eagerly desires to recall them as soon as that can be done without disturbing the tranquillity of the country and the authority of the Pontifical Government, in whose prosperity his August Sovereign the Emperor takes so lively an interest.

The chief Plenipotentiary of France noted how desirable it was, for the European equilibrium, for the Roman Government to become strongly enough consolidated so that the French and Austrian troops could evacuate the Pontifical Estates without inconvenience, and he believed that an express statement in this sense could not be without usefulness. He did not doubt, in any case, that the assurances given by France and Austria respecting their true intentions in this regard would exercise a happy influence.

Pursuing the same line of thought, Count Walewski asked whether it was not to be hoped that certain Governments of the Italian Peninsula, by acts of well-conceived clemency and by rallying the support of spirits which are misguided but not perverted, might put an end to a system which leads in a direction quite contrary to what is intended, a system which instead of reaching the enemies of the public order has the effect of weakening governments and creating partisans of demagoguery. In his opinion it would be a signal service to the Government of the Two Sicilies, as well as to the cause of order in the Italian Peninsula, to enlighten that Government as to the false path it has taken. He thought that admonitions conceived in this sense and issuing from the Powers represented at the Congress would be the better received by the Neapolitan Government inasmuch as the latter could not doubt the motives which had dictated them.

[Walewski then passed to the excesses of the Belgian press; he invited the Congress to lay the bases for a uniform maritime law in case of

war. Then CLARENDON began to speak; and after a few words on the
situation in Greece, continued as follows:]

The chief Plenipotentiary of Great Britain recalled that the Treaty
of 30 March opened a new era; that just as the Emperor had said to
the Congress when he received them after the signature of the Treaty,
it was to be an era of peace; but that to be consistent, nothing should
be neglected to make that peace solid and durable; that, representing
the principal Powers in Europe, the Congress would be derelict of its
duty if it should consecrate, by breaking up without saying anything
about them, certain situations prejudicial to the political equilibrium,
situations which are far from safeguarding the peace, in one of the
most significant countries of Europe.

"We have just provided," continued Count Clarendon, "for the
evacuation of different territories occupied by foreign armies in time
of war; we have just solemnly engaged to effectuate that evacuation
without the briefest delay; why should we not take up the question of
occupations which occurred before the war; why abstain from seeking
out means of putting an end to them?"

The chief Plenipotentiary of Great Britain did not believe it useful
to inquire into the causes that had brought foreign armies to several
places in Italy, but he thought that even admitting that these had been
legitimate causes, it was nonetheless true, he said, that the outcome
was an abnormal, irregular situation, which could only be justified by
extreme necessity, which ought to cease as soon as the necessity was
no longer felt overwhelming; and that, meanwhile, if no efforts were
made to terminate this necessity, it would continue to exist; and that
if those concerned were content to rely on armed force instead of
seeking to remedy the reasonable causes for discontent, they were
certain to make permanent a system hardly honorable to the governments and regrettable for the people. He thought that the administration of the Roman States had demonstrable disadvantages which could
give birth to dangers which the Congress had the right to try to efface,
that to neglect them would run the risk of working in favor of the
revolution which all governments condemned and wished to prevent.
The problem which urgently needed solution consisted in combining,
he thought, the withdrawal of foreign troops with the maintenance of
tranquillity; and the solution resided in the organization of an administration which, by reestablishing confidence, would render the government independent of foreign support; and as foreign support never
succeeds in maintaining a government to which public sentiment is
hostile, the result would be, in his opinion, a role which neither France

nor Austria would like for their armies. For the well-being of the Pontifical States, as well as in the interest of the sovereign authority of the Pope, it would be useful, according to him, to recommend the secularization of the government and the organization of an administrative system in harmony with the spirit of the century, whose goal would be the good of the people. He admitted that this reform would present certain difficulties at Rome itself, at this time, but he thought that it could easily be accomplished in the Legations.

The chief Plenipotentiary of Great Britain pointed out that for eight years Bologna has been in a state of siege, and that the countryside has been tormented by brigandage: one could hope, he thought, that by constituting in that part of the Roman States a regime which was both lay and separate, and by organizing a national armed force there, security and confidence could rapidly be restored and the Austrian troops could shortly retire without any danger of the return of new agitation; this was at least an experiment which in his mind ought to be made, and this proposal, offered as a remedy to undeniable evils, ought to be submitted by the Congress for the serious consideration of the Pope.

In the matter of the Neapolitan Government, the chief Plenipotentiary of Great Britain desired to follow the example given him by Count Walewski, passing over in silence the acts which have had such vexatious repercussions. In his view one must undoubtedly recognize in principle that no Government has the right to interfere in the internal affairs of other States; but he believed that there were cases which made exceptions to that rule correct and even a duty. The Neapolitan Government seemed to him to have conferred that right and imposed that duty on Europe; and since the Governments represented at the Congress all wished, in the same degree, to sustain the monarchic principle and prevent revolution, one must raise his voice against a system which maintains revolutionary ferment among the masses instead of seeking to pacify it. "We do not," he said, "want the peace to be troubled; and there can be no peace without justice; therefore we must apprise the King of Naples of the desire of the Congress for an amelioration of his system of government, a desire which cannot remain silent, and must ask of him an amnesty in favor of persons who have been convicted or held without trial for political offences."

[Clarendon then discussed the observations of Walewski regarding the Belgian press and maritime law in case of war. The Russian delegate,

Orloff, declared that he was unable to participate in discussions for which there was no provision in his instructions. Then Austrian Foreign Minister BUOL spoke:]

Count Buol was gratified to see that the Governments of France and England were disposed to end the occupation of Greece as promptly as possible. He gave assurances that Austria most sincerely desired the prosperity of that Kingdom, and similarly desired, as did France, that all the countries of Europe might enjoy their political independence and full prosperity under the protection of public law. He had no doubt that one of the essential conditions for so desirable a state of affairs was legislation so contrived as to prevent or repress the excesses of the press which Count Walewski had rightly condemned in speaking of a neighboring State, and whose repression must be considered a European necessity. He hoped that in every continental State where the press raised the same dangers the Governments would find legislative means to contain them within reasonable limits, and thus guard the peace from new international complications.

[He could make no pronunciations on the question of maritime law, for want of instructions.]

But here, he said, the task must end. He found it impossible, in fact, to discuss the internal situations of independent States which were not represented at the Congress. The Plenipotentiaries had received no other mandate than that of treating the affairs of the Levant, and had not been called together to give independent Sovereigns their views on the internal organizations of their countries; the full powers lodged in the acts of the Congress bear witness to that. The instructions of the Austrian Plenipotentiaries, in any case, had defined the mission confided to them, so that they were not permitted to take part in any discussion for which their instructions did not provide.

For the same reasons, Count Buol felt obliged to abstain from getting involved in the order of ideas injected by the chief Plenipotentiary of Great Britain, or to give explanations for the duration of the occupation of the Roman States by Austrian troops, while yet he associated himself completely with the words pronounced by the chief Plenipotentiary of France on that subject.

COUNT WALEWSKI pointed out that it was not a matter of making specific resolutions, nor undertaking obligations, nor least of all of mixing directly in the internal affairs of Governments represented or not represented at the Congress, but only of consolidating and completing the peace by dealing in advance with new complications which could arise, whether from the indefinite or unjustified prolongation of certain foreign occupations, or from a system of inappropriate and impolitic rigor, or from a disturbing license contrary to international obligations.

BARON HÜBNER answered that the Plenipotentiaries of Austria were authorized neither to give any assurances nor express any views. The reduction in number of the Austrian army in the Legations was a sufficient indication, according to him, of the intention of the Imperial Cabinet to recall its troops whenever such a measure may be deemed opportune.

[The Prussian delegate MANTEUFFEL pronounced himself in favor of a solution of the problem of maritime law, and then called the attention of the Congress to the situation in Neufchâtel, which represented a particular interest for Prussia.]

As for the actions judged useful in what concerned the state of affairs in the Kingdom of the Two Sicilies, Baron Manteuffel made the observation that such action could create several inconveniences. He said it would be wise to ask whether views of the kind which had been proposed would not arouse in that country a spirit of opposition and of revolutionary activity, instead of fulfilling the purposes which with obvious good will had been intended. He did not feel obliged to get into an examination of the present state of affairs in the Pontifical States; he limited himself to expressing the desire that it might be possible to place that Government in circumstances which would thereafter render superfluous any occupation by foreign troops. Baron Manteuffel concluded by declaring that the Prussian Cabinet perfectly recognized the evil influence which the subversive press exercised on all regular order, and the dangers it sowed with its preachings of regicide and revolt; he added that Prussia would willingly participate in an examination of what measures might be judged appropriate for putting an end to these plots.

COUNT CAVOUR had no intention of contesting the right of every Plenipotentiary to abstain from the discussion of any question not provided for in his instructions; yet it was, he thought, of the highest importance that the opinions manifested by certain Powers concerning the occupation of the Roman States be placed on the record.

The chief Plenipotentiary of Sardinia declared that the occupation of the Roman States by Austrian troops was assuming, every day more and more, a permanent character; that it had lasted seven years, and that meanwhile there had been no evidence for supposing that it would end in the near or distant future; that the causes that had brought it about still existed; that the condition of the occupied countries had certainly not been improved, and that to be convinced of this it sufficed to observe that Austria found it necessary to maintain the state of siege in Bologna in all its rigor, even though it dated back to the very time the occupation began. He pointed out that the presence of Austrian troops in the Legations and in the Duchy of Parma upset the political equilibrium of Italy, and constituted, for Sardinia, a genuine danger. The Sardinian Plenipotentiaries, he said, thus believed it their duty to call the attention of Europe to so abnormal a state of affairs as that resulting from the indefinite occupation of a large part of Italy by Austrian troops.

As for the question of Naples, Count Cavour entirely shared the opinions enunciated by Count Walewski and by Count Clarendon, and he thought that it was of the highest importance to suggest moderations which by calming passions would render less difficult the regular progress of things in the other States of the Peninsula.

BARON HÜBNER said, for his part, that the chief Plenipotentiary of Sardinia had spoken entirely of the Austrian occupation, and kept his silence on that of France; that these two occupations, however, had come about for the same reasons; that the argument which Count Cavour had based on the permanence of the state of siege in Bologna was unadmissible; that if exceptional measures were still necessary in that city while it has long ceased to exist in Rome and Ancona, then that seemed to prove all the more that the attitudes of the populations of Rome and Ancona were more satisfactory than those of the city of Bologna. He recalled that it was not only the Roman States in Italy that were occupied by foreign troops; that the communes of Mentone and Roquebrune, in the Principality of Monaco, have been occupied by Sardinia for eight years; and that the only difference there was between these two occupations was that the Austrians and the French had been called for by the countries' Sovereigns, whereas the Sardinian troops had entered the Principality of Monaco contrary to its wishes, and that they maintained themselves there despite the protests of the country's Sovereign.

In answer to Count Hübner, COUNT CAVOUR said that he was as anxious to see the end of the French occupation as he was the Austrian, but he could not help considering the one far more dangerous than the other for independent States of Italy. He added that a weak army corps, at a great distance from France, menaced nobody, whilst it was very disturbing to see Austria, based on Ferrara and on Piacenza (whose fortifications it is building up in contradiction to the spirit if not the letter of the Treaties of Vienna), extending its reach along the Adriatic clear to Ancona.

As for Monaco, Count Cavour declared that Sardinia was ready to withdraw the fifty men who occupied Mentone whenever the Prince was in a position to reenter that country without exposing himself to very great dangers. For the rest, he did not think that Sardinia could be accused of having contributed to the overthrow of the old Government so as to occupy these States since the Prince had been able to preserve his authority only in that one Monacan town which Sardinia had occupied in 1848, by virtue of treaties.

. . .

COUNT WALEWSKI was gratified to have engaged the Plenipotentiaries in an exchange of their views on the questions discussed. He had supposed that it might have been possible, and perhaps useful, to make more complete pronouncements on certain of the subjects which had drawn the attention of the Congress. But such as it was, he said, the exchange of ideas that had taken place was not without usefulness.

The Chief Plenipotentiary of France stated these conclusions:

1) That no one contested the need for deep concern for the amelioration of the Greek situation, and that the three protector Courts had recognized the importance of mutual consultations in that regard;

2) That the Plenipotentiaries of Austria had associated themselves with the wish expressed by the Plenipotentiaries of France to see the Pontifical Estates evacuated by French and Austrian troops as soon as that could be done without risk to the tranquillity of the country and the consolidation of the authority of the Holy See;

3) That the majority of the Plenipotentiaries had not contested the efficacy which measures of clemency might have if taken in an appropriate manner by the Governments of the Italian Peninsula and especially that of the Two Sicilies;

4) That all the Plenipotentiaries, including those who reserved the principle of the liberty of the press, did not hesitate strongly to stigmatize the excesses which the Belgian journals allow themselves with impunity, recognizing the need of remedying the real inconveniences which result from the unbridled license of which so great abuse is made in Belgium;

That finally the reception given by all the Plenipotentiaries to the idea of concluding their labors with a declaration of principle on the matter of maritime law permitted the hope that by the next session they would have received from their respective governments authorization to adhere to an act which, crowning the work of the Congress of Paris, would mark progress worthy of our times.

Cavour to Urbano Rattazzi, Interior Minister at Turin

Dear Colleague,   Paris, 12 April 1856
I am sending a courier to Chambéry, so I can write you without being guarded.

From your dispatch of yesterday I see you share my opinion on the chance to accept the resignation of Cibrario. I tell you frankly that I provoked it on purpose with a deliberately insulting letter. This means seemed to me more appropriate than to say to him on my return: "Go take a steamboat to St. Moritz."

I come now to the second part of my letter, and the most important.

Convinced that the impotence of diplomacy and of the Congress will produce serious consequences in Italy and will place Piedmont in a difficult and dangerous position, I have thought it right to see if there were not a way of arriving at a satisfactory solution by heroic means: by arms. And accordingly yesterday afternoon I had the following conversation with Lord Clarendon:

"My lord: what has happened at the Congress has proved two things: 1st, that Austria is determined to persist in her system of oppression and violence towards Italy; 2d, that the efforts of diplomacy are incapable of modifying her system. For Piedmont this brings consequences which are overly vexatious. Faced by the exasperation of the parties on the one hand and the arrogance of Austria on the other, there are only two courses she can take: either reconcile herself with Austria and the Pope, or prepare herself to declare war on Austria in the very near future. If the first course were preferable, I should upon my return to Turin counsel the King to appeal to the power of the friends of Austria and the Pope. If on the contrary the second hypothesis is the better one, my friends and I are not afraid to prepare ourselves for a terrible war, a war to the death, 'the war to the knife,' *la guerre jusqu'avec les couteaux*." Here I stopped. Lord Clarendon, showing neither surprise nor disapproval, then said: "I think you are right; your position is becoming quite difficult; I think a clash is becoming inevitable, but the time to speak of it formally has not come."

Cavour, *Lettere*, II (1st ed.), 216–20.

I answered: "I have given you proofs of my moderation and my prudence; I think that in politics it is wise to be very reserved in words and very decisive when it comes to action. There are situations where there is less danger in a course of audacity than in too much prudence. With La Marmora I am persuaded that we are in a condition to begin the war, and however briefly it lasts, you will be forced to assist us." Lord Clarendon answered with great animation: "Oh! certainly, if you are in difficulty you can count on us, and you will see with what energy we come to your aid."

After that I did not press the discussion further and limited myself to friendly and sympathetic words toward Lord Clarendon and England. You will judge the importance of these words spoken by a minister who is famed for his reserve and his prudence.

England, disliking the peace, would I am sure see with pleasure an opportunity arise for a new war, a war as popular as one which had the liberation of Italy as its goal would be. Why then should we not profit from this situation and make a supreme effort to fulfill the destiny of the House of Savoy and of our country?

But since these are questions of life or death, it is necessary to proceed very cautiously; it is for that reason that I think it opportune to go to London to talk with Palmerston and the other heads of the government. If they share Clarendon's point of view, we shall have to prepare quietly, float a loan of 30,000,000, upon La Marmora's return give Austria an ultimatum which she cannot accept, and commence the war.

The Emperor could not be against this war; at the bottom of his heart he wishes it. He would be certain to help us, if he saw England decide to enter the lists.

Also I shall present the Emperor with an argument analogous to the one I directed to Lord Clarendon. The last conversations I had with him and his ministers were of a kind to prepare the way for a warlike declaration. The only obstacle I foresee is the *Pope*. What will he do in the event of an Italian war?

I hope that after you have read this letter you will not think me the victim of fever of the brain, or fallen into a state of mental intoxication. Quite on the contrary, I am in a state of perfect intellectual health; and I have never felt myself more calm. I have even acquired a great reputation for moderation. Clarendon told me so repeatedly; Prince Napoleon accused me of lack of energy; and even Walewski praised my restraint. But I am truly persuaded that we could adopt a course of audacity with a great probability of success.

You can be quite sure I shall undertake no commitment, immediate or remote; I shall collect the facts, and when I return the King and my colleagues will decide what to do.

Today again there was no conference. The minutes of the stormy session of Tuesday are not ready. Lord Clarendon is quite prepared to recommence the hassle with Buol, but perhaps the latter will try to avoid it by making no observations on the minutes. Meanwhile Clarendon has sent Lord Cowley to Hübner to tell him that England would be quite irritated by the words of the Austrian Minister when she learned of them.

I have seen the martyr*; he manifested complete approval of my conduct at the Congress. He gave me a certificate as super-Italian [*mi ha dato una patente d'Italianissimo*], and declared himself an ardent supporter of our policy. The poor man was moved and dissolved to the point of shedding abundant tears.

I have at this moment received your letter of the 10th instant. I see with regret that I have given too heavy a dose to poor Cibrario; give him my sincere regrets. I shall write him not so as to depress him, but to placate him.

Today I dine *monstre* with the Emperor. It will be difficult for me to talk with him; I shall ask him the favor of a private audience.

I beg you to keep the political part of this letter to yourself alone. Your aff.

[Excerpts from Cavour's dispatches to Rattazzi of 12 and 14 April 1856, as reproduced above and below, were leaked to the press in January, 1862, provoking the following statement from Clarendon in the House of Lords on 17 February, 1862. (Hansard, *Parliamentary Debates*, CLXV, 347–51.)]

*The allusion is unclear; probably Marquis Giorgio Pallavicino.

The Earl of Clarendon and Count Cavour

Personal Explanations

The Earl of CLARENDON: My Lords, although I am afraid it is somewhat late, I hope your Lordships will allow me to trespass on your attention for a short time on a subject which, though personal to myself, is yet of great public importance, and which I regret that, owing to my unavoidable absence, I have not been able sooner to bring under the notice of the House. Your Lordships have probably read some

letters of the late Count Cavour which have recently been published
in the newspapers; and I can assure you that if any of you in reading
those letters have experienced any surprise, it could not have equalled
my own. I know not whether those letters are genuine or not, or into
what hands they have fallen, nor do I know by whom or with what
objects they have been published. With that I have nothing to do. But
in those letters certain sayings are attributed to me with respect to
which your Lordships and the public have a right to expect some explanation, because at the time those letters purport to have been
written, and the conversations are said to have taken place, I had the
honour to be Her Majesty's Secretary for Foreign Affairs and the first
British Plenipotentiary at the Congress of Paris. In that capacity I
think it was my duty to have expressed no opinion, and to have given
no advice, without the sanction of the Government of which I formed
a part, or which I did not think would be in accordance with the
views of the Government. I am therefore, prepared to take upon
myself the entire responsibility of everything which I did say, but I
cannot be made responsible for things attributed to me which I did
not say. In offering the explanation, however, which you have a right
to expect from me, I find myself in a two-fold difficulty—first, that of
separating what is true from what is incorrect in Count Cavour's
letters; and, secondly, the pain and repugnance I feel in contradicting
the late Count Cavour. If he had been alive, it would have been
comparatively easy for me to have corrected any inaccuracy in his
correspondence, and to have accompanied it with such explanation
as might be necessary, and the publication of his letters, if authorized
by him, would have justified. But as Count Cavour is, unfortunately,
no more, I will say nothing beyond what I think strictly necessary for
clearing myself from the absurdity—I may say the palpable absurdity
—with which, although not directly, yet by implication I am charged.
It amounts to this, that I encouraged Count Cavour to pick a quarrel
with Austria—in fact, to declare war against her, by an assurance that
in such a course of policy Piedmont would have the material support
of England. There is much that is true in Count Cavour's letters, and
I say so with reference to his account of what fell from him in the
Congress when Italian affairs were discussed. From the first meeting
of the Congress Count Cavour had constantly urged upon the British
and French Plenipotentiaries the necessity of bringing before it the
affairs of Italy. We had remarked to him that the Congress was assembled for the purpose of negotiating a treaty of peace with Russia;
that to introduce any other subject would be irrelevant and even im-

possible; in fact, that even after the treaty of peace was concluded it might meet with serious obstacles, because the other Plenipotentiaries might protest, as they did, against the introduction of any other subjects; they might declare their powers limited to the matters for which the Congress was assembled, and that their instructions would not permit them to enter into the subject. Nevertheless, when the treaty was signed, the French and English Plenipotentiaries did bring on a discussion of Italian affairs, and Count Cavour's account of what I said with respect to the Neapolitan and Papal Government is perfectly correct. I neither regret, nor do I wish to retract, one word of what I said, because I felt, as every other Englishman did, the profoundest sympathy for the misgoverned Italians, and an ardent desire to see an alleviation of that system of oppression and tyranny which obtained from one end of the Peninsula to the other, and I thought the Congress in which the principal Powers of Europe were represented was a fitting place for the expression of those opinions. But the result of a long and angry discussion was only that the Austrian Plenipotentiaries agreed with the French Plenipotentiaries that the Pontifical States should be evacuated by the French and Austrian troops as soon as it could be effected without danger to the tranquillity of the country and the consolidation of the authority of the Roman See, and further that most of the Plenipotentiaries did not question the good effect might arise from measures of clemency [sic]. This meagre result not only did not satisfy Count Cavour, but it greatly disappointed him. With his views, looking as the matter both as an Italian and a Piedmontese, his irritation was not unnatural, for his whole heart and soul were set on freeing the North of Italy from the domination of Austria. He did not conceal his irritation from me. He constantly told me that he could not present himself before the Parliament of Turin unless he proved that he had produced some effect by his presence at the Congress. I was in the habit of seeing him daily, and I willingly listened to him upon the only subject upon which he would converse, and on which he was always earnest and eloquent. But those conversations never appeared to me to be of a character sufficiently practical to make it necessary to report them to Her Majesty's Government. Consequently there is no record of them, though I have searched, nor of those repeated assurances which I gave him that our invariable principle was to maintain our treaty engagements, and to be guided by the principles of international law. At the same time, I did not disguise from him, what he knew and what everybody else knew, that our object at that time was to free Italy from foreign occupation, and to reform the Papal and

Neapolitan Governments, and that towards that end the moral support
of England would be always forthcoming. Out of the numerous conversations that I had with Count Cavour, the only one I can remember
which could—I will not say justify—but give rise to his assertion that
I said "If you are in a strait, we shall come to your assistance," had
reference, not to a war by Piedmont against Austria, but to an invasion
of Piedmont by Austria, which was a fixed idea in Count Cavour's
mind. He always thought that the free institutions of Piedmont—her
freedom of the press and freedom of debate—even her very prosperity
under such a system, would always make her an intolerable neighbour
to Austria. I assured Count Cavour that my conversations with Count
Buol, though certainly not very satisfactory in general with respect to
Italy, entirely confirmed my impression that no such apprehension
need be entertained by him; and, upon Count Cavour asking me what
course we should take in such an eventuality, I remember saying, "If
you ask my opinion, I should say that if Austria invaded Piedmont
for the purpose of suppressing free institutions there, you would have
a practical proof of the feeling of the Parliament and people of England on the subject." Of course I cannot pledge myself to the exact
words, but I do feel quite sure about the spirit and scope of my
answer. It was a personal opinion given upon an hypothetical case,
to which I did not then attach any importance, nor did I know that
Count Cavour attached any importance to it until I read these letters,
in which he says—

> England, grieved at peace, would with pleasure see an op-
> portunity for a new war, which would be popular because it
> would be a war for the liberation of Italy.

He then goes on to say—

> If they (Lord Palmerston and his Government) share
> Clarendon's views, we must make secret preparations, contract
> the loan for 30,000,000f., and, upon Della Marmora's return,
> offer to Austria an *ultimatum* which it will be impossible for
> her to accept, and open hostilities.

In another letter Count Cavour says—

> Talking with him (Lord Clarendon) as to the means of
> acting morally and even materially upon Austria, I said to him,
> 'Send your troops upon men-of-war to Spezzia, and leave your
> fleet there.' And his answer was, "The idea is excellent."

Now, my Lords, upon my honour I have not the slightest recollection
of any such conversation, and, therefore, I cannot deny it; but I
think so wild a notion cannot have been seriously entertained even
by Count Cavour himself. Bearing in mind the enthusiasm of Count
Cavour in favour of his own views, and his ardent desire to make
known his activity in the Congress of Paris, and to keep up the spirits
of his friends at Turin, I for one—though I have the most reason
to complain—can make allowance for these imaginative reports of
private conversations contained in letters to his friends and colleagues,
but which were evidently not intended for publication. But that I, as
one of Her Majesty's Secretaries of State, without any communication
from my colleagues, and contrary to the dictates of common sense,
knowing that the French Emperor at that time had not the slightest
thought or intention of making war against Austria, that he did not
then even require her to withdraw her troops from the Legations,
until he had withdrawn his own troops from Rome—that I, under
such circumstances, should, even in the most indirect manner, have
recommended a country to which he heartily wished well to commit
such a suicidal act as going to war with Austria, with her large army
under Radetzky, and having the support of Tuscany, Parma, Modena,
and Naples—and that, without the shadow of authority for doing so,
I should have given any pledge for the support of England in such
a policy as would have imbroiled us in war with half Europe—is an
absurdity so palpable that I hope your Lordships will think it carries
with it its own refutation, without my laying claim to that character
for extreme reserve and discretion for which Count Cavour rather
paradoxically on that occasion informed his correspondent I was
notorious.

Cavour to Urbano Rattazzi at Turin

Dear Colleague,   Paris, 14 April 1856
At dinner yesterday with Count Clarendon and Prince Napoleon, I
had a long conversation with these two personages. Both said that on
the day before they had had a long discussion with the Emperor on
the Italian question, in which they had told him that the conduct of
Austria placed Piedmont in so difficult a position that it was necessary
to help her get out of it. Lord Clarendon said frankly that Piedmont
could be led to declare war on Austria, and in that case it would be

Cavour, *Lettere*, II (1st ed.), 223–24.

necessary to take her side. The Emperor seemed quite impressed, became thoughtful, and expressed a desire to confer with me.

I hope to convince him of the absolute impossibility of remaining in the situation created by Austria's obstinate and provocative conduct. Knowing his sympathy for Italy and for us, recognizing the need to act, he will do so with the resolution and firmness which so distinguish him. If the English government shares the sentiments of Lord Clarendon, we shall not lack the support of Great Britain. When the latter minister met Buol at the Emperor's he said to him: "You are throwing down the gauntlet to liberal Europe; be aware that it may be picked up, and that there are powers which, though they have signed the peace, are ready and willing to recommence war." When he discussed with me ways of putting moral and material pressure on Austria, I said to him: send your soldiers on warships to La Spezia, and leave a fleet of yours there. He answered promptly: "a perfect idea." Prince Napoleon does as much as he can for us. He openly shows his antipathy for Austria; at yesterday's dinner all the plenipotentiaries were invited except the Germans. When he was asked the reason for this exclusion he answered: *"Because I do not like them, and I have no reason to hide my dislike."*

The Congress meets today and perhaps again on Wednesday. Thursday I shall leave for London, where I shall stop as briefly as possible. But perhaps on the way back I shall have to stop to see the Emperor. After careful consideration, I think you can without inconvenience show my letters to Durando, in whose coolness, firmness, and good sense I have much confidence.

Believe me your aff. friend.

Note on Italian Affairs Submitted by the Sardinian Plenipotentiaries to Lord Clarendon, 16 April 1856

The undersigned, Plenipotentiaries of H. M. the King of Sardinia, fully confident of the just sentiments of the Governments of France and of England, and of the friendship they profess for Piedmont, have not ceased to hope since the opening of the Conferences that the Congress of Paris would not break up before giving serious consideration to the state of Italy, and without having consulted on the means to remedy it, by reestablishing the political equilibrium which is dis-

Valsecchi, ed. *L'unificazione italiana*, pp. 221–26.

turbed by the occupation of a large portion of the provinces of the Peninsula by foreign troops. Sure of the support of their allies, they were loath to believe that any other power, after having shown so lively and generous an interest in the fate of the Eastern Christians belonging to the Greek and Slavic races, would refuse to consider peoples of Latin race who are more unfortunate still, because, on account of the higher degree of civilization they have attained, they feel the consequences of bad government more sharply. This hope has been deceived.

Despite the good will of France and England, despite well-meant efforts, the persistence of Austria in insisting that the discussions of the Congress remain strictly circumscribed within the sphere of questions drafted before we met is the reason why this Assembly, with all the eyes of Europe turned upon it, is going to dissolve, not only without having brought the slightest softening of the evils of Italy, but without having let a glimmer of hope for the future shine beyond the Alps, which might calm troubled spirits and make them bear the present with *resignation*.

The special position occupied by Austria in the Congress perhaps made this deplorable result inevitable. The undersigned are forced to recognize this. However, without addressing the slightest reproach to their allies, they believe it their duty to call their serious attention to the evil consequences which can result for Europe, for Italy, and especially for Sardinia.

It would be superfluous to draw here an exact description of Italy. What has been happening in these countries for many years is too notorious. The system of repression and of violent reaction inaugurated in 1848 and 1849, which perhaps was justified at the beginning by the revolutionary troubles which had just been put down, continues without the slightest softening; one can even say that with certain exceptions it is carried out with redoubled vigor. Never have the jails and prisons been more filled with men condemned for political reasons; never has the number of outlaws been greater; never have the police been more annoying, nor the state of siege more vigorously applied. What is happening at Parma proves it only too well.

Such governmental methods must necessarily keep the population in a state of constant irritation and revolutionary fermentation. Such has been the state of Italy for seven years.

Nevertheless in recent times the popular agitation seemed to be growing calmer. When the Italians saw one of the national Princes allied with the great Western Powers in quest of the triumph of the principles of right and of justice, and the amelioration of the lot of their coreligionists of the East, they conceived the hope that peace would not be made without an alleviation of their troubles. This hope made them calm and resigned. But as soon as they recognized the negative results of the Congress of Paris; as soon as they knew that Austria, despite the good offices and the well-meant intervention of France and England, refused any discussion of the matter; that she was not even willing to consider means of remedying so sorry a state of affairs—then there could be no doubt that their dormant antagonism would revive more violent than ever. Convinced that nothing more could be expected from diplomacy or from the efforts of the Powers who had taken an interest in their lot, they will pour back into the ranks of the revolutionary and subversive party with Mediterranean ardor, and Italy will again become a hot-bed of conspiracy and disorder, which redoubled severity may perhaps suppress, but which the slightest European commotion will make break out in the most violent manner. A state of things as unpleasant as this, if it is important enough to attract the attention of the Governments of France and of England, who are interested both in the maintenance of order and the regular development of civilization, must naturally preoccupy the Government of the King of Sardinia in the highest degree. The rise of revolutionary passions in all the countries that surround Piedmont, caused by things of a kind to arouse a lively popular sympathy, exposes it to excessively grave dangers, which could compromise that firm and moderate policy which has had such happy domestic results and has brought Piedmont the sympathy and esteem of enlightened Europe.

But that is not the only danger that menaces Sardinia. Still a greater one is the consequence of the methods employed by Austria to repress revolutionary ferment in Italy. Summoned by the Sovereigns of the petty States of Italy, who were incapable of containing the discontent of their subjects, this Power occupies militarily the greatest part of the valley of the Po and of Central Italy, and its influence is felt irresistibly even in those countries where it has no soldiers.

Based on one side on Ferrara and Bologna, its troops spread out to Ancona, so that the Adriatic has become a kind of Austrian lake; on the other side, as mistress of Piacenza, which contrary to the spirit if not the letter of the Vienna Treaties she has worked to transform into a base of the first order, she has a garrison at Parma, and is in position to deploy forces along the whole length of the Sardinian border, from the Po to the summit of the Apennines.

This permanent occupation by Austria of territories which do not belong to her make her absolute mistress of almost all Italy, destroying the equilibrium established by the Vienna Treaty, and is a continual menace to Piedmont.

So to speak encircled everywhere by the Austrians, seeing forces developing quite openly on the eastern frontier belonging to a Power that cannot be animated by friendly feelings toward her, Piedmont is held in a state of constant apprehension, which obliges her to stay armed and to undertake defensive measures too onerous for a fiscal system burdened by the consequences of the events of 1848 and 1849 and by the war in which she has just participated.

The facts which the undersigned have just stated suffice to make clear the dangers of the position in which the King of Sardinia finds himself.

Domestically troubled by the effects of revolutionary passions which are stirred up all around by a system of violent repression and by foreign occupation, menaced by the extension of Austrian power, Piedmont might at any moment be forced by unavoidable necessity to adopt extreme measures, whose consequences it is impossible to calculate.

The undersigned do not doubt that such a state of affairs arouses the concern of the Governments of France and of England, not only because of the sincere amity and real friendship which these Powers profess for the Sovereign who, quite between us, openly declared himself on their side at the moment when success was most uncertain, but above all because it constitutes a true danger for Europe.

Sardinia is the only Italian State which has been able to raise an insuperable barrier to the revolutionary spirit and still remain independent of Austria; it is the sole counterweight to her invading influence.

If Sardinia collapses, drained of strength and abandoned by its allies, if it too were forced to submit to Austrian domination; then the conquest of Italy by that Power would be achieved. And Austria, having obtained without the slightest cost the immense benefit of the liberty of navigation of the Danube and the neutralization of the Black Sea, would acquire the preponderant influence in the East.

That is what France and England cannot wish; that is what they will never permit.

The undersigned are thus convinced that the Cabinets at Paris and at London, when they seriously consider the state of Italy, will take counsel together with Piedmont for ways of applying an effective remedy.

Cavour to Urbano Rattazzi at Turin

Dear Colleague,   Paris, 16 April 1856
I have seen the Emperor; I used on him language analogous to what I used with Clarendon, but a little less vigorous. He received it very well, but suggested that he hoped to bring Austria back to milder ways. He told me how at the dinner on Saturday he had said to Count Buol that he regretted finding himself in direct opposition to the Emperor of Austria on the Italian question; that as a result of this declaration Buol had come to Walewski to assert Austria's desire to please the Emperor in all things; he hinted at having no ally other than France, and that therefore it was necessary to make Austrian policy conform with her desires.

The Emperor seemed satisfied with these protestations of affection, and repeated to me that he would make use of them to get concessions from Austria. I showed my incredulity, insisted on the necessity of taking decisive action, and as a start told him I had prepared a protest which I would give to Walewski on the next day. The Emperor seemed very hesitant. He ended by saying: "Go to London; have a good talk with Palmerston; and stop to see me on your way back." The Emperor must in fact have talked with Buol, because the latter, at the end of the session, came to me and made a thousand protestations of Austria's good intentions toward us; he said they wanted to live in peace, not to attack our institutions, and more such eyewash. I answered him that he had given no proofs of this desire during his stay in Paris, and that I was convinced our relations were worse now than they had been before. It was a long and quite animated conversation; it would take too long to report it in detail; many a truth was exchanged, in an urbane and genteel manner. As we parted he said: "I leave with regrets at seeing our political relations deteriorate; but that does not keep me from hoping that you will retain remembrances as kindly as mine of our personal relations." He pressed my hand affectionately, saying: *"Let me hope* that politically too we shall not always be enemies."

Judging by these words, Buol has been frightened by the manifes-

Cavour, *Lettere*, II (1st ed.), 225–26.

tations of sentiments in our favor, and perhaps also by what the Emperor must have said to him.

Orloff made me a thousand protestations of friendship, agreed with me that the condition of Italy was insupportable, and almost gave me to understand that his government would willingly cooperate in ameliorating it. Also the Prussian spoke critically of Austria. In sum if nothing practical was accomplished, with respect to public opinion the victory was complete.

Buol told me he had made a request that *Espero* be sued because of an old article. It would be good if the journal were condemned; that would make more effective the things I shall have to say about Austria and the other states of Italy in Parliament.

This letter was to have been brought you by Sommeiller, but since I was unable to finish it, I consign it to Signore Nigra,[1] who is returning directly to Turin.

I think it wise to have the treaty of peace printed at the royal printing office, with all the protocols, so as to distribute it to the Chambers, as soon as notice of the exchange of ratifications has arrived in Turin. Please see that Cibrario has that done.

When you write me send your letters to Paris, under seal, care of Villamarina.

Believe me your affectionate friend.

1. Cavour's personal secretary.

Cavour to Michelangelo Castelli, Deputy in Parliament, at Turin

Dear Castelli,   Paris, April 1856

. . . I cannot enter into many particulars, but I assure you I have no complaints to make of the Emperor. France wanted peace; he had to get it and therefore he had to get Austrian concurrence. Hence he could not treat that power as an enemy; rather he was obliged to treat her in some degree as an ally. In such a situation he could not use threats on the Italian question; only exhortations were possible. He applied them, and as it turned out they were in vain. Buol was not to be moved, neither in great nor in small matters. This rigidity, which brings present harm, will bring future advantage to Italy. The Emperor is very irritated about it, and does not hide his irritation.

Cavour, *Lettere*, II (1st ed.), 227–28.

The other evening he said to me: "Austria is unwilling to yield a thing; she is ready to make war before consenting to cede Parma to you, for I cannot make a *casus belli* with her out of that; but be easy; I have a presentiment that the present peace will not last long."

The Emperor proposed to Austria that she take the Danube Principalities and give up Venetia and Lombardy, and in my presence he said to Clarendon: "This is the only reasonable solution in Italian affairs." This is enough to prove to you the Emperor's good intentions and the need not to irritate him with epigrams which can do no good and might do great harm. . . .

Our enemies are sending to Paris every number of journal X which contains such allusions to the Emperor, and every one comes before his eyes. The journal denounces the ministers, denounces me; I lament it not on my own account, but it should leave alone the man who whether you like it or not has the key to politics in his hands.

Believe me, etc.

Cavour to Urbano Rattazzi at Turin

Dear Colleague,   Paris, Thursday, 17 April, 6 p.m.
At the moment of departure for London and of facing the English Channel, which they say is very rough, I write to share with you a long conversation I had with Clarendon, who spent two hours with the Emperor today. When Clarendon had expressed his distress at the futility of efforts made in Italy's favor, the Emperor said to him, "I authorize you to declare to the Parliament that it is my intention to retire my troops from Rome, and to force Austria to do the same," speaking with appropriate full formality. He said Buol had made him the finest promises; and finally he promised to join with England in asking the King of Naples to issue an amnesty in such a way that he cannot refuse; that is, by threatening to send a squadron.

Clarendon said to me that the Emperor seemed to him to be speaking in good faith, and that certainly if Austria did not change or at least modify her system, within a year France and England would make her do it, by force if necessary.

It is certain that the Austrian plenipotentiaries are downcast and discontented. Even they are complaining about Walewski, and make jokes about his incapacity.

The Emperor has made me the gift of a Sèvres porcelain vase of

Cavour, *Lettere*, II (1st ed.), 229–30.

great value. If X . . . finds out about it, poor me; he'll accuse me of having sold Italy out.

I leave you to start for the train.

Love me and believe me your aff. friend.

Cavour to Urbano Rattazzi

Dear Colleague,   London, 20 April 1856

Here I have been in London for almost three days without doing anything important. I found Lord Palmerston in deep mourning over the sudden death of his wife's first son, Lord Cowper, so that none of Azeglio's efforts got anywhere. Nevertheless I saw Lord Palmerston, but couldn't get going on the argument I had to present. He told me that the latest letter from Lord Clarendon contained better news, and that I need not despair. I see very well that there is no chance for serious conversations before Lord Clarendon's arrival.

The Queen invited me to dinner the day after my arrival, was very polite with me, and manifested the warmest sympathy for the affairs of Italy. Even Prince Albert was quite outspoken, even respecting Austria. The Queen invited me repeatedly to stay and see the grand naval review which will take place on Wednesday. I could not refuse, considering the great store the English set by their demonstrations of gigantic power at these affairs. I shall leave then on Thursday evening or Friday morning, quite dissatisfied at having made this trip.

I have already seen many politicians. All declare themselves favorable to our cause. The Tories seem no less certain than the Whigs; the most animated are the zealous Protestant captains of Lord Shaftesbury. If they had the say, England would launch a crusade against Austria.

I shall not write you again from London unless something extraordinary happens.

Believe me your aff. friend.

Cavour, *Lettere*, II (1st ed.), 230–31.

Cavour to Rattazzi

Dear Colleague,   London, 24 April 1856

I send one or two lines to tell you that tomorrow morning at eight I leave for Paris, where I shall arrive in the evening. If I can get an

Cavour, *Lettere*, II (1st ed.), 231–32.

audience by Saturday, I shall start for Turin on Sunday. I intend to stop a few hours in Chambéry to finish up the Aix affair, so I shall not be in Turin before Tuesday evening. . . .

Today I was at the naval review, which was a stupendous success; I think I have never seen such an assemblage of ships. The English showed lively regrets at not being able to use them right away.

I have not been able to see Lord Palmerston, and only today shall I see Clarendon. Instead I have talked with the most influential members of the Opposition, Tories and Radicals. I have found them well-disposed in our favor. Old Lord Lyndhurst, who despite his eighty-three years is still the leading orator in the House of Lords, is all fired up for us. He promised me a most explicit speech. . . .

Believe me with affectionate sentiments your most devoted friend.

IV

THE INTENTIONS

WILLIAM R. THAYER ON CAVOUR AND THE ITALIAN QUESTION

Legitimizing the Revolution

While defending Piedmont from foreign intriguers, bent on robbing her of the prestige he had won for her at the Congress of Paris, Cavour was busied with equally important negotiations with one of the great bodies of Italian patriots that had outlined a new plan for the redemption of Italy. The stability of the little Subalpine Kingdom was now fairly well assured; but Victor Emanuel's subjects numbered only five millions, against twenty other millions calling themselves Italians and parceled out among six detested rulers. How could the non-Piedmontese be brought to work together for a National end?

The first difficulty lay in the choice of a leader. The Party of Revolution, which, after 1849, the Mazzinians dominated, was Republican. When it split up in 1853, its dissident sections still clung to Republicanism, holding very tenaciously Mazzini's doctrine of unity. The groups outside of his influence either professed Unitarianism, or they limited their plans to local or provincial reform. The inveterate Italian sectionalism was tested in the recent revolution, when the wave of national enthusiasm quickly spent itself, leaving behind the old warring elements, amid which feuds as ancient as the days of Guelf and Ghibelline smouldered, and the old dynastic jealousies, and the discredited, terror-stricken princes still lived. And yet, every Italian who could analyze his deepest political sentiments recognized

From William R. Thayer. *Life and Times of Cavour* (2 vols., Boston, 1911), vol. I, pp. 422–41. Copyright 1931 by Houghton Mifflin Company. Reprinted by permission. Footnotes omitted.

that it was the National Spirit which mysteriously impelled him to unite with his brother Italians, no matter what dialect they spoke or what differences had separated their ancestors from his. The hated Austrian might be driven out; the cruel and corrupt governments of Pope and Bourbons might be purged; each province might enjoy the best products of modern civilization: and yet the National longing would still be unrealized. Without that realization no political victory, no social betterment, could satisfy. The Italians had reached the stage where the Spirit of Nationality, become for them the Spirit of Truth and Duty and Desire, exercised upon them such a compulsion as Religion, or Chivalry or Individualism had exercised upon other men in earlier epochs.

Independence and Liberty—two of the requisites of national existence—Piedmont possessed, and she had proved strong enough, in spite of crushing defeats and unceasing dangers, to guard and develop them. Piedmont, however, was not Italy, but the least Italian of all the provinces of Italy. The monarchical tradition bound its people and its sovereign together. Whenever the princes of Savoy cherished expansion to the eastward, they dreamt of aggrandizing Piedmont, not of creating Italy. Victor Emanuel himself, though he usually blurted out his opinions with little regard for discretion, had never whispered the Unitarian program. And now the Party of Revolution, which obeyed Mazzini, hated Piedmont as an obstacle to the Unitarian and Republican hopes: for Victor Emanuel's government was demonstrating that under a constitutional monarchy five millions of Italians were enjoying those very benefits which the Mazzinians declared could be secured by the Republic only.

Nevertheless, all except the hopeless doctrinaires began to ask themselves whether Piedmont might not become the agent of Italian Nationality. Gioberti, shortly before his death in 1852, pointed to the Subalpine Kingdom as the heaven-sent champion of the down-trodden Peninsula. Ten years earlier, he hailed a Liberal Pope as the spiritual guide and Charles Albert as the sword of Italian independence. The revolution blasted his Neo-Guelf dream, but not his trust in Piedmont. Gioberti had not been dead two years before a greater than he arose to be the prophet of Italian nationality.

This was Daniele Manin, the spotless citizen, the heroic defender of Venice, the dictator who preferred justice to victory, the man whom prosperity could not unbalance nor poverty embitter; Manin, who converted sorrow into spiritual incentive, and who allowed exile neither to cloud his vision, swallow up his hopes nor poison his heart.

Since the autumn of 1849 he had lived in Paris, earning a precarious pittance for himself and his invalid daughter by giving lessons in Italian. He listened to the plans of his fellow-refugees, but held aloof from premature action: for he had a most judicial mind, which men and their opinions could not take by storm. Of all the Italian exiles he was the sanest, just as he was the loftiest of all the leaders in the Revolutionary year. Like Cavour he felt patriotic enthusiasm more intensely than any other emotion, but it did not effervesce in dithyrambic eloquence; like Cavour, he was nobly practical, content to model in the clay of today the ideal which may be sculptured in marble tomorrow. He was too grave, too reasonable, to be popular in the meetings of the exiles at Paris: but the members of all parties treated him with profound respect; and he gathered round his hearth at No. 70, Rue Blanche a little flock of zealous disciples.

During the first year of his exile, he devoted himself almost entirely to watching the course of events; taking care, meanwhile, to establish intimate relations with several of the most influential journals in Paris, London and Turin. He preached the gospel of unity, discouraged spasmodic outbreaks, and permitted himself to hope, though still cautiously, that Piedmont might redeem Italy. On March 13, 1854, when England was trying by every device to persuade Austria to join the Western Allies against Russia, Lord John Russell said in Parliament that if the Italians, instead of revolting against the Austrian government could remain quiet, the time would come when this government would be more humane and would grant more popular privileges than Italy could hope to secure by insurrection. Ten days later Manin printed in the *Presse* of Paris the first of many articles which made the round of Europe, in so far as the newspapers under despotic oversight were allowed to quote or criticize them. "We do not ask," he said, "that Austria be humane and liberal in Italy,— which, after all, would be impossible for her even if she desired; *we ask her to get out*. We have no concern with her humanity and her liberalism; we wish to be masters in our own house." No declaration could be clearer than that, and it was final: for it placed the Italian aversion for Austria on the unarguable grounds of the hatred of a conquered people for its conquerors. Whether Austria were cruel or kind, despotic or liberal, was not the question.

Manin went on to utter this warning: "The end we set before us, and which we all, without exception, desire, is the complete *Independence* of the entire Italian territory, and the *Union* of all the parts of Italy in a single political body. In that, we are all of one accord, we are unanimous. The different views which subdivide Italian patriots into several political ·parties (Republicans, Royalists, Unitarians, Federalists) concern secondary questions, about which we are ready to make all the concessions and compromises which may be required by circumstances. But, as to *Independence* and *Union* we cannot make concessions, we cannot compromise. . . . No, we will not remain quiet so long as we have not reached the goal we pursue, so long as we have not obtained the *Independence* and the *Union* of Italy. . . . Let the world take heed: the Italian Question is henceforth a European Question of the first magnitude. It must be solved in a way satisfactory to our indomitable aspirations of nationality. Till then, no matter what is done, we will agitate unceasingly; there will always be in Italy a hotbed of trouble, a cause of war, which will menace the repose of Europe and will not allow her to count upon a durable peace."

His platform included *Independence,* which implied the expulsion of Austria; *Unification*, which, whether Unitarian or Federalist, would secure for all parts of Italy equal liberty; friendship towards France, no matter who ruled her, if she would attack Austria; alliance with Piedmont, if she stood loyally by the National Cause; hands off Rome, until France should withdraw her support of the Temporal Power. He insisted that Mazzini, for whose patriotic intent he had great respect, but whom he now regarded as a marplot, must retire from directing Republican conspiracies; because, whether Mazzini wished it or not, his presence, Manin candidly stated, always stirred up irreconcilable sectarian passions. The ultimate political form of Italy—Republican or Monarchical—ought not to be even discussed until independence and unification had been achieved. By defining Nationality as the main issue, Manin attracted many to his plan; but when it came to deciding how the national cause could be won, differences of opinion cropped out. Few of the exiles possessed his patience. Most of them clung to their old belief that a local explosion, let it begin where it might, would touch off the revolution which they all desired, nor could they easily put aside their distrust of the House of Savoy, which dated from the disastrous close of Charles Albert's career. For a moment, when Piedmont joined the Western Alliance, Manin himself felt "dispirited as well as angry," because he feared that Victor Emanuel had deserted the Italian cause. He soon perceived, however, that the Crimean Expedition was really a flank movement against Austria. Thenceforth, he redoubled his exhortations.

Manin's most energetic lieutenant was Marquis Giorgio Pallavicino,

the Lombard noble who in youth expiated his complicity in a patriotic
plot by fourteen years' imprisonment in the Spielberg. He bore his
part in the rising of 1848, was banished when the Austrians returned,
and found a refuge in Piedmont. Although hard hit by the law of
sequestration, he still was rich compared with most of his fellow
Lombards, and to Italy he consecrated his wealth and his own unusual talent for effective agitation. A devoted friend of Gioberti, he
became Manin's confidant; but he retained with both of those great
men his individuality. He criticized frankly, differed openly, and
treated them as comrades rather than as masters. At Turin his rank
and early associations gave him entrance to the highest circles. He
was particularly drawn to the King; but towards Cavour he at first
felt hesitation, suspecting both his methods and his Italianism. His
own double rôle of aristocrat and democrat was so paradoxical that
he found his best opportunity as a free lance. He had the doctrinaire's
persistence, but an elasticity and a practical sense that saved him from
the defects of his class. Having once been taught by Gioberti to believe in the "hegemony of Piedmont," he never ceased to assert that
Italian independence could somehow be attained by that means. "I am
infected by a folly which resists every treatment," he said.

In September, 1855, Manin published another statement, the pith
of which lay in these words: "The Republican Party, so bitterly
calumniated, again performs an act of abnegation and sacrifice in behalf
of the National Cause. Convinced that before everything *Italy must
be made*, it says to the House of Savoy: *'Make Italy, and I am with
you! If not, not.'* It says to the constitutionalists: *'Plan to make Italy,
not to aggrandize Piedmont; be Italian patriots, and not exclusively
Piedmontese, and I am with you! If not, not.'* " The manifesto produced
a deep impression. Its phrase, "if not, not," became a catch-word, and
found an echo in many hearts. But Manin was grieved because the
Liberals in Piedmont gave his proposition no welcome.

That they drew back from such an offer of support seemed ill-
considered, if not impolitic; but they held, first, that since whatever
gain had come to the Italian Cause had been secured by the royal
constitutional régime in Piedmont, it was for that régime to determine
what would best promote that cause in future. To bind itself to the
guidance or dictation of the element which had continuously opposed
the monarchy and engineered abortive but damaging outbreaks would
be foolish. Again, many Piedmontese shrank from jeoparding the
existence of their little nation by competing openly for the Italian
crown; some there were, indeed, who already dreaded the possibility

that Piedmont might be merged in Italy, and would have rejected that consummation if it had been proffered to them. Finally, the Ministerialists were too wary to consent to an official connection with any group of the Party of Revolution: such an imprudence would at once alienate the goodwill of France and England and give color to the charge of the Italian Absolutists that Piedmont was in league with the conspirators.

Manin, though disappointed, was not discouraged. Throughout the autumn and winter of 1855–56 he printed his political epistles in the French and English papers, and Pallavicino and the Turinese editors translated and expounded them. He set up "Independence and Unification" as the watchword of Italian patriots, and acknowledged Victor Emanuel as the standard-bearer of the national cause. Cavour's achievement at Paris convinced him that the Piedmontese statesman, although he still appeared to be bounded by Subalpine rather than by Italian frontiers, could be depended upon. Cavour had several conferences with Manin, for whom he had great personal respect. "He is still somewhat Utopian," Cavour wrote to Cibrario. "He has not abandoned the idea of a war frankly popular; he believes in the efficacy of the press in stormy times; he desires the unity of Italy and other trifles; but nevertheless, if the practical issue should arise, all this might be made use of."

While official Piedmont, for common-sense reasons, held Manin off at arm's length, he was actively assailed from two opposite quarters: Mazzini deemed the time ripe for another Republican enterprise, and the promoters of Lucien Murat were getting ready to try their chance. Muratism, the offspring of French Imperialism, like its parent lusted for dominion. From the days of his presidency, Louis Napoleon had dreamed of making France paramount in Italy. His garrison in Rome served as an entering wedge. His friendliness towards Piedmont, involving jealousy of Austria, might lead to an unofficial protectorate over Northern Italy. The Crimean War made fashionable the discussion of territorial changes in the Italian Peninsula not less than in the Orient. Among the many suggestions of the map-remodelers, two found especial favor at the Tuileries: one was that Central Italy should be patched up into a Kingdom for Prince Napoleon (Plon-Plon); the other was that Lucien Murat should occupy the throne of Naples. The first scheme had to be deferred until a victory over Austria should enable the French Emperor to expel the Austrian princelings from Tuscany and the Duchies and to take a part of the Papal States. But the sooner Murat organized his conspiracy, the better. He was a vulgar and disreputable fellow, without brains, courage, or character; but he had a name to conjure with, and Louis Napoleon, eager to rake out, revamp and gild every battered transmittendum of the First Empire, bestowed upon him a large pension and a princely title. Both the French Imperialists, who pushed him forward, and the Neapolitans, who took him up, regarded him merely as a symbol.

Bomba's ferocious suppression of the Liberals checked for a while active plotting in his capital and the neighboring provinces. But the Neapolitan exiles in Malta, Paris and London kept busily weaving and unweaving their Penelope's web, and by 1854 they had reopened communications with their friends at home. As the government went from bad to worse, Bomba's subjects grew desperate. In their eagerness to throw off the Bourbon incubus, the old sectarian lines began to be blurred among them. Many Neapolitan patriots of the highest type—Poerio, Settembrini, Spaventa—were in prisons. Their comrades at liberty were tending towards Liberalism of the Monarchical Piedmontese sort: indeed, Massari, La Farina and other vigorous exiles from the Two Sicilies had found shelter at Turin, and were Cavour's followers. But the Mazzinians were still the most vehement, not to say efficient conspirators, and their creed was Republican. Murat drew recruits from both of these parties, because they thought that he would do something soon. He found favor among the survivors of his father's admirers and their children, who looked back to the reign of Joachim as to a Golden Age, when compared with what had come after it. He also enticed to his cause Bomba's courtiers and officials, a venal throng, who either accepted bribes outright or cast anchors to windward in order to save themselves in case their Bourbon King should go overboard in the coming storm. Just how far the Muratist undermining extended cannot be known. The party's headquarters were at Paris, where Neapolitan grandees like the Duke of Cirella and his brother, and exiles like Trinchera, Mazziotti, Stocco and Romeo declared their adherence to it. Aurelio Saliceti, ex-Republican agitator, ex-Royalist minister and pamphleteer, was engaged as tutor to Murat's sons and gave in return his pen and his influence as a veteran plotter to his employer. A pamphlet setting forth Murat's claims was attributed to him. Louis Napoleon ordered the pamphlet to be suppressed,—after it had been circulated so widely that its contents were generally known,—but he imposed no restraint on the Prince. The Muratists conspired openly at Paris, and the Claimant himself made no secret of his candidacy.

Muratism added a disturbing factor to the already intricate Italian

Question. If it prevailed, it would upset the plans of Cavour, Manin and Mazzini; whatever its outcome, it had to be reckoned with. As early as the spring of 1854, Cavour wrote to Oldofredi at Paris to follow the Napoleonic intrigues, which were aimed especially at Southern Italy. Count Pepoli, Murat's nephew, had just spent two months in Genoa, looking over the ground. The arraignment made at the Congress by Clarendon and Walewski of Bourbon misrule naturally gave a great impetus to Bomba's opponents, especially to the Muratists, who almost flaunted their hopes in public. Murat himself held conferences at Aix-les-Bains. A crisis seemed imminent. Although Cavour had no desire to see a "Napoleonid" replace Ferdinand on the throne of Naples, and convert the lower half of the Peninsula into a French dependency, he could not antagonize Napoleon III, on whom he counted, soon or late, to expel the Austrians. His first concern was Piedmont; his next, the liberation of North and Central Italy: as usual, he allowed nothing to divert him from his main purpose. For months he tried in vain to learn the Emperor's real intentions. Gramont declared that Murat had no Imperial sanction; but his official denial meant nothing, because French Ambassadors could not speak with authority unless they had their cue from the Emperor instead of from Walewski. Until the doubt was cleared up, Cavour directed Villamarina to say to Walewski: "We are for Murat if France desires him; but Murat, without the support of France, does not suit us at all." Walewski's reply seems to have been inconclusive; and more time elapsed before Cavour finally learned that the Emperor would like Murat to be King of Naples, but that until a war with Austria should create a favorable occasion, he would not openly support the enterprise. Thus relieved of the obligation of helping the Muratists, Cavour merely let them plot as they would in Piedmont, while he himself pursued other lines. He encouraged England, always jealous of French territorial acquisitions in Italy, to take umbrage at the proposed election of Murat. He hinted that, if the French got Naples, they must, at least, be kept out of Sicily, for which island, since the days of Nelson and Lady Hamilton, England had shown a peculiar interest. Cavour would have welcomed an English protectorate in Sicily then, because that would not only curtail the French power in Southern Italy, but introduce into the contest a rival of the first magnitude who might be pitted against either France or Austria in the coming struggle for Italian independence. He probably believed that it would be easier to deal with three foreign masters, mutually discordant, than with two. He saw also the chance that, if England should decline to occupy

Sicily, Piedmont might be permitted to take it to counterbalance French aggrandizement. Sicily and Naples, natural antagonists for centuries, would be more comfortable if they could live under different rulers.

Immediately after the Congress of Paris, Marquis Antonini, Bomba's minister at the French Court, protested to Walewski against the hurling at the Neapolitan government of calumnies which had been manufactured in Piedmont. Walewski assured him that Cavour was not their author; and he advised the King to start the reforms which the outraged conscience of Europe demanded. King Bomba, far from being chastened, entered a protest against the charges, and against any attempt to interfere with his internal affairs, being satisfied that they were conducted according to the dictates of justice and conscience. He declared, further, that he would resist to the end, rather than compromise with the Party of Revolution which Count Cavour was abetting. Here is a striking parallel: Cavour warns Europe that Piedmont will perish rather than concede an inch to Austria; Bomba, with equal solemnity, vows Naples to destruction rather than suffer the pollution of Piedmont! Posterity reads the similar declarations with very different emotions.

To Bomba's curt message, Walewski replied that he did not suggest interfering, but that it would be well for the Neapolitan King to govern more mildly, and to accept the friendship of France, before England grew urgent. To this Bomba retorted, with the least possible diplomatic veneer to his words, that England and France might mind their own business and let him alone. Thus piqued, the Western Powers decided, after deliberations which dragged on from May till September, to employ the most stringent diplomatic means to bring Bomba to his senses. Their purpose, they advertised, was moral, inspired by a regard for humanity. Even on political grounds they justified their move: for Bomba's shocking government made his realm the hotbed of conspiracies which threatened at any moment to shatter the peace of Italy and perhaps of Europe: such a calamity they, warders of peace, must prevent if they could. Nations or individuals, in order to produce an edifying "moral effect," must themselves be moral. In 1856, what nation had a record so spotless, a heart so free from guile, a policy so unselfish, that it could set itself up to administer moral reproof to its neighbors? Certainly not Imperial France, begotten by the Crime of December 2; nor Royal England, which had allowed a million Irish to die of famine and was busy in all parts of the world bullying and exterminating black, brown and yellow men to promote the sacred interests of British trade; nor the Republican

United States, recently engaged in the immoral Mexican War and still responsible for five million slaves. Small nations upon which large nations were pleased to exert moral pressure could not fail to observe that when the giants dealt with each other they carefully refrained from mounting a high moral pedestal. That would have been too comic! But the pygmy states had to submit both to the overwhelming brute force and to the cant which it indulged in.

So the Western Powers in the name of humanity pressed Bomba closer and closer. There is no doubt that they had excuse enough for their interference. A large number of the most conscientious people of Britain, who had no selfish interest at stake, approved the action of their government. Likewise in France many noble-minded men longed to have an end put to the Bourbon horrors; but in France it was taken for granted that every public project had a dynastic aim. Bomba relied on the support of Russia, which did not fail him. He stood up firmly to his contention that he could not with dignity yield to the demands, for that would be equivalent, in his opinion, to surrendering to the Party of Revolution. He knew, of course, that at the very time when France was promising to become his advocate against England, the Muratists, with French connivance, were plotting to overthrow his throne; and perhaps he believed those who attributed England's ill-will to the anger of English railway promoters to whom he had refused charters. The chasm opened, and neither party would bridge it. On October 21 the British and French ministers presented their ultimatum to Carafa, the Neapolitan Minister of Foreign Affairs, received their passports, and with little delay sailed out of the Bay of Naples on their men-of-war, which had lain at anchor in the harbor for some time past in order to intimidate the King. The Western Powers urged Piedmont to join in their diplomatic and naval demonstration, but Cavour, having sounded them and perceived that they intended to be satisfied with "milk-and-water measures," prudently decided to "hold aloof from their diplomatic imbroglio." Reactionists applauded Bomba for his "heroic resistance." Canofari, his diplomatic agent in Turin, wrote: "The noble figure of our august master becomes majestic and imposing above those of all his contemporary monarchs"; and Carini at Paris predicted that the time would come when the "Emperor Napoleon would thank the King of Naples for having saved the independence of the monarchical principle." Perhaps Canofari and Carini, being courtiers, exaggerated; still, the fact remained that Bomba, despite the threats of the Western Powers, had conceded nothing. Even the intrigues of the Muratists could not bend him. He was sealed to his idols as surely as Cavour to his ideals. The degradation of the ideal into the idol constitutes the real fall of man.

Whatever might come of Muratism, therefore, Cavour prepared against injury. He made no secret of his dislike of the Muratist project, nor of his determination not to traverse it so long as the Emperor gave it his support. But he did not hesitate to whisper in Downing Street that if France took Naples, the English ought to take Sicily, and he even suggested very privately to the Neapolitan *chargé d'affaires,* that if Naples would join with Piedmont, they two might control Italy, regardless of Mazzini, or Murat, or the meddling of foreign governments. To this suggestion Chevalier Canofari replied haughtily that it was not for his sovereign to retrace his steps towards Piedmont, but for Piedmont, by ceasing to be a hotbed of assassins, calumniators, and revolutionists, to return to Naples: another proof that the two governments could no more be brought together than the antipodes.

The Muratist spectre caused Mazzini great anxiety. With Murat king at Naples and with Southern Italy virtually French, his dream of Independence and Unity would be dashed. Not only that—Austrian domination in the North would be so strengthened that Italians could not hope to shake it off. Mazzini, therefore, refused to parley with the Muratists at Paris, and frowned when upright patriots like Montanelli and Sirtori joined them. He believed that some of his own followers had also been coaxed over; and he was doubtless right: for in every sect there were conspirators who threw in their lot with the leader who seemed to offer the speediest occasion for action, and besides these, men of irresolute character, sharpers and turncoats even, could be purchased cheap. For such, Murat had the chief qualification —money. Mazzini finally crystallized his policy in a single phrase— "Whoever sides with Murat betrays Italy."

By a similarly logical course the venerable Venetian was led to declare war on Mazzini. Both stood for unity; both stood for independence: but Mazzini insisted that he could accept only a republic: whereas Manin, although a fervent democrat, recognized that in the Piedmontese monarchy lay the Italians' best hope of national existence. The Mazzinians charged Manin with being unconsciously the dupe of the Italian princes, who used his "unhappy program" as a veil to their Federalist designs. 'We can never have a United Italy,' the Mazzinians said in substance, 'so long as the several provinces are ruled by monarchs; the only genuine unity must be that of the Republic, before which the Piedmontese Kingdom will be swept away along with its monarchial neighbors. Manin proposes to keep royalist Piedmont, royalist Naples and the rest—a palpable absurdity!' With unabated persuasiveness Mazzini still preached insurrection as the surest weapon. Manin agreed with him in this, but regarded insurrection as the only signal which would bring Piedmont and possibly France to the aid of the volunteers in their third War of Independence, while Mazzini expected by it not merely to drive out the Austrians but to constitute Italy a republic. As for stubbornness, Mazzini displayed on paper not less self-abnegation than Manin. "We, Republicans today as yesterday," he said, "do not wish to impose the Republic, and we acknowledge the country to be the supreme arbiter; you, Republicans yesterday, wish today to impose the Monarchy: which of us is exclusive?"

Mazzini was too able a disputant not to give his rival as good as he sent. In his replies to Manin, he tries not to forget that he is addressing a patriot who, though evidently mistaken now, fought nobly earlier and sacrificed all for his country: but an apostle cannot allow personal considerations to stifle his zeal. He freely admits that Italians must be friends, brothers, workers in a common cause, and that the questions which divide them must wait: and yet, so ingrained was the dictatorial spirit in him that it dominated even his conciliatory lapses. Mazzini was sincere when he protested his willingness to allow the nation, after its independence was won, to choose its form of government; yet when the moment came to concede or postpone, he remained intractable, thereby giving color to the charge that he wittingly deceived. Detailed evidence of his personal dealings with the leaders of other parties does not exist: we must judge, therefore, by the published correspondence and documents, generally written with publication in view, and accordingly not really intimate. The fact that his opponents, whether Royalists or Republicans, almost unanimously report between 1848 and 1860 that he attempted to carry out a rule-or-ruin policy, more than counterbalances his own protestations of good-will.

Manin hastened a crisis by sending (May 25, 1856) to the London *Times* an appeal to Italians to abandon the "theory of the dagger." The "great enemy of Italy," he said, "is the doctrine of political assassination," which horrifies decent persons everywhere and alienates from the cause of Italy the sympathy, the indispensable sympathy, of foreign governments. "Consider how much authority the Catholic Church has lost and loses," he urged, "especially in Italy, because in order to protect temporal interests it does not blush at employing means which the universal conscience condemns, and to avail itself of the work of so many of its perverted and perverting ministers. . . . Our hands ought to be clean. Let this be one of the principal signs for distinguishing the noble defenders of the country from the polluted instruments of her enemies. . . . Let us leave the theory of assassination to the Jesuits. Let us leave the dagger to the Sanfedists."

Mazzini hoped to diminish the effect of this appeal by issuing three open letters to Manin, in which he denied that any group of conspirators adopted political assassination as a tenet. The fact of assassination existed, not because patriots were blood-thirsty, but because the rulers of Italy created an environment in which desperate remedies could not fail to be used. "The *theory of the dagger* lives," he said, "in the insane, incessant, savage persecution of thought, of the least suspicious acts, of the property, of the life of those who are guilty or believed guilty of love of country—in the rod, made the law in Central Italy—in the perennial insolence of foreign masters—in the feverish irritation caused by surveillance and shameless espionage —in the hatreds bred by purchased accusations—in the acts of violence performed, under the shield of an abhorred government like the Papal, by petty, tyrannical subalterns, known to every person in our smaller cities—in the absence of popular education—in the involuntary contempt for every existing institution—in the impossibility of finding justice against the frauds of oppressors—in the contempt of human life, the inevitable consequence of wholesale uncertainty concerning tomorrow—in a condition of things which has no basis save the will of the powerful—in the culpable indifference of official Europe for the thought of a common Country, for an immense aspiration, nourished and inexorably repressed for half a century." With such causes for fury, what wonder that occasionally some overwrought victim broke out into violence?

Mazzini stated that he could not find it in his heart to censure regicides. "In the hands of Judith," he wrote, "the sword which cut short the life of Holofernes was holy; holy was the dagger which Harmodius crowned with roses; holy was the dagger of Brutus; holy the poniard of the Sicilian who began the Vespers; holy the arrow of Tell. When and where all justice is dead, and a tyrant denies and blots out by terror the conscience of a nation and of God who wished it to be free, a man, innocent of hatred and of every low passion and devoted only to the religion of Country and of Eternal Right incarnate in him, rises up before the tyrant and cries to him: 'You torment millions of my brothers; you withhold from them that which God designed for them; you destroy the bodies and corrupt the souls; because of you my Country agonizes every day; in you an entire edifice of servitude, dishonor and guilt has its head and front; in destroying you, I overturn this edifice'—I recognize, in this manifestation of the tremendous equality between the master of millions and the single individual, the finger of God. Most men feel as I feel: I dare to say it. So that I would not, like you, Manin, cast anathema on those stabbers; I would not say to them, with patent injustice, 'You are cowards.' "

A zealot who thought in these terms, necessarily regarded political assassination as a mere accident, compared with the vast campaign of revolution which he was planning; and he might assert, with perfect honesty, that *he* did not teach the theory of the dagger; for he held the wickedness of despots responsible for their slaying. The point may seem casuistical to straightforward moralists; to Mazzini it was unanswerable. None of his enemies has brought sufficient proof to convict him of having directly connived at assassination: nor, on the other hand, did he himself ever express more than a lukewarm disapproval of it. An inflamed patriot, hesitating whether or not to kill a tyrant, would hardly have been deterred by Mazzini's words which we have just quoted.

Political assassination in the middle of the 19th century sprang either from desperation, or from the desire to be rid of a cruel official, or from what we may call the Brutus motive. The example of antiquity had an immense hold on the young devotees of Liberty, who offered their lives to the cause, even when they did not hope by killing the tyrant to kill tyranny itself. They ignored the fact that ancient tyrants differed fundamentally from modern: the former were, indeed, individuals, so that when one of them was cut off, there might be a complete change of conditions; but the latter, whether Bourbon or Hapsburg, Romanoff or Papal, were but the figure-heads of a system which would survive their death. In no modern instance has political assassination accomplished a reform: almost every attempt has resulted in making tyranny more cruel. The Italian votaries of the dagger, against whom Manin inveighed, were for the most part impelled by the Brutus motive, and they are to be judged accordingly, and not to be confounded with the recent Anarchist enemies of society, who destroy for the love of destroying, or for greed, or for vanity, or for envy, or because they find the restraint of civilized life galling. Mazzini believed so thoroughly that the blood of the martyrs is the seed of the church, that he could not condemn a patriot who, having tried to rid Italy of a tyrant, paid for his daring on the scaffold.

But Manin's repudiation of the theory of the dagger produced a great effect. It had the advantage of filling only two pages of print, and of being widely copied by the European press, whereas Mazzini's replies filled thirty, and were restricted to a clandestine circulation. The leading Liberal paper in Piedmont, the *Opinione,* significantly took issue with Manin on the ground that he wronged Italy by assuming that political assassination was a crime peculiar to Italians.

Nevertheless, Cavour welcomed in secret every indication that a large number of patriotic Italians, detaching themselves from the Party of Action, were convinced that the redemption of Italy lay in rallying to the banners of Piedmont. Among the Sicilian exiles at Turin was Giuseppe La Farina, a vigorous writer who had made his mark as historian, editor and publicist. Once a Republican, he had learned that to be an Italian was the first necessity. Neither the habits of conspiracy nor the heart-burnings of exile had spoiled him. In August, 1856, he issued a pamphlet on "Murat and Italian Unity," which approved him both to the Nationalists and to the Liberals. A few weeks later he requested an interview with Cavour, who asked him to call "tomorrow, 12 September, in his house, Via dell'Arcivescovado, at six o'clock in the morning." From that meeting dates a new stage in the Risorgimento. Although no written evidence of its purport exists, we can safely infer what each said. La Farina declared that the Nationalists would do their best to prevent the Muratist designs in Naples, if they could be assured that Victor Emanuel's government would not intrigue against them. Cavour must have replied that he had no liking for the Muratist project, towards which, however, while the Emperor backed it, he must, for policy's sake, remain officially neutral; but that he would not oppose the efforts of the Nationalists to defeat it. The two understood each other. La Farina came soon again; and before long he was given access by the private staircase, which only intimates used, to Cavour's little study and chamber. The interviews took place very early in the morning, in winter long before daybreak, and Cavour had La Farina's promise of secrecy. "Go ahead and prosper," he is reported to have said to his accomplice: "but if you fail, or if I am molested on your account by the Chamber or by Diplomacy, I shall be forced to deny you like Peter."

With this encouragement, La Farina devoted himself to organizing the Italian National Society. Manin was its prophet and Pallavi-cino its sponsor. La Farina himself, its head and hands, wrote its correspondence, conducted its business, and served as link be-tween official Piedmont and inchoate Italy. Evidence is lacking, but we may assume that he took no important step without consulting the Prime Minister as soon as Cavour felt sure that he could trust him. At the outset, and indeed throughout the year 1857, La Farina and his associates believed that a revolution in the Two Sicilies was both feasible and necessary: and to this end they worked to forestall the Muratists, but for good reasons, their plans hung fire. The Na-tional Society accomplished something much better in drawing into its fold many of the recognized patriots from every province of Italy. Above them all Garibaldi towered. No one could suspect him of joining a party which was likely to be inactive or provincial. The Piedmontese government not only tolerated the Italian National So-ciety, which ere long made no secret of its existence, but allowed it to organize after the pattern of the Corn Law League in England, to hold meetings, collect subscriptions and to agitate through the press. On December 27, 1857, the Society adopted a sound constitution, and established at Turin a central committee of which Pallavicino was president and La Farina secretary. Manin, worn out by his labors, had died three months before (September 22) at the age of fifty-three. His last patriotic duty was to sign the *credo* of the Society which La Farina drew up. Thus Venice, also, through her greatest modern son, had her share in creating free, united and independent Italy.

The National Society was the confirmation from within of Pied-mont's claim to Italian hegemony as outlined at the Congress of Paris. It gave Cavour the assurance that a large body of Italians would support his national policy. It clinched the Unitarian ideal among the Monarchists and the Monarchical ideal among the Unitarians. Above all, it withdrew many desirable men from the ranks of the Reds, widened the line of cleavage between legal and violent agita-tion, and deterred from sporadic, futile outbreaks. The Society con-tinued to preach insurrection, which Manin had urged as the means to be used when all the conditions were favorable: but as its leaders fell more under the influence of Cavour and understood the intricacy of the problem, they recognized that insurrection alone would not avail: and so they prudently postponed action. It must not be sup-posed, however, that the National Society deliberately adopted Cavour's program, or even consciously followed his suggestions. La

Farina, Pallavicino, and perhaps a few others took counsel with the Prime Minister: but most of the members, who supposed that the Society pursued its own policy, chafed at delays. Cavour had always to be prepared for the danger that they might grow uncontrollably impatient: men who have once had the revolutionary fever, do not easily settle down to accept the slower methods of legality.

Cavour to William de la Rive

Turin, October 1857

. . . Politics is causing me much anxiety . . . . Abandoned by England, faced by a malevolent and hostile Austria, obliged to struggle against Rome and the other Italian princes—you will understand how difficult our position is. For all that I am not discouraged, for I believe the country is with us. The general elections will prove it. It will be a fierce struggle, for the clerical party will deploy all its forces. But I believe it will be beaten, for the moderate right absolutely refuses to join it and seems disposed to support the ministry. . . .

Cavour, *Lettere*, II (1st ed.), 227–78.

Cavour to William de la Rive at Geneva

Turin, January 1858

. . . . The results of the election are in certain respects very vexatious, though they have their good side. The friends of free institutions can congratulate themselves that the entire aristocratic class, which until now had stood aloof, entered frankly into the political arena and adhered most explicitly to the Constitution.

Party chiefs are perhaps playing games, but the mass is of good faith. The country is honest and an oath still has full validity with us. Also it troubles me not at all to see on the benches on the right a dozen marquesses, two dozen counts, not to speak of a great number of barons and chevaliers. Most of the ones that come into the Chamber as clericals come out of it as plain conservatives. This transformation, in a given time, will make a ministry of the right possible, which could perhaps be good for the country, while of course being an immense advantage for me because it would give me a chance to come spend some time with you.

Cavour, *Lettere*, II (1st ed.), 288–89.

The vexatious side of the question comes from the role which religion has been made to play in this affair. The prelates, pressed by Rome and by Paris, have organized a regular conspiracy, Mazzini style. Secret committees and various groups have been organized with the help of bishops and priests throughout the kingdom. Orders issued by the central committee spread with the speed of light into every commune, by way of episcopal palace and presbytery.

The committee has decided to use every spiritual weapon to influence the voters. The confessional has become a pulpit for the indoctrination of the people in blind faith. The priests have been authorized to draw heavily on heaven and hell. Rome has opened up, in this way, unlimited credit in the other world. The result of this is that the liberal party is extremely irritated against the clergy and that it will take a lot of trouble to restrict it to fighting its adversaries.

I do not depair of success, but I do not hide from myself the perils which the ministry runs; the slightest false step toward left or right could upset the boat. . . .

I shall say nothing of Savoy. I must tell you that its ingratitude toward the government has annoyed me profoundly. To a policy of conciliation, to our efforts rapidly to develop its resources, Savoy has answered by choosing whatever men it could dig up. . . .

Trial of Felice Orsini

Judicial Debates before the Court of Assizes of the Seine District. M. Delangle, Chief Judge, Presiding

Hearing of 25 February 1858

Today appeared before the jury Orsini, Gomez, Rudio, and Pieri, accused of the crime committed on the evening of 14 January.

At a very early hour, the entries to the Palais-de-Justice were filled with throngs of the curious. All these people could have no hope of getting inside the building, but they hoped to get some news, some sense of the powerful debates which were about to begin.

The doors were opened at nine, and soon all places were filled. The interior of the palace, the space reserved for the public, for wit-

Textuel procés Orsini, contenant par entier les débats judiciares . . . le tout recueilli et mis en ordre par M. C.–A. Dandraut, Avocat près la Cour impériale de Paris, Secretaire de Jules Favre (Turin, 1858), pp. 1–6, 10, 27–28, 67–73, 97–98.

nesses, the reserved seats behind the Bench—every spot was occupied in an instant; but all this took place in a very orderly fashion.

Among the distinguished personages who attended these debates we note, says the *Gazette des Tribunaux,* in the Court semi-circle: Prince Joachim Murat, General Fleury, aide-de-camp to the Emperor, Viscount Walsh, Count de Laferrière, chamberlain to the Emperor, M. de Valebrègue, Lord Cowley, English Ambassador, the Ministers Plenipotentiary of Denmark, Württemberg, Saxony, and Sardinia, Duke Beauffremont, and senators and deputies.

Many Magistrates of Court and of Tribunal are placed behind the seats of the Bench. Among the magistrates one notes M. Dupin, Prosecutor-General of the Court of Appeals.

The benches reserved for the bar are occupied by members of the council of the order of advocates, and by many other robed advocates.

At eleven-twenty, the guards bring in the accused Orsini, Gomez, Rudio, and Pieri.

Orsini is of middle height; he is dressed in black; he has a high and handsome forehead; his black eyes are fiery, but the fire is tranquil and contained; his nose, slightly arched, is a little too sharply pointed, but it is especially remarkable for the mobile and expressive nostrils; his mouth, lips pressed together, expresses disdain; his hair, which is starting to fall and to turn white, especially at the temples, is thrown back with a certain art; his black sideburns contrast harmoniously with the pallor of his features; his hands, in black gloves, are small and seem well-made.

Gomez has a common face, clean-shaven; his forehead is low, and the lower part of his face very elongated.

Rudio is small and compact of body; his neck is sunk into his shoulders; his eyes have a certain vivacity. He would be unbearded like Gomez except that his lip bears a thin black moustache; his skin is olive-colored.

Pieri is heavily bearded; his head is covered with thick hair, brush-cut, which stands up straight in a way which lengthens his head, which is already long; the beard and hair of this fifty-year-old man are completely black; his features are gaunt; his face, like his body, is in perpetual movement; there is nothing distinguished in the person or the bearing of this accused, who declares himself lettered and able to speak all the languages of Europe.

The Court sits. The Chief Judge proceeds to the summary interrogation intended to establish the identity of the four accused.

The Prosecutor-General, Chaix d'Est Anges, requests that in view of the presumed length of the arguments, two supplementary jurors be drawn, and that the court add a third advisory assistant.

After a decision favorable to this, the Court retires to the council-chamber, whither the accused are also conducted, so that the jury may be drawn.

While this is taking place, Marshal Magnan comes and occupies one of the reserved seats in the semi-circle.

When the hearing is resumed, the order in which the accused had first been placed is modified. They are now in the following order:

1st.   Antoine Gomez, aged 29 years, domestic servant, born at Naples, Italy, living ordinarily in England, lodged in Paris on the Rue Saint-Honoré, Hotel Saxe-Cobourg.—M. Nicolet, defense.

2nd.   Charles de Rudio, aged 25 years, teacher of languages, born at Bellune, Venetian States, living ordinarily in Nottingham, England, lodged in Paris on the Rue Monmartre, No. 132, Hotel de France et Champagne.—M. Matthieu, defense.

3rd.   Félix Orsini, man of letters, aged 39 years, born at Meldola, Roman States, living ordinarily in London, England, lodged in Paris on the Rue Monthabor, No. 10.—M. Jules Favre, defense.

4th.   Joseph-André Pieri, teacher of languages, born at Lucca (Tuscany), living ordinarily in Birmingham, England, lodged in Paris on the Rue Montmartre, No. 132, Hotel de France et Champagne.—M. Nogent Saint-Laurens, defense.

To these accused present must be added, in the terms of the decree of assignment and the indictment:

5th.   Simon François Bernard, former naval surgeon, born at Carcassonne (Aude),—fugitive.

Prosecutor-General Chaix d'Est-Ange occupies the seat of the public ministry. He is assisted by Advocate-General Sallé.

After the jury has been sworn, the clerk rises to read the indictment.

THE CHIEF JUDGE.—Accused, the indictment that concerns you is about to be read; be attentive to the reading.

Commerson, Clerk, reads the charge, as follows:

A new attempt has been made against the life of the Emperor. His Majesty was untouched; but numerous victims were struck all about him. Nothing, indeed, stems the fury of demagogic passions. Pistol and dagger are not enough for them. These instruments of murder have been succeeded by machines conceived and prepared with an infernal art. A band of assassins, some from abroad, emerging last from England, whose generous hospitality is put to the profit of execrable designs, determined to hurl these new instruments of destruction against the Emperor. To strike at his sacred person, it was necessary to doom to death an august princess known to all for her benefactions; it was necessary as well to strike at random into the midst of the assembled crowd. The assassins did not hesitate; but Providence watched over the welfare of the country. It preserved the precious life of the Emperor; it protected too his noble lady companion who shares his perils; finally it permitted the immediate authors of the attempt promptly to be seized and brought forth to answer to justice for a crime directed against the greatness and prosperity of France, no less than against the life of the sovereign she has chosen for herself.

On Thursday, 14 January 1858, Their Imperial Majesties were to attend the performance at the Opera. The visible preparations customary in these circumstances made it apparent that they were expected.

Their party arrived about eight-thirty. The first carriage, occupied by officers of the Imperial Household, had passed the peristyle of the theater. It was followed by an escort of lancers from the imperial guard, which preceded the carriage containing Their Majesties and with them General Roguet.

When the imperial carriage arrived at the crest of the main entrance, it slowed down to enter the private passage at the end of the peristyle. At that moment, three successive explosions like cannonshots took place at intervals of several seconds. The first, in front of the imperial carriage and among the last rank of the escort of lancers; the second, nearer the carriage and a little to the left; the third, under Their Majesties' carriage itself.

Amidst the general confusion, the single response of those attendants who had not been too cruelly hit was to announce by their shouts that the Emperor and the Empress had been preserved. Heaven had, indeed, most clearly enveloped them in its protection; for the danger they had escaped was frightfully apparent all around them.

The numerous gas lights illuminating the facade of the theater were extinguished by the very force of the blast of the first explosions. The windows of the peristyle and of the buildings nearby were almost all shattered. The great marquee over the entrance was perforated in several places, despite its extreme thickness.

Finally, on the walls and even in the pavement of the Rue Le Pelletier there were deep scars left by projectiles of all shapes and sizes.

The imperial carriage was literally riddled; it had been struck in various places by 76 projectiles. Of the two horses drawing it one, wounded in 25 places, died instantly; the other, seriously wounded, had to be killed. Several fragments had penetrated to the interior of the carriage; and General Roguet, on the forward seat, received a very serious contusion on the upper part of his neck, on the right side, beneath the ear, which caused an enormous flow of blood, and which extended to the clavicle and was accompanied by considerable swelling.

The Emperor and the Empress did not leave the carriage until after the last explosion. They never ceased to be calm, and showed themselves mainly concerned with giving aid to the victims. On a ground strewn with debris and flooded with blood there lay many wounded, several mortally. The judicial report, which is surely an understatement, declares that 156 persons were struck, and the number of wounds reported by medical experts is no less than 511. On the long list of victims one notes 21 women, 11 children, 13 lancers, 11 Parisian guards, and 31 policemen.

To complete the scene on the Rue Le Pelletier at that moment, it must be added that apart from the two horses from the imperial carriage, 24 horses of the lancers were hit, among which two died on the spot and three more succumbed on the following day. . . .

The atrocity of the crime foretold that its authors were men of the savage exaltation of demagogues in revolt against all laws; and investigation has only confirmed that these were the sentiments of all of them.

Orsini has long been involved in anarchist enterprises. After being marked as an emissary of Mazzini, he broke or gave the appearance of breaking with him. He was condemned to the galleys for life in February 1845 by the Supreme Tribunal of Rome for conspiracy against the pontifical government, and then was amnestied on 13 July 1846.

In the month of May 1847, he was expelled from Tuscany for violence and anarchist dealings. In 1849, he turns up again as deputy to the Roman constituent assembly. Named commissioner extraordinary to Ancona, then to Ascoli, he committed excesses which later, in the month of April 1853, brought about his condemnation in absentia, pronounced by the Supreme Tribunal of Rome, for theft with violence and for peculation and usurpation of authority. The restoration of the pontifical government having obliged him to flee, he sought refuge first in London. Then he journeyed through Piedmont, Switzerland, and Lombardy, everywhere concocting revolution-

ary intrigues, traveling with false passports, hiding under the name of
Tito Celsi.

In 1855, he was arrested in Vienna under the name of Herway
[Herwegh]. He was suspected of having planned an attempt on the
life of the Emperor of Austria. Imprisoned at Mantua, brought before a special court for the crime of high treason, he managed to
escape during the night of 29 to 30 March 1856. Three months later
he reappeared in Marseille and embarked for Genoa on 30 June
1856. Then he returned to London, where he seems regularly to
have resided since that time. . . .

Interrogation of the Accused Orsini

THE CHIEF JUDGE: Accused Orsini, rise. After your arrest you were
interrogated several times; you have constantly changed your scheme
of defense. After first denying any participation in the attempt of
14 January, you then made several admissions. These admissions you
then retracted; then you repeated them at greater length; and finally,
in your interrogation of 9 February, you made a complete confession,
which confession did not keep you from writing a letter a few days
ago to the Prosecutor-General in which you seem to wish to return
to your earlier admissions. Now, what scheme are you going to settle
on?

ORSINI: Let me go back a bit. Since my youth, my thoughts and all
my actions have had but one object, but one goal: the deliverance of
my country, and vengeance against the foreigner, against the Austrians who shoot us down, who plunder us, who butcher us. It was
with this object that I was in all the conspiracies before 1848, and
after the fall from power of Pius IX, I was named member of the
Roman Convention.

When the French, whom we had always considered our friends,
debarked in Italy, we thought they would reach out their hands to us.
But they promptly became our most implacable enemies. In one of
the many assaults they made on us, they were repulsed and we took
some of them prisoner. We thought still that France was first among
civilised and liberal nations; that if Frenchmen acted against us it
was because they could not help it; and we set the prisoners free with
cries a thousandfold of *Vive la France! Vive la liberté! Vive l'Italie!*
That was a national holiday for us.

How did they answer our generosity? They suspended hostilities
for a month, but that was to await reinforcements. Then they re-

turned to the attack, a thousand against ten, Messieurs! and we were judicially assassinated; the elite and the youth of Italy were made sacrifice.

THE CHIEF JUDGE: Our respect for the liberties of the defense is all that makes us tolerate such language.

THE ACCUSED: Then I went to Piedmont; our annoyance with the French had passed, and we kept writing to Rome, to all the conspiracies that took place there, that they should respect the French garrison. If the papers seized by the papal government still exist, you will see if I am lying. I have always conspired against Austria, only against Austria. In 1853 I fell into the hands of the Austrians, in Hungary; they tried me, they convicted me, and I was about to be hanged when I found means to escape.

Then it was that I went to England, still with that idea, with that mania if you like, of being useful to my country, of delivering her and endangering only myself. I was convinced that it was useless to expose ten, twenty men to the danger of being shot, as Mazzini has uselessly done for so long. I wanted to use legal means. I addressed myself to English nobles; I drafted a petition to the government on the principle of non-intervention, in favor of the cessation of the French and Austrian intervention. I had already attracted their sympathy when the revolt in India broke out, and you realize that that question took precedence over the affairs of Italy, in England; that is natural. When I saw all my efforts lost, I had a moment of despair.

When I examined the political condition of all the governments of Europe, I came to the conclusion that there was only one man in a position to bring an end to the occupation of my country by foreigners, and that that man was Napoleon III, who is all-powerful in Europe. But all his past led me to the conviction that he would be unwilling to do what he alone could do. I admit frankly that I considered him an obstacle. Then I said to myself: he must disappear. I acted as Brutus did. He killed my country; I decided to kill him. . . .

THE CHIEF JUDGE: In the event that your abominable attempt had succeeded, what consequences did you expect in Paris?

ORSINI: I said to myself: if something happens in Paris, that will destroy the policy France follows toward Italy; that will without doubt bring about a rising in my country.

THE CHIEF JUDGE: And it was in the hope of a rising in Italy to give her the liberty of 1849 that you became an assassin in France?

ORSINI: I wanted to give Italy independence, for without independ-

ence no liberty is possible. I wrote in this sense to M. Cavour, and
I said to him: I offer you my daring and the energy God has given
me; he did not answer.

THE CHIEF JUDGE: You wished, I repeat, to give Italy the liberty
she had in 1849, a liberty of murder and robbery, under a triumvirate; and you did not recoil before the frightful disorders which
your attempt might precipitate. Sit down.

ORSINI: You are free, M. le Président, to make your interpreta-
tions; I cannot stop you. . . .

[After an emotional and eloquent summing up by the prosecution, the
turn comes for the defense to speak.]

JULES FAVRE for the Defense

. . . .There was really no need, gentlemen of the jury, for the
Prosecutor-General to make that eloquent appeal to pity, that strong
invocation of respect for human life; for we like the prosecutor are
seized by horror at the recitation of the bloody tragedy in which so
many victims fell mutilated. Who among us did not shudder at the
picture of that new hecatomb, offered up to political fanaticism?

Before hearing all this, we were all ready to lament the destinies of
our nation should she be too often exposed to the repetition of such
crimes.

To be sure, different opinions are to be met with here on many
things, and for my part, if the Prosecutor-General will permit me to
say so, I am far from accepting all the principles, all the acts, all
the men that he defends. Yes, gentlemen of the jury, despite the
times in which we live, which hinder the free expression of my
thought, in the depths of my heart, I cherish no less with proud
jealousy, the sacred receptacle of my sentiments and my beliefs. But
their symbol has never been sword or dagger. I am among those who
hate violence, who condemn force whenever it is not used in the
service of right. I believe a nation regenerates itself morally and not
by blood. Should she be so unfortunate as to fall under the yoke of
a despot, it is not the blade of an assassin that breaks her chains.
Governments perish by their own faults; and God who counts their
hours in the secrets of his wisdom makes ready for those who ignore
his eternal laws unforeseen catastrophes, more terrible yet than any
deadly machine invented by conspirators.

There is my faith, gentlemen, my profound faith—and yet, when
Orsini appealed to me, I did not turn him away. I felt the weight of

that terrible burden. I measured the size of the effort and its futility. I saw rise before me those tragic shadows, whose phantoms importuned me. Yet I realized that so great a crime could not have as its motive greed, nor hate, nor ambition. The cause of such an attempt must be found in the distortion of an ardent patriotism, in that feverish yearning for the independence of the fatherland which is the dream of every noble soul. I said to Orsini: I condemn your crime; I shall say so openly. But I am touched by your misfortunes and by your constancy in the struggle against your country's enemies, the desperate struggle you undertook, the sacrifice of your life—I understand these things; they go to my heart. Had I been an Italian, I should have liked to suffer with you for my country—to offer myself up thus in a holocaust; to shed my blood for her liberty—all, save these murders, which my conscience does not allow. But you confess your crime, you expiate it, you give your head to the law you have violated; you are ready to die to pay the price for your attempt on the life of another; well then, I shall aid you at that supreme hour . . . not just to make a useless defense, not to glorify you, but to try to make shine upon your immortal soul as it returns to the bosom of God a ray of that truth which may protect your memory against unwarranted accusations.

So here I am before you, gentlemen, once more not to excuse, but to explain the guilty web which this unfortunate could not escape. It is not my task, nor have I the liberty—it is not my task, I mean, to lay before you a work of history and to delve into the causes why such acts have so frequently recurred in our country. But in this solemn moment, when society is about to strike, allow me to throw my feeble light on the mind of the unfortunate Orsini and examine with you the aims and the motives of the act for which expiation is demanded, and I do not despair of making some of the sentiments which stir my heart penetrate yours.

The Prosecutor-General errs; no, gentlemen, the crime of Orsini was not dictated by greed, nor hate, nor ambition; it is not that he wished to attain power by sowing death and destruction around him; it is not that he wished to climb to power by these bloody stairs. Just whose story is this, Mr. Prosecutor-General? it is not Orsini's—What did he want? To free his country. He tells us so; accuse him of folly, but do not question the honesty of his declaration; we have his whole life to prove it, I know not with what more inflexible logic. He used his life unsparingly in an energetic, incessant struggle against the enemies who oppressed his country. It could not be otherwise; hatred of the foreigner, gentlemen of the jury, he had in his infancy from his mother's milk, his father's blood.

Orsini's father was a captain in the Italian army organized by Napoleon I; he followed our legions into the Russian ice; he mixed his blood with ours on every battlefield; he did not lay down his arms until he had seen the last soldier fall of the Bonapartist cause, which was, at that time, the cause of independence.

When the last soldier of that noble cause had fallen, what did he do? What his son did after him. After putting his sword in its sheath, he turned to conspiracy. In 1831 we find him attacking the pontifical power in the company of illustrious accomplices whose names history knows and of whom one fell under the bullets of the law's lackeys.

Félix Orsini was hardly twelve years old when he was witness to these misfortunes; he saw his home destroyed, his father a fugitive, cast into exile, condemned to a life of wandering. And you do not expect him to feel born in his heart that ardent, burning, inflexible hatred which drives him against the enemies of his country! All the other passions of his soul made way before this profound emotion, which was like a torch that kindled his heart. Only a moment ago the Prosecutor-General was depicting Orsini as a vulgar conspirator, working for the fall of governments only so that he might rise to power and give himself over to the intoxications of luxury and power. I repeat, the Prosecutor-General was not telling the history of Orsini. I do not want to discuss this point with him further, nor to enlarge [agrandir] this debate. I only ask him: Had he been Italian, would he not have suffered from the evil which devoured his country, would he not have felt the weight of his country's chains, would not all his efforts have been devoted to casting off the odious yoke of the foreigner? Orsini tried; his whole life was consecrated to that noble end. The independence and unity of Italy were also the aim of Napoleon I. To attain them, what was necessary? Destroy the temporal power of the pope. That was Orsini's belief too; led by that belief into a plot, he was condemned in 1845 by the pontifical government. When he was amnestied they made him take an oath never to undertake anything else against the papal regime. Whatever has been said to us, it was not he who violated his oath; he left the Roman States to conspire, indeed, but in Tuscany, against the Austrians.

The events of 1848 broke out. It is not for me to describe those events here, nor to repeat the story of the expedition to Rome, which has been so variously judged and which has caused such violent debate, and such disastrous consequences. I limit myself to describing the atmosphere of that time. Lamartine's manifesto had raised hopes for independence in Italy; and those hopes had been hailed by many men who nowadays take quite a different line. A dismayed Austria had pulled her colors back behind the Tagliamento. All France applauded this liberation. Such were our promises at that time. The pontifical government had been overthrown. Orsini had not changed; but he did not violate his oath; you cannot accuse him of having conspired then for the overthrow of the papal power. Though he entered the Constituent Assembly, it was by universal suffrage that he got there. And how was it that he left? God preserve me, gentlemen of the jury, from giving way to bitter or imprudent statements; but can one avoid saying that this assembly, which like our institutions of that time rested on universal suffrage, was overthrown by Europe? And who dispersed it? French cannon.

What was this man to do then, condemned to the life of the proscribed, pursued by violence? Should he submit to the ancient enemies of his country? The patriotism of the old soldier of the Empire, that ardent patriotism fired within him by his father's example and his father's misfortunes—would it die out now in his heart? No; it would blaze all the higher; henceforth Orsini will have no peace, no truce until he has broken his country's chains. What does he do? He conspires; he travels through Italy; he restores courage; he organizes resistance. In Piedmont, in Tuscany, at Lucca, Modena—everywhere the same. He is arrested in Genoa in 1853, then set free but exiled. He travels through Switzerland and France, then heads for London. In March 1854, under the name of Tito Celsi, he starts an expedition to the Duchy of Parma; it fails; he is arrested in Switzerland and escapes by a miracle. In 1855 he goes to Vienna under the name Herwag, still pursued by the same demon—by the same folly, prudent men of the times will say. He goes seeking support, preparing uprisings; but he is discovered, arrested, put in chains, and thrown into the citadel at Mantua, a veritable tomb. For ten months without flinching he sees death, an ignominious death, hanging over his head. Even his judges privately recognize the nobility of his soul and the purity of his patriotism. Yet he is condemned. But generosity and devotion are watching nearby. A woman, hearing that a young Italian patriot is about to die, takes an interest in this unfortunate. . . . Thanks to the miracles of tenderness and the prodigies of intuition of which only women are capable, the means of rescue are prepared, and communications established within the prison. Finally, the hour of rescue arrives . . . eight bars are cut . . . The instruments of escape miraculously supplied! Shall I describe to you, gentlemen of the jury, the time and patience required for all this? It would be vain to try. Orsini, with the help of a weak rope, tries to climb down from a height of forty yards; the line breaks, and the fugitive falls half-shattered into the moats of the fortress; still he drags himself away and hides for twenty-four hours in an icy pool while pursuers hunt for him. It is clear, gentlemen of the jury, that Providence did not want him to die. Why not? But is it right for us, feeble vermin that we are, to be allowed to question Providence? What do we know, what can we know of its designs! Meanwhile here he is, still captive of the same ideas, victim of the circumstances of all his life; here he is again precipitated into the horrible enterprise which I condemn, but which I have just explained.

After what I have been saying to you, do I need any further defense? Should I still discuss proofs and witnesses? Will you not henceforth be persuaded that Orsini had in mind only one single thing: the rescue, the liberation of his noble and beloved country? Once again, this thought and this desire cannot excuse such an attempt, nor excuse the deaths of those sorry victims to whom Orsini, as he said to you yesterday, would wish to give life back at the cost of all his blood; but they explain; imperious sentiments of force strengthened his arm.

We ourselves, gentlemen of the jury, have not suffered from the power of these redoubtable sentiments. Sometimes, in the cabinets of kings, it happens that their counsellors try to dispose over the lives and power of nations. Our own was the object of one of these attempts at a time not yet long past. In the pages of our recent history, do we not find the bloody memories of 1815? Was not Napoleon I, despite his prestige, despite his power, thrown from power by the allies? And was not the government which replaced his unpopular because it was imposed; was it not attacked by conspirators; did they not wage a steady and bitter war; and has not the country in the end, if not glorified, at least lamented the victims fallen in that patriotic struggle? Well! gentlemen, you have before you one who wanted to do for Italy what they did for France. Look into his heart, and you will see the motive for his crime; you will not scorn it; and above all you will not add to this crime the blood of the unfortunate victims caught up in that horrible attempt. The responsibility for this bloodshed he will bear before God; but it cannot weigh upon him before the justice of men; the law forbids it; in the eyes of the law, as you know, crime lies only in the intention. The Prosecutor-General understands this as we do; besides, in his

loyal indictment, he laid little weight on this point. I myself shall
speak no more of the subsidiary accusations.

Need there be more discussion of the evasions with which Orsini
thought he must envelop his explanations? of the contradictions, the
denials that came out in his interrogations? What, gentlemen, can
be in doubt here when this unfortunate has offered his head in
expiation for his crime? At first, it is true, he denied the crime; but
that was in the company of the other accused who denied it too;
they had denied it, and he went along with them. You think he was
afraid? Oh! no; no, do not believe it! Here finally is the day of justice,
the day when he finds himself faced by a jury; this is the day when
he must present to you and does present his final explanations. All
right! Does he dissimulate, and did you hear in his testimony a single
word of bravado or weakness? Once more, he frankly and courageously avows his fault and his purposes. There he is, gentlemen,
before you, ready to die . . . but hopeful still that his blood may serve
the cause of Italian independence; he has formulated that prayer in a
high testament, in a letter he addressed from the depths of his
dungeon to the Emperor. In this document which I am about to read
you, having received permission from him to whom it was addressed,
you will see revealed anew, gentlemen of the jury, the thought of
Orsini's whole life:

Orsini to Napoleon III, Emperor of the French
The evidence I have given against myself, in the political trial
occasioned by the attempt of 14 January, is sufficient to send me to
death, and I submit without asking mercy, as much because I shall
never humble myself before him who has killed the liberty dawning
in my unfortunate country as because, in my situation, death is a
blessing.

Though the end of my career is near, I desire to make one last
effort to come to the aid of Italy, for whose independence I have
to this day faced every peril and been ready for every sacrifice. This
was the constant object of all my affections; and this is the last
thought which I wish to record in these final words which I address
to Your Majesty.

To maintain the present equilibrium in Europe, either Italy must
be made independent, or the chains by which Austria holds her in
bondage must be tightened. Do I ask that the blood of Frenchmen
be shed for Italian liberation? No, I do not go that far. Italy asks
that France prevent Germany from assisting Austria in the struggles

which perhaps soon will begin. Now, this is precisely what Your Majesty can do if he chooses. On his will, then, depends the well-being or misery of my country, the life or death of a nation to which Europe in great part owes its civilization.

This is the prayer I dare address Your Majesty from my dungeon cell, despairing not that my feeble voice may be heard. I entreat Your Majesty to render to Italy the independence which her children lost in 1849 through the fault of the French themselves.

May Your Majesty remember that Italians, among them my father, joyfully shed their blood for Napoleon the Great, wherever he chose to lead them; let him remember they were faithful until his fall; let him remember that as long as Italy is not free the tranquillity of Europe and of Your Majesty will be but a chimera; may Your Majesty not turn away the supreme prayer of a patriot on his way to the scaffold; may he deliver my country, and the benedictions of 25 million citizens will follow him throughout posterity.

Signed: Félix Orsini

Mazas Prison, 11 February 1858

These, gentlemen, are the last words of a man who is resigned to his fate. They are, as you see, consistent with all the actions of his life.

Still I acknowledge there is a sort of boldness about turning in this way to the very person he had sought to destroy as an obstacle to his designs; but once more, still faithful to the conviction and the passion of his whole life, he wished the shedding of his blood to be useful to his country. Yes, gentlemen of the jury; Orsini, engaged in an enterprise in which he has tried and by the grace of God failed, adapts himself to this; he ignores the fact that he is about to die! From the edge of the grave he addresses this solemn prayer to one against whom he has no feeling of personal hatred, to him who was the enemy of his country, but who can be its savior. Prince, you glorify yourself as having risen from the hearts of the people; come succor the oppressed nationalities; succor a people beloved of France; raise again the banner of that Italian independence which your valiant predecessor once restored. Prince, permit not so beautiful, so noble, and so unfortunate a land to be the eternal prey of the children of the North who grasp her; do not be taken in by the hypocritical poses of old royalty. Prince, the origins of your house are revolutionary in their deepest roots; have the strength to give Italy independence and liberty; be great and magnanimous, and you will be invulnerable.

This, gentlemen of the jury, is what he says; it is not my part to comment on it; I have neither the power nor the right [liberté] to do so; but these last words of Orsini tell you clearly the thought and the goal of his act. I am finished, gentlemen; my task is done. You do not need the urging of the Prosecutor-General to do your duty without passion and without weakness. But God who judges us all, God before whom the great of this world appear as they are, stripped of their coterie of courtesans and flatterers, God who alone measures the greatness of our sins and the power of the circumstances that lead us into them and the expiation that erases them—God will give his verdict after yours; and perhaps he will not refuse a pardon which men find impossible on earth.

Orsini and Pieri were beheaded in the Place de la Roquette on the morning of 13 March.

Here is how the *Gazette des Tribunaux* . . . reported the facts.

Orsini and Pieri paid their penalty today at seven in the morning, in the Place de la Roquette.

During their stay at the Roquette prison, where they had been transferred after making their appeal from judgment, Orsini and Pieri kept the character and attitude they had maintained during the whole course of the trial.

Orsini, impassive and calm, spoke little and remained almost constantly plunged in silent meditation; in his rare conversations, when he spoke of his trial, he said he had no complaint to make of French justice, and that all the magistrates had loyally done their duty. He received with respectful deference the visits of the Abbé Hugon, chaplain of the prison, and listened in the same way to the exhortations of this honorable ecclesiastic. He ate only one meal a day, and asked as a favor to have his wine ration slightly increased.

Pieri was prey to continual overexcitement; he talked and gesticulated incessantly, talked on every subject with his guards, and even sought subjects for argument in the words addressed him by the chaplain.

Yesterday the order for execution was given. For a week a great crowd of the curious had come every evening to the Place de la Roquette. Many of them even spent the night there waiting for the execution. As the news of the rejection of jurisdiction by the Court of Appeals had spread on Thursday evening, the crowd became much larger yesterday. This morning at five o'clock it was already immense, and it grew steadily until seven o'clock.

The scaffold was prepared overnight by torchlight. At five in the morning, several squadrons of cavalry arrived and took up positions around the gates of the prison. Pickets from the Paris guard were placed at the accesses of the streets perpendicular to the Rue de la Roquette, from the Rue Basfroi to the Rue Popincourt.

Yesterday evening an examining magistrate and a surrogate of the imperial prosecutor went to the prison to hear the statements of the condemned in case they had any to make.

This morning at six o'clock the director of the death section and Abbé Hugon, chaplain of the prison, presented themselves at the cell of Orsini and informed him that the fatal moment had come. The director and the Abbé Nottelet, chaplain of another prison, went then to the next cell, that of Pieri, and informed him he must prepare to die. At that news Pieri made a movement like a convulsion, and, with a forced air of assurance, asked for breakfast and expressed a desire for coffee and rum. He took these aliments amidst feverish agitation, which he showed by his jerky motions and by a breaking voice. After he had drunk the coffee and rum served him, he asked emphatically and as though angrily to be given more rum or wine. Pieri responded to the words of Abbé Nottelet with interruptions that showed the confusion of his thinking. Orsini, who had refused any food, asked only for a glass of rum and begged the director to let him drink to his health and good fortune. The condemned two were then conducted to the chapel, where they stayed briefly. Orsini, whose confession had been heard the evening before by Abbé Hugon, kneeled in meditation beside the chaplain. Pieri kneeled as well, and for that moment he was calm and silent. Soon thereafter they were brought to a room near the registry and delivered to the executioner of Paris, who was assisted by the executioner of Rouen.

Orsini preserved his calm and impassiveness in his last preparations. He said only one word in Italian, to tell Pieri to be calm. Pieri, more and more overexcited and trying to give himself assurance and artificial courage, did not cease to talk and gesticulate.

Soon the funereal procession got under way; the condemned, barefooted, enveloped in long white smocks, their heads covered by black veils, emerged from the prison. Pieri came first, led by Abbé Nottelot and the executioner of Paris. Orsini followed, accompanied by Abbé Hugon and the executioner of Rouen. When he entered the prison courtyard Pieri, whose features had contracted convulsively and whose feverish excitement had become even greater, tried to sing the song of the Girondins, and he kept it up in a cracking voice until he was outside the prison. The prisoners ascended the steps of the scaffold. When they reached the platform they stood exposed while a bailiff read the order of execution.

When this had been read, the executioners took hold of Pieri, who was still trying to murmur his song after a moment's interruption, and whose voice was stopped by the knife.

Orsini, who until then had been silent, now cried: *Vive l'Italie! Vive la France!* and then he gave himself over to the executioners.

At seven o'clock all was finished and the abominable crime which had shocked France and Europe had had its lawful expiation.

Diary of Count Joseph von Hübner, Austrian Ambassador in Paris

Friday, 26 February 1858—Yesterday the four accused of the attempt of 14 January appeared before the jury-court of the Seine district. Orsini is the hero of this sorry drama. He is neatly dressed and has the appearance of a well-bred person. He boldly acknowledges having been the head of the conspiracy and treats his co-defendants, who look like regular villains, with deepest contempt. All the Polish and Russian ladies, who sit crowded together on the benches of the courtroom, are mad about him. They admire his beauty, his courage, his composure. Even the Empress is in raptures over this murderer in white gloves.

Saturday the 27th—The *Moniteur* has published the transcript of the second and last session in the trial of Orsini and his accomplices. Jules Favre was the lawyer for the chief defendant. He took this opportunity to make a very political speech in favor of a free Italy and against Austria. He read aloud a letter from Orsini to the Emperor, which the Emperor should have forbidden. It contained the following sentence: "May Your Majesty reflect that as long as Italy is not independent, the peace of Europe and that of Your Majesty will remain but a chimera." If that isn't clear!

Sunday the 28th—I was given the following explanation of Orsini's letter. My source was Rouher, Minister of Public Works. The members of the cabinet were at table together at Fould's last Friday—

Joseph A. von Hübner, *Neun Jahre der Erinnerungen* (Berlin, 1904), II, 71–72, 74–76, 81–85.

they eat together every Friday—when they were informed of Jules
Favre's scandalous defense speech and of Orsini's letter to the
Emperor. Two of the Ministers went immediately to Favre to
find out how he had got hold of the letter and whether his reading
it aloud has really been approved. They learned that it was Pietri,
prefect of Police, who had given it to him. The letter being already
out, the Emperor thought that to refuse to let it be read at the trial
would infringe upon the freedom of the defense; and, after it was
read aloud in open session, he could not suppress it in the report
and in the official transcript. So it happened that the *Moniteur* published the testament of this murderer, who consequently by the jury's
verdict was labeled a political martyr, who sheds his blood for the
same cause that was once Napoleon's but which he now betrays.
Never has such a scandal been tolerated.

The Ministers however, who are trying to find a half-acceptable
excuse for the master, are trying to shove the blame onto the
"stupidity" of Court President Delangle, who allowed Jules Favre
to play politics before the assembled court instead of shutting him
up and calling him back to the point, and onto the "stupidity" of
Pietri, who delivered this letter to the Emperor without the knowledge of the cabinet. But Delangle is a man of considerable intelligence, and Pietri is a sly customer [*Schlaukopf*]. It is a suspicious
business, but it will come to light. Meanwhile Orsini has become the
hero of the day. The Empress' head is completely turned; she spends
her time weeping and appealing to her husband's mercy, to save the
life of this pitiful figure.

Monday, March 8—A Faubourg-St. Germain dinner at my house
this evening. Nuncio Sacconi, his advocate Mgr. Meglia, the Princess
Theodora de Beauffremont, the Marquis and Marquise de Vogüé,
the Marquis and Marquise de la Ferté, Duke Rohan, Duke and
Duchess Pozzo, Count and Countess de Bryas, Marquis de Nadailhac,
Count and Countess Hippolyte de Larochefaucauld, Count and
Countess Charles de la Ferronnays, Count Werner de Mérode, Count
Stanislas de Blacas and my secretaries and attachés. An ambassador
who permits himself to assemble the titled social and political
eminents of the old parties at his table puts his courage to the test.
Without wishing to set myself up as a hero, I think I am really the
only one among my colleagues who has not let himself be intimidated
by the faces made by certain Tuileries personages. One evening when
I sat next to the Empress at dinner she forgot her place as Empress,

which sometimes happens to her, and engaged me in a lively conversation about my guest-lists. "You very much frequent," said she loudly, "the society of our enemies." "Say rather," answered I, "the society of my friends, who are too well-bred to make politics in the salon of an ambassador. My relations with them reach back to the year 1832. Besides, I am told that the Empress often honors Madame Delessert with visits. Surely one breathes no imperial atmosphere in the company of this lady." "That is true, and I think it honors me. The Delesserts were very good to me when I was still in society" (her customary way of saying: before my marriage). "I never forget my friends." "For that very reason," answered I, "perhaps the Empress will permit me to follow her example." She began to laugh: "Of course; from now on I shall protect you against the ill will of certain persons."

A republican disorder has taken place at Châlons. The appearance of troops was enough to restore order. The *Wiener Zeitung* has announced that the Empress Elizabeth is expecting a happy event.

Thursday the 11th—The dispatches of the 9th, which I received via courier in the course of the evening, indicate to me that Buol after his fashion—that is, in the way most inimical to Napoleon III—has taken over my ideas. His thesis is the following: The Emperor of the French finds himself embarrassed; this suits us, because it will make him compliant; but we should not make too much trouble for him, for we and he are in the same situation with regard to the struggle against anarchy. Accordingly we should not add to his embarrassment. Thus too we shall not protest against the publication of Orsini's letter. And all this the good Buol puts in writing, in a dispatch that is to be put before the Foreign Minister of France.

Friday the 12th. With my dispatches to Walewski, to read them to him. He regrets the publication of Orsini's letter; his feelings about this matter, he told me, are like Count Buol's, except that he cannot concede that the French government has as many embarrassments hung around its neck as seems to be the belief in Vienna. That was the only possible answer. Yesterday the appeals court rejected the appeal of Orsini and accomplices. Dupin, president of this supreme court, took the opportunity to condemn the way in which this murderer was tried at the trial court. That is a satisfaction to public opinion, which unanimously disapproves the abuse made of the freedom of the defense, and allowed to be made of it. The privy council met today, I think for the first time. The Emperor's intention was to get its opinion on the execution of the condemned.

Saturday the 13th—Orsini and Pieri were excused early this morning. Rudio was pardoned and his death penalty changed to life imprisonment at forced labor. The government thought a considerable body of troops, six thousand men, was necessary; but the crowd remained quiet, and order was not disturbed. High society [*die schöne Welt*] has been charmed by the dignity, the resignation, and the magnanimity of the murderer Orsini. Especially the grace of his bearing, and the air with which he swept back his thick black hair as he turned himself over to the executioner. When you hear this kind of talk out of the mouths of elegant young men and lovely ladies you ask yourself if it isn't a hallucination. But it appears that in this day and age the ideas of good and bad are confused and logic has evaporated from people's hearts. The detailed history of this trial, if it is ever written, might make very interesting reading. When I went to see Walewski yesterday I found him pale and depressed, not to say in a state of complete collapse. He told me the Empress was like one bewitched. She pleaded with her husband to pardon Orsini; and it took a great deal of trouble to keep her from going to see him in prison. "At this moment," he added, "the privy council is at the Tuileries to put an end to the Emperor's indecisiveness; for he too wants to save the murderer's head. All the council members are determined to hand in their resignations if the execution does not take place. The rest of us (the Ministers)"—this with a sigh— "we shall do the same."

Friday, 9 April—There is no doubt that in these wearing days the Emperor's thinking wavers between opposite views, and that the most contradictory decisions, or rather the most extreme impulses, are churning around in his head. It is my duty to keep Count Buol in touch with these oscillations. I do this conscientiously by trying to keep the fearful from becoming too discouraged and the optimistic from becoming too bold. So I write to him in this way: "In my last conversation with Count Walewski it seemed to me that while in form his language was very conciliatory, he nonetheless betrayed a certain reserve, not to say mistrust and antipathy toward Austria. This increasingly bad mood I explain to myself as follows. There can be two reasons for it: first, the stubborn and independent policy which the Imperial government follows in the Eastern Question. The second reason for dissatisfaction is rather an indirect one. The Orsini trial and this murderer's letters, which set up Napoleon as master of Italy's fate; the continuous efforts of the Italian nationalist party to draw the Emperor into a policy of intervention in the affairs of the peninsula—these have for the moment confused the Emperor's thinking, flattered his ego, and awakened thoughts and memories from another epoch of his life, from which he has not yet entirely freed himself. Thus on the one hand there is mistrust of the so-called Austrian intervention in the East and on the other hand an easy pretense for making trouble for us, for unsettling us; a way to prevent us from carrying out our alleged plans for seizing Turkish territory. Accordingly he is keeping alive the doubtless temporary excitement which the Orsini trial has caused in Italy and which the Sardinian government is trying to take advantage of, or at least he does nothing to calm it down. This is my reading of the turn of things which I think I have caught sight of. It seemed to me appropriate to compare my impressions with those of my English colleague before submitting them to you. From the following you will see that he judges the situation as I do. Lord Cowley has given me permission to put before you in a private letter the information which he kindly gave me.

"He believes the that Emperor, who is by nature proud and who is vulnerable to people who declare they have put their trust in him, let himself be talked into prospective support for the Montene-grins when their chief visited here a year ago. But now Turkey is sending troops to the Montenegrin border with the approval and indirect support of Austria. The hard-pressed Danilo has probably reminded the Emperor, who can do nothing for him, of his fine words; and this is one reason for Napoleon's annoyance and ill-will against Austria—which, Cowley says, is very great right now. The Emperor also believes that we plan an invasion or at least unilateral intervention in Turkey. Lord Cowley, who saw him just recently, tried to correct these errors. He told him that it showed poor understanding of Austria to attribute these sorts of plans to her.

"The Emperor also descussed Italian affairs with him. He much regretted, he said, that he had had to let Orsini be executed, and he admired the calm and the coolness with which this assassin died. The ambassador contested these sympathies for a man who far from being a hero, as Pietri tried to make the Emperor think, was only a common murderer, who tried to save himself during the official investigation by turning in his accomplices and who after his con-

viction, as we know, tried to surround himself with the shining aura
of hero and martyr in his letters to the Emperor.

"Lord Cowley thinks just as I do that these letters and the influence
of the Italian nationalist party, among whom the Emperor has many
friends, have upset His Majesty, temporarily drawn his attention
to Italy, and now have awakened this ill-will toward Austria, because
he feels it impossible to fulfill the hopes of the Italian nationalists
as long as Austria is in control of the Lombard-Venetian Kingdom,
and because he is just as unable to get it out of our possession.

"I asked my colleague what he thought the plans and private
thoughts of the Emperor Napoleon were respecting Italy. Without
hesitation Lord Cowley answered that it was his firm conviction
that the Emperor had no intention of bringing about changes on the
peninsula, not because he would not like to justify the confidence
the Italian party has or gives the appearance of having in him, but
because he realizes that any effort to change the territorial organization of Italy would call Austria to arms, which would be the signal
for a European war; and he realizes that a war is not in his interests.
In Lord Cowley's opinion there are many people who are convinced
the Emperor is thinking of cutting himself loose from England,
forming a close alliance with Russia, and then falling on Austria
and England. Lord Cowley is convinced that these people are mistaken. The alliance with England, though for the moment shaken
and a little quiescent, still constitutes the basis of Napoleon III's
policies.

"Respecting the special problem of Rome Napoleon does not deceive
himself about the insuperable obstacles the Pope would put in his
way should the Emperor seek to bend him to his will. You have no
idea, he told Lord Cowley only last Friday, how hard it is to deal
with the Pope. Before we brought him back from Gaeta to Rome
we wanted to make him conditions. He said to us: 'Leave me on these
cliffs, or banish me to a desert island; I shall always remain Pope.'
In the end we were obliged to beg him please to come back to Rome
under the protection of our troops and with no conditions. The
Emperor also seems to regret very much that he was obliged to leave
troops in the Papal State. That is bad politics, he said, but the Pope
needs support in Rome and if I do not supply it Austria will. Lord
Cowley thinks that the best way of getting through the difficulties
caused by the Emperor's present mood would be for us to show no
distrust of him, but on the contrary to agree readily and with a
good will to his proposal to resume the negotiations with Rome, and
to keep out of the newspaper war over Italy as much as possible."

Count Walewski to the Prince de la Tour d'Auvergne, French Minister at Turin

Paris, 22 January 1858

Monsieur le Prince,

Among the sentiments which the attempt of 14 January have aroused, and which have been expressed to me in the correspondence of the Emperor's envoys everywhere, none is manifested with more force and unanimity than the dangers which this odious crime has let loose on all Europe.

The Governments have never appreciated better than in this moment the solidarity that unites them, nor have they ever more resolutely declared how the maintenance of order in France is a matter of common interest.

It is in the name of this solidarity that the Emperor's Government believes itself entitled to call upon the cooperation of the Cabinet at Turin in warding off the dangers the extent of which this last attempt has demonstrated.

This is not the first time, as you know, that His Majesty's Legation has been instructed to represent to the Piedmontese Government how desirable it was for the security of neighboring States, as well as for their own, for them to put an end to the enterprises or demogogic demonstrations for which its territory is the foyer or even the theater. The events at Genoa have recently justified our apprehensions; but if doubts still remained in some minds of the designs of Italian demagoguery, such can no longer be the case today. What the governments are faced with are not just partisan political opinions more or less hostile to existing constitutions; these are adherents to a savage and anti-social doctrine, openly professing regicide and assassination. Such men place themselves outside all political and social order, and cannot invoke its protection when they flout all its laws.

Count Cavour, I am convinced, has perfect knowledge of this situation; and I have no doubt that he is already occupied with the obligations which it places on all governments, and more particularly on those who have up to the present exercised the right of asylum very liberally.

Still I ask you to confer with the President of Council and represent to him how regrettable it would be if the Sardinian States and particularly the city of Genoa continued to offer refuge to the enemies of European society, and if the commander-in-chief of these perverse men, Mazzini, should be able to come and go with impunity

Nicomede Bianchi, *Storia documentata della diplomazia europea in Italia*, VII, 659–60.

in that city, as he does with impunity all the time at this very moment, reheating the zeal of his initiates.

We have no particular measures to suggest to the government of King Victor Emmanuel. We leave it to his prudence and his loyalty to take care to undertake those which will seem to him the most appropriate for attaining that end, persuaded that he will not fail in a task commended to him at once by a friendly government, his own dignity, and, I say again, the public opinion of all Europe.

The Turin Cabinet, we are sure, will at the same time direct its attention to the criminal abuses committed in the name of liberty of the press by certain journals in the Sardinian States. There is one above all, *L'Italia del popolo,* whose existence is a continual outrage to the public conscience. It is in fact notorious that this sheet is Mazzini's mouthpiece, and that it is its custom to publish the manifestos that prepare his conspiracies or defend them. Just a few days ago *L'Italia del popolo,* faithful to its infamous role, did not fear to open its columns to a publication emanating from that very pen, destined to give instructions to the Italian demagogues, in preparation for the attempt of the 14th of January. That fact alone should doubtless suffice to make understood the necessity of advising at least the suppression of a paper from which, as though on a permanently open high grandstand, Mazzini and his accomplices can gird themselves for the most criminal attacks against the Governments, and for the spread of their detestable doctrines.

I beg you, Prince, to read this dispatch to Count Cavour and to have a copy sent to His Majesty.

Receive, etc.

Cavour to the Marquis S. Di Villamarina, Sardinian Minister in Paris

Turin, 5 February 1858

My Dear Marquis,

M. de la Tour d'Auvergne came looking for me again yesterday; he talked with me at length in the name of Walewski about what measures we intend to take respecting the press and respecting the emigrés, showing himself little satisfied. But after I had again enumerated to him the measures taken and to be taken, he was obliged to agree that they were sufficient and that we could scarcely do more;

Cavour, *Lettere,* II (2d ed.), 527–32.

he would only have wished: 1st that emigrés be forbidden to write for the newspapers; 2d that Bianchi-Giovini be expelled from the country.

The first measure is absurd; and among the writers for the ministerial journals are several emigrés of great merit. How shall we forbid Farini, Oldofredi, Achille Mauri, etc., to take up the pen, who are more conservative than we! As for those emigrés who write for ill-disposed newspapers, I don't need a new law to silence them; it takes only an order to the police to shut them up by showing them the door. A new law, however severe, could only diminish the powers with which the government is now invested. Surely it is not reasonable to tie one's hands in order to give the impression of acting forcefully. As far as Bianchi-Giovini is concerned, I did not deny that he has published two disagreeable articles on the assassination attempt and sneaked in some very malicious dispatches from Paris. It would have been easy to have him penalized if M. de la Tour d'Auvergne had consented to file suit against him; I should have been charmed to see him punished; but expulsion, which would have ruined him completely, seemed to me too rigorous a measure for a man who has rendered real services to the country and is still, in his own way to be sure, one of the most ardent partisans of the French alliance. I cannot forget that in 1848 and 1849, when the Revolution triumphed in several Italian countries, Bianchi-Giovini was one of the few writers who dared attack Mazzini openly and who did it with unprecedented vigor. Since then he has never ceased to combat the deadly apostle of the Revolution and of crime, and nobody has done it more successfully.

No more can I forget that after the Treaty with France and England, Bianchi-Giovini was one of the few journalists who supported the ministry. Besides, I repeat, Bianchi-Giovini is at bottom a sincere partisan of the alliance, I am not saying with France, but with the Emperor Napoleon. Despite certain regrettable deviations, his journal on the whole tends to popularize here the Empire and its Chief. His expulsion to please the minister of France would produce the most inopportune effect from the point of view of the French alliance. I do not know whether M. de la Tour d'Auvergne was convinced by my reasoning, but he no longer insisted on this.

As I am about to treat the question of the emigrés, I think I must remind you of what I have told you about our main cause for embarrassment. A subject which I treated at length with the Prince de la Tour d'Auvergne.

Since the Austrian amnesty the number of political emigrés has greatly declined. The emigration that is tormenting us is that from the countries where amnesty has not been given; for it is very difficult for us to get rid of them. But patience still, if these were only persons seriously compromised from the political point of view. What makes this emigration so numerous is that it is increased every minute by individuals expelled from their own countries simply on suspicion, or even from causes remote from politics. The Romagna constantly sends us new emigrés that we do not know what to do with.

Even though they are provided with passports regular in appearance, Roman consuls will not give them visas for the return home; we cannot send them to France; we would not wish to if we could, for this would be an unfriendly procedure with respect to her. Switzerland does not want them and besides it is scarcely in our interest to increase the number of dangerous men collected in Geneva and in the Canton of Ticino: thus it is necessary to keep them willy-nilly, all the more because most of the time these men behave well enough.

Though expelled, often on flimsy grounds, they are far from being vicious men.

But since once they are here, finding themselves without support and without resources, they fall into the clutches of compatriots affiliated with Mazzinianism who really are dangerous; after a while they become Mazzinians themselves. One might in all conscience say that it is the Roman government itself that by its imprudent expulsions is guilty of furnishing Mazzini with the means of recruiting his army. If we could get the Pope to keep his bad subjects at home and to reopen his doors to those who are uncompromised, three-quarters of the job would be done, and the emigration would be reduced to insignificant proportions. Thus if the French government wants to dry up the fatal source from which so many murderous infamies flow, it should address itself to the Pope and not to us.

But we come to the second subject treated by the Prince de la Tour d'Auvergne: the *press*. On this point he was mightily insistent without formulating anything precise; he repeated in every key that something more had to be done than we had announced ourselves prepared to do. Amid the haze of his discourse, it appeared to me that he would have liked: 1st the suppression of *L'Italia del popolo;* 2d prosecution before ordinary courts for attacks on foreign governments; 3d the prohibition of foreigners from writing in the newspapers; 4th official prosecution of offenses against sovereigns. The first demand is for the equivalent of a *coup d'état.*

The law does not permit the government to suppress a journal; if it did so, the courts would condemn it and public opinion would violently censure it. If M. de la Tour d'Auvergne had followed the Gramont system and had consented to file suit against it [the paper], it would have perished under the battering of repeated adverse judgments. But M. de la Tour d'Auvergne proclaimed upon his arrival here that he would refuse to file suit *because that would render less evident the necessity of modifying the press laws.* The journalists, assured of a kind of impunity by that declaration, took off the brake. The results obtained by Gramont in four years of perseverance and struggle were compromised in an instant by the ill-will of his successor. This may be the way M. de la Tour d'Auvergne operates, but I should try to reach the same goal by other means.

The second point cannot be granted at a time when we are radically reforming the jury system. We cannot simultaneously improve the jury system and narrow its jurisdiction; that would be a flagrant self-contradiction. We have preferred jury reform because we consider this a more effective measure, with a much greater scope. It is for the sake of repression that we have resolved upon the more extended and more effective measure.

I shall not discuss the third point because I have already treated it fully at the beginning of my letter.

I come to the fourth: official prosecution of offenses against foreign sovereigns is immensely inconvenient to us; because of our position *vis à vis* Austria, the Pope, and the King of Naples, this can become an endless source of difficulty and annoyances; but still it is a measure which is not contrary to the principles I have consistently professed. The treacherous conduct of the Pr. de la Tour d'Auvergne toward us makes it, in my eyes, almost necessary. I shall try to bring my colleagues to share this opinion. If I succeed, the law we shall propose will consist of 3 parts:

1. More precise definition of what can incite outrages or political assassination;
2. Radical modification of the law on the composition of juries;
3. Official prosecution of slanders against foreign sovereigns.

I hope that these measures will be considered satisfactory by the French government; in any case I shall refuse to do more. I repeat to you: I took up the portfolio of Interior to combat Mazzini and Revolution, I am determined to do so with the greatest vigor, but at the same time I intend to remain faithful to my principles; I should resign the ministry a hundred times before renouncing them.

It may be that by bringing pressure to bear the French government will force me to quit power; but let it beware the consequences of this senseless action. It will lose a friend who is not without value. Instead of supporters of the Empire, power will be in the hands of more or less disguised legitimists. The edifice of the French alliance, which took such pains to build, will be wrecked. The prestige of the moderate party will be destroyed, and the influence of Mazzini will grow to an immense proportion.

If that is what the Emperor desires, he need only follow the inspirations of Walewski and of de la Tour d'Auvergne.

Believe, my dear Marquis, in my devoted sentiments.

(P.S.) I am sending you the statistics on the emigration to Genoa and information on measures taken in this regard.

General Enrico Della Rocca* to King Victor

Paris, 5 February 1858

Sire,

Having finally had the honor of a long conversation with H. M. the Emperor, I hasten to communicate the result to Y. M.

The arrival of the Prussian Princes, the reception of Prince Lichtenstein, envoy extraordinary from Austria, the dinners and hunts accorded him, and above all the acquittal of the journal *La Ragione*, which has produced bad effects here, were the reasons why our official dinner was delayed until this evening.

Seeing that no opportunity to talk with the Emperor had come, these recent days, I had decided to ask M. the Duc de Bassano to obtain for me a special audience, as Y. M. had indicated in his instructions. H. M. the Emperor had me told that he would talk with me in his cabinet after the dinner.

Actually this evening after the official dinner (at which M. the Marquis de Villamarina and I were accorded the first places, and for which the Emperor wore the neck-piece of the Order), I was bidden into the Emperor's cabinet by a sign of his hand.

It was the Emperor who opened the conversation, saying that he had found Y. M.'s letter most friendly, and that he would answer you soon. After I had told him all that Y. M. had done me the honor of instructing me to tell him, he took charge of the conversa-

*Chief aide-de-camp to the King.

Il carteggio Cavour-Nigra, I, 59–61.

tion again, asking me to pay close attention so as not to forget anything and so as to be able to report his thoughts to you quite entire.
I shall endeavor, Sire, to repeat this long discourse to you with
frequent quotations, not entirely sure of his exact words, but as
accurately as I can.

"I have infinite liking and esteem for the King and very great
respect for M. de Cavour. I want them to be quite certain that I
have always been very well-disposed toward Piedmont, which I
should like to see prosper; but I know positively that you have no
policing, particularly in Genoa and in Savoy, where officials have no
effective means of carrying it out. The Press is much too free. It
shows no respect for morality, religion, for order, for persons. You
do not have laws adequate to suppress it. You have just absolved
and acquitted *La Ragione* and this has affected me painfully. One
must have the strength and the energy to propose and promulgate
the needed laws, and to modify existing ones. I do not claim that all
emigrés should be turned back at the border; but the bad ones should
be rooted out and the others kept under surveillance. What I say to
Piedmont I say also to Belgium, to Switzerland, to England, that very
England that is a great Nation. I should have to have no blood in
my veins to tolerate assassins on my frontier, to tolerate the preaching and the defence of assassination in the countries of my neighbors.
Consider: England and France have an equal interest in remaining
united, and yet if there too nothing is done, the amity will start to
cool; and you know that from coolness to hostility, my dear M. de la
Rocca, is only one step. So I say to Piedmont. I love your country,
I love your King, I am sympathetic toward your colors, toward the
cause it represents in Italy; but if nothing is done, if no way is
found to restrain the press, protect morality and religion, if there
is no law and order, my friendship will cool and I shall be forced to
align myself closely with Austria. Then what will happen to Piedmont? So let this be well considered. Make sure you realize that I
am your only ally; do not imagine that England will help you! What
can she give you? Some money perhaps, but not a single man. There
must be a choice between France and England; and the choice cannot
be in doubt. I insist that everything necessary be done, everything I
have the right to demand. Belgium is beginning to take action with a
good grace (though I do not think with too much belief in the actions
taken). The Government at Berne has sent two commissioners to
Geneva to verify the number and kind of emigrés, but they won't
find them any longer, because they have gone over to Savoy, where

the police have taken no trouble. When the commissioners have gone, these gentlemen who have been so well-received by you will return to Geneva. You read the newspapers; you must have read the petitions from all the corps of my army; I have even had suppressed a number of them which were much stronger than those you have read. I need only raise a finger and my army, like all France, will march delightedly to wherever I tell them is the sanctuary of assassins."

Sire, if I were to report to you completely all the Emperor said to me, I should never finish, though he concluded by repeating himself over and over. Naturally I did my best to calm H. M.; I repeated to him what he had heard many times from the Marquis de Villamarina; I assured him of the good intentions of Y. M. and of the Count de Cavour; but the Emperor, even while assuring me that he had full and entire confidence in the loyalty and the good character of Y. M., finished by repeating to me the same phrase he used with Villamarina on the evening of the grand ball at the Tuileries: "If he does not do what I wish, then I can no longer count on him."

The Emperor dismissed me by asking if I could promptly lay what he had just said before Y. M.; and when I answered that I had a courier at my disposal whom I could send express, he requested me, if I was staying in Paris, to let him know Y. M.'s response.

I did not think it my duty to say that I was leaving, and I have felt I must await your orders. Before concluding this letter I think I am also obliged to inform you, Sire, that the Ministers, Statesmen, Marshals, Presidents, etc., with whom I have had occasion to converse were badly informed about our country. Almost all of them asked if things were getting better, if the troubles had ceased. We have thought it our duty to answer the plain truth: that tranquillity reigns at home, that there was not the slightest disorder during the elections and that everything proceeded lawfully.

It is not without very painful sentiments that I fulfill my duty by addressing this letter to Y. M.; meanwhile all it contains, or very nearly, you have already been informed of by the Minister the Marquis Villamarina, to whom the Emperor expressed the very same sentiments.

I lay at Y. M., feet the homage of my profound respect, and in the expectation of your orders I have the honor to declare myself Y. M.'s

P. S. I ask Y. M.'s pardon if I add a few more lines; but upon rereading I perceive I forgot an essential phrase of the Emperor's. One of these days, he said to me, I shall order a regiment into Geneva and I shall settle the question of that republic that way.

This leaves tomorrow by express and will arrive in Turin on Monday.

Marquis Villamarina to Cavour

(Private)

My dear Count   Paris, 6 February 1858
Yesterday I had the honor of dining with the Emperor, along with General La Rocca and Count Robilant. After dinner the Emperor took La Rocca aside, conversed with him privately for a long time, and then came to me, took me by the arm, and led me to a corner of the room. His Majesty informed me succinctly of his conversation with La Rocca immediately, asking me to note that he had wished thereby to give testimony of his sympathy and special affection for the King, saying that he had used only the language of an open heart, Sovereign to Sovereign.

It would only be repetitious for me to report word for word the arguments the Emperor used in his conversation with La Rocca; he has always followed the same theme since the unhappy event of 14 January. Yet there is one circumstance that seems to me quite remarkable, which I hope La Rocca will not forget in his report to the King. That very circumstance seems to me of a kind to merit the attention of an eminent statesman like yourself, being animated by sentiments of the warmest patriotism. Permit me then, dear Count, to give you here the precise words of the Emperor.

"I can assure you, dear Marquis, that the language I address to Sardinia is the same as that which I address to other powers, including England. Thus you must not believe that I claim to exercise any sort of pressure on your Government; that is far from my purpose, for, unlike so many other sovereigns, even in the serious vicissitudes of my life, I have appreciated and respected the dignity of small States, in the most difficult of circumstances. But just what is it that I ask? . . . to be accorded the easiest thing in the world by a government, let me not say allied, but simply fair, honest, and of good faith.

Il carteggio Cavour-Nigra, I, 61–63.

"Consequently I say to you openly that if England refuses to do justice to my reasonable requests, my relations with her will weaken bit by bit, and from that state of affairs to hostilities in only a step.

"In that case, let us, *entre nous,* look frankly at the position in which Sardinia will find herself. There are two possibilities. Either be with me or against me. Have no illusions; your real support is France. So to be with me, you must unavoidably consent to do what I have asked you to do, or else be against me. What real advantages can an English alliance offer you? No material support, that goes without saying; for England has no army at all, and what is more, she will have India and China on her hands for a long time yet; so it will come down to the dispatch of a few warships to the ports of Genoa and Spezia, with no profit to you if England persists, as she has done so far, in upholding the treaties of 1814–1815. Add that in this latter case I should be obliged despite myself to count on the support of Austria, and once entered into that orbit, I should be forced to renounce all that has been until now my private dream, my heart's desire. Even I, who have always wanted the well-being and independence of Italy, should be forced to ally myself with a cabinet for which I have always felt, and feel at this very moment still, the strongest repugnance."

Now that I have been chronicler of what happened yesterday evening, dear Count, allow me to give you my personal impressions of the physical and moral state of the Emperor.

I have found him weighed down, dominated by thoughts of assassination, and his face and his body show it clearly. Every word he says, and the expression he gives to them, betray this intimate and permanent feeling in his soul; one can see how the idea of assassination pursues without cease, and that it agitates him terribly.

I must also tell you of an incident which occurred in the course of the evening, concerning the Empress. Her Majesty, surrounded by a group of ladies (among whom were Mme. Villamarina and my children, my daughter and my daughter-in-law), said that on that very day the accused Pieri had confessed that at first the plan of the conspirators had been to get admitted with false invitations to a ball at the Tuileries which took place the night before the assassination attempt, and to kill the Emperor in his apartments in the very midst of the festivities. Pieri and Orsini had decided to sacrifice their lives. The Empress told of this infernal plan with such accents of woe and of emotion that her lamentations attracted the eyes of everybody. It was then that the Empress added: are we indiscreet, are we too de-

manding or too violent if after such things have happened we ask
our neighbor states and friends to expel conspirators from their territories, and to make proper laws against the licentiousness of the
press? . . .

I cannot conclude this report without expressing to you the satisfaction I have found in the candor and loyalty of La Rocca, who
repeated to me the whole of the conversation he had with the Emperor.

I am desolate, dear Count, that the strict observation of my duties
obliges me, in telling you of all that has just happened, perhaps to
increase your difficulties; but what shall I do? Think well on all I
have sent you today and you will perceive, I am sure, that the Emperor, like myself and all the sane and enlightened party in our
country, wants to maintain you in power; because everyone believes
it is Piedmont's good fortune for you to be head of the government
at this moment, for you *alone* in the country have acquired, with
just title, the eminence necessary to bring the parties to do what circumstances imperiously demand that they do. For the rest believe it,
my dear Count, your poor representative in Paris has no bed of roses,
and is not free of sleepless nights . . .

Napoleon III to King Victor

                              Palace of the Tuileries, 8 February 1858
          Monsieur mon frère
I am very sensible of the interest which Y. M. has shown for the
Empress and me on the occasion of the attempt of 14 January. Your
letter genuinely touched me and I thank you for sending it to me by
General de la Rocca. What has given me great pleasure as well is
to see Y. M. has resolved no longer to tolerate in his State the fomenters of disorder and the instigators of assassination. You know
how devoted I am to Your Person and your cause; so you will permit
me to speak frankly. If Piedmont gives an example of a Government
which is liberal but firm and master in its own house, it will be able
always to count on the support of France. If on the contrary one
comes to see a deplorable weakness in the places of power in favor
of demagogy, if one sees the incendiary journals openly preaching
assassination and contempt for religion, if one knows that your Government does not dare take action against your most loyal allies, then,

Il carteggio Cavour-Nigra, I, 63.

I say with regret, in self-defense I shall be obliged to repress within myself all my sympathies and no longer regard Piedmont as anything but a source of agitation, dangerous for all the world. I receive letters from Genoa, from Nice, from Chambéry; they complain everywhere of the total lack of order and of license left to the worst people to say and do whatever they please. Such a state of affairs, I beg Y. M. to believe me, does more harm to the cause of Italy than all the political attacks of Austria. I much esteem and like M. de Cavour, but there is only one honorable road to follow, and that is to break sharply with the ultra-radical party and to put oneself frankly at the head of the ideas of order, of justice, of morality, without abandoning the national cause. A chief who *governs* is followed; that chief is repudiated who puts himself in the train of any party whatever.

There, Sire, is what I had to tell you; I hope Y. M. will see in my frankness only the sincere desire always to maintain with Him and his Government the most intimate and most affectionate relations.

The Empress charges me thank Y. M. for his good remembrance and I renew my assurance to you of my sentiments of high esteem and amity. *De V. M. le bon frère*

King Victor to General Della Rocca (in Cavour's hand)

My dear de la Rocca   (9 February 1858)
I received your letter yesterday evening; I answer it this morning at 5:00 o'clock after having let the night pass and I think I was right to do so, for I must confess the effect it had on me was not very agreeable, for aside from the personal compliments which the Emperor was good enough to render my person and that of Count Cavour, from your letter one may perceive in the words of the Emperor you report to me something which resembles reproaches or threats (something to which I am very little accustomed) especially where the Emperor speaks of joining with Austria against us if we *do not immediately carry out his wishes.* This seems to me a little violent especially because I deserve nothing of the kind, neither myself nor my [crossed out: "people"] country. The Emperor says he lets this country be spoken to in the same way that he lets England, Belgium, and Switzerland be spoken to: I hope he will not wish us to be compared with those Gentlemen in every way, especially as

Il carteggio Cavour-Nigra, I, 64–65.

it is a question of the loyal and frank affection and sympathy which I and my country have always shown on every occasion, for no King and no country have loved him nor do love him so frankly as we.

So I fear, dear de la Rocca, that you must have made the case seem more grave than it really is and that you have not accurately reported the Emperor's words, for I know from experience the nobility and steadfastness of his heart and I know that he sees clearly in all things.

We come to details: Press, Police, Émigrés, England.

Press. The Emperor knows that the press is free here, but there is also a repression law which, though it is not very severe, has always served us well in the past, serving to condemn always or almost always with good strong penalties journals which talked against religion, against foreign sovereigns (after the request had been made by their representatives) and against morality, so well that some journals, convicted several times with heavy fines, had to close.

Now the jury, in a way I much deplore but could not prevent, has absolved the *Ragione*: without the Emperor's saying anything to me about the subject, I immediately spoke to Cavour and we are putting together a law which will completely prevent any such thing from ever happening again; I shall send it to you and you will see it is forceful. It will be brought before the parliament.

Police. Although our policing has not been brought to the perfection of the French, still we have always had it, and it has served us in the interior of our country, foreseeing and preventing revolutionary movements of whatever kind. And no matter what they say in France, since the '49 this country has enjoyed the most perfect calm. This country is so good and so affectionate that you know, dear General, that I travel by night and by day everywhere, all alone, and neither I nor my ancestors have had to fear the smallest attack; even the most heated émigré party is quite respectful. I cannot set myself to torturing everybody. The Emperor must have seen the circular from Cavour to the Prefects, and then I wrote them myself that I was as interested as Cavour, most specifically, in a more energetic reorganization of the police, and I would give them proof of it. But one cannot do everything in 24 hours.

Tell the Emperor for me that not so long ago, Mazzini made a longer visit in Paris than he has made in Piedmont, and the police did not find him. Felice Orsini was surely in Paris for several days too before the frightful event; one does what he can.

Émigrés. We regularly expel a great number of émigrés; when we know they are dangerous we make up cargoes of them for America. But tell the Emperor that the greatest part of them, at least a great number, come to us via Marseille. Now Cavour has written a very strong note to Rome asking that she take back those Roman subjects of which she has complained to us from time to time.

England. Someone is talking here of an intimate alliance we are supposed to have with England. If the Emperor believes that, he is deceived. We have certainly been friendly to England whenever our policy has demanded it; but the Emperor must know how little liking I in particular have for England, her policy, and her Lord Palmerston. I have only one single and true ally, and that is himself.

From what I have just said to you, dear La Rocca, the Emperor must be quite persuaded of my good intentions and see that things have been done before he asked for them. If he wanted violence here, I should lose all my power, and he would lose the sympathy and affection of a generous and noble nation. Do not play the imbecile, dear General; tell him all this in my name, and *if the words you have transmitted to me are the exact words of the Emperor,* tell him in whatever terms you think best that one does not treat a faithful ally in this fashion; that I have never tolerated physical violence, that I am the soul of honor, never blemished; and that for this honor I am answerable only to God and my people; that for 850 years we have carried our head high and no one has made us bow it; and that for all that I desire nothing but to be his friend. Adieu, do your duty and tell me by courier what the Emperor says and if he wants something different from me. Your affectionate

Cavour to Villamarina

(Written on the back, in Cavour's hand: "Letter to the M's. Villamarina, which accompanied the answer of the King to G'l. La Rocca.")

My dear Marquis,   9 February 1858
Tonight the King sends the courier Roveda with his answer to the letter from La Rocca. The King desires that you take cognizance of it so that you can understand exactly his sentiments and his intentions.

The letter from La Rocca has excited his profound indignation and lively irritation. The blood of the counts of Verd, of Emmanuel-Philibert and of Amadeus, that flows in his veins was repelled by the Emperor's unseemly language. After having treated him as a faithful ally, a devoted friend, he could not expect to see accusations and threats directed against him.

The letter he sent back to La Rocca is noble and dignified; it is the kind of letter his noble ancestors would have written, not hesitating to risk their crowns to preserve the honor of their country. I should not think it unfitting if La Rocca committed the indiscretion of reading it to the Emperor; but he must avoid leaving it in his hands, for fear he make a copy of it; for it contains an item on England which I regret, but which could cause no inconvenience provided it cannot be used as written proof of his lack of sympathy for perfidious Albion.

The King's language is very amicable toward the Emperor; it must show him that the King still considers him a sincere ally and a true friend; but at the same time it shows that the Emperor would deceive himself in an extraordinary way if he thought to intimidate him. Charles Albert went to die at Oporto sooner than bow his head to Austria. Victor Emmanuel would let himself be swallowed up twenty times by Alpine gorges before making a humiliating concession to France. These sentiments must pervade your speech. While carefully avoiding anything that could be interpreted as a provocation or as bravado, you must make the Emperor and his ministers understand that we are determined to risk everything before compromising our dignity or our National honor.

La Rocca wrote the King that the ministers and the high functionaries of the Empire talked to him of Piedmont's troubles, of the excessive agitation in the country, etc. But just where are these gentlemen fishing out their information from? No country in Europe is more tranquil than ours. Despite tremendous interest in the elections, there was not the slightest disorder when they took place. The Genoa trial started a week ago, and foreigners passing through that town would have a hard time seeing any sign of it. Really, if the French police reports on everything the way it reports on our country, it is a hundred times stupider than ours. Lose no opportunity to deny these absurd rumors and to establish the true facts concerning us.

Even though we are determined to concede nothing to the unreasonable demands of France, we shall continue to apply vigorously the measures I told you about in my last letter. At Genoa the screening of the émigrés goes forward with an energy *that leaves nothing to be desired.* Two émigrés, the Pezzi brothers, relying on the protection of the municipality in whose service they were, did not obey orders to leave and were put into prison in the full light of day. The syndic of Genoa has written me several letters in their favor; in my answers I have restricted myself to saying that in the matter of émigrés, as in all the rest, the government is *unmovable.* The look of Genoa has changed remarkably; wait another two weeks and it will no longer be recognizable, without coup d'état, without any arbitrary measures. If the French consul in that town is an honest man, he must inform his government of this.

As for the press, I have undertaken to have two consecutive days of *L'Italia e Popolo* seized, in expectation of confirmation of the telegraphic report which indicates that the French government will consent to make us a general request which will serve in all cases. You promised me a letter for this purpose via Roveda, but he has brought me only your special note of the 6th, which does not touch upon this question.

I repeat, you can assure the French government that nothing will be left undone to satisfy what is legitimate in its requests; and that we shall obtain by honest and legal means far greater results than we should by violence and arbitrariness.

Our policing system is getting organized. Perhaps we have known what was going on at Geneva longer than the French police itself. A highly placed and very reliable agent has offered to get Pescantini, the habitual host of Mazzini, to come to Piedmont, assuring me that once he is here, we could by fair means or foul discover important secrets. I have not made up my mind about it yet, but I let you know of this fact so that if you hear we have let Pescantini come make an excursion here, you will know there are *good reasons.*

The Emperor is unjust toward the Intendants of Savoy. It is possible that some émigrés have entered illegally, but none has taken up residence there and certainly none has got into Piedmont that way. A small number of émigrés crossed Savoy, but that was so as to re-enter France via Seysell.

As I have been writing you at length these days, I have nothing to add for today, except to urge you not to let yourself be downcast. Courage, dear Marquis; walk with your head high as the representative of a generous sovereign, and of a loyal and energetic government which knows its duties as well as its rights, which will never compromise with the spirit of disorder or of revolution any more than it will let itself be intimidated by the menaces of neighboring powers.

Strong in your conscience, you will carry on the struggle at Paris so far as you have hope of seeing justice done to your country; and should that have to be given up, then you will turn away from diplomatic processes and don your colonel's uniform to come defend at the King's side the honor and independence of our country.

Believe me, etc.

P. S. The Genoa trial has not commenced badly. The prosecution witnesses show much courage; the prosecutor-general hopes for good results from this.

I reopen this letter to repair an oversight. Judging by the discourse of the Emperor to La Rocca, and by certain remarks of M. de la Tour d'Auvergne, it is apparent that there is a belief at Paris that since the attempt of the 14th we have sought rapprochement with England, while loosening the tie of the French alliance. Nothing more false. Strong in our right, in our loyalty, we have so far solicited support from nobody. I have not written a line to D'Azeglio* on the subject of the French demands respecting the press and refugees, and I have only said a few casual words to Hudson. Certainly if France joins Austria we shall seek support from England, just as we shall seek auxiliaries from among the ranks of oppressed peoples. But as long as the Emperor does not desert the cause of the nationalities, as long as he is faithful to his old program, we shall be with him. To avert the dangers that menace him, let him unfurl the banner of the cause of peoples and he shall find us at his side or better as his vanguard, whatever the adversaries he may have to combat, even if the whole continent aided by England should join against him.

*Piedmontese ambassador at London.

General Della Rocca to King Victor

Sire,   Paris, 13 February 1858, 4 o'clock
The second telegraphic dispatch, of the contents of which M. de Cavour will tell you, can only be explained by this letter, which I have the honor to address to you, Sire, to bring you up to date on what the Emperor told me during an audience with which he has just honored me.

At half-past one the Emperor had me enter his study and received me with his customary affability. I told him all about the painful effect which my dispatch had had on you, and after several explanations I let him read your letter; and as it contains a passage where Y. M. seems to doubt the accuracy of my report of the Emperor's words, I asked him to read also what I had the honor to write to you. When that was done, he assured me that I had faithfully reported his thoughts and almost his words.

The Emperor infinitely regrets that Y. M. has been pained by that letter, and he is distressed that at that moment you were receiving his letter, in which, he told me, he repeated the same things to Y. M., before receiving this explanation. He charges me assure you that he does not wish to contradict in any way the procedure of the Government; he does not wish and he has never thought of pretending to change our legislation. He does not want anything that would contradict you or risk forcing you to change ministries. He respects our liberty of press, our institutions, and all he wants is that it be not permitted to preach assassination, to make apologies for it, and to allow journalists continually to attack order and preach revolution. In short, he repeated to me several times, I desire nothing other than to conduct myself as one should with a genuine friend. So say to your King that I have always believed and that I believe perfectly now in his good intentions and that I am persuaded that he is taking action and will do so, and that I regret that he could think that I wanted to exert any kind of pressure. He is king in his country as I am the sovereign in France.

He added an infinity of other phrases which I shall have the honor to repeat to you upon my return, which would be too long to write down this evening before the departure of the courier. All in all, the Emperor seemed to me much calmer than at the other audience.

I had the honor to observe to him that H. E. M. the Count de Cavour has already done a good deal in the way of police since becoming Minister of Interior, and that you intend to do all you think wise and appropriate, as soon as the reopening of the Chambers, i.e., in a few days. He seemed to me quite satisfied and he added that he had full confidence in M. Cavour. Before letting him read Y. M.'s letter I took care to warn him that it had been addressed to me and that naturally it contained phrases and expressions dictated by the bad humor resulting from my letter. In response he assured me that he understood this remark quite well, but that for that matter one should never be vexed by more or less strong phrases among friends.

On the matter of the Austrian alliance he wished to explain anew: "I love Italy and especially Piedmont, and I shall always be her ally against Austria; so my thought is that I should never like to be pushed toward an alliance with Austria. My background and the constant policy of France itself must reassure you, and if in 1849 I had occupied the place I do now, I would have aided Charles Albert."

H. M. the Emperor wanted to know from my point of view the state of the other countries of Italy. My response was as laconic as possible, but I thought it my duty to say to him that the number of malcontents was steadily growing; and speaking particularly of the Roman State, I said to him that I did not think anybody could pretend that subjects so badly governed and administered were contented. He answered that I was right and that in fact Rome was the real stumbling-block for Italy.

As Y. M. has ordered me to wait here until the arrival of the law which will be presented to the Chambers, I shall not leave Paris yet, hoping to receive Y. M.'s orders with the law.

I have the honor to be, with profoundest respect, Y. M.'s

P.S. I forgot to say, Sire, that in my explanations to the Emperor I let him think I had received several other letters from Y. M.

General Della Rocca to Cavour

My dear friend,   Paris, 13 February 1858
This is the first time I have been charged with a diplomatic mission and I have got through it in the way I could, which is to say like an *imbecile.* Yet the Emperor was much calmer and seemed to me content with what is being done and what it is proposed to do.

I had imagined that the King's letter would be badly received or badly interpreted by him, but there was no fuss, and I even think that this somewhat strong language did not displease him.

To excuse my clumsiness and at the same time to have one more excuse for having him read the letter, I protested that I had never been a diplomat and that I am only a soldier, fully devoted to my King and my country for more than 33 years. Then he answered me: it is exactly the non-diplomats who make order of the tangles diplomats have made, so don't stand on ceremony, and talk to me as soldier to soldier.

From my correspondence I already know about all the ridiculous things published about me in the little journals, but Villamarina's answer will let you know the whole truth. Naturally Pr. Lichten-

Il carteggio Cavour-Nigra, I, 70–71.

stein was more ceremoniously received than all the other envoys, but that is easily explained. You will see the letter I have just hastily written to H. M., which I shall send together with this. It does not contain all the Emperor could say to me in an audience of a full hour, but the essentials are there.

Since I am writing you, I warn you that I have seen a very reliable person who said he had received a letter from the French consul at Nice, and that he talks of the quantities of Mazzinians there are in that town. I do not know whether the French consul at Nice is a capable man or not, but presumably there was some truth in what he wrote to a friend.

The King has ordered me to stay here until he has sent me the law you plan to present to the Chambers, so as to give a copy to the Emperor. I am awaiting new orders.

Do me the kindness of making excuses to the King for my letter, which I have just sealed without even rereading it, so that it could still get off this evening. Aff.

Cavour to Villamarina

My dear Marquis,   Turin, 14 February 1858

M. Thomas d'Aquin brought yesterday the response of the Emperor to the autograph letter of the King which had been sent him by way of General La Rocca. This letter repeated in a slightly more courteous form the principle points the Emperor raised with the general in the conversation he reported to the King. It is a question of the absence of any policing, the alliance of the Government with the ultra-radicals, and a thousand absurdities of that sort. You can complain sharply to Walewski about the kind of accounts his agents give him of what happens in Piedmont. If our policing is not perfect, it is no worse than the French, which permits to live at our gates, despite our requests, a number of Mazzinian Committees, and which knows of the existence in France of an enormous number of secret societies without managing to get hold of the thread that unites them.

After these recriminations, you will repeat that I am engaged in improving the police, and that I think I have already done a great deal in that regard, especially at Genoa.

The Emperor cites Chambéry as a center of disorder, where a great number of refugees has collected. I believe that there are no

Il carteggio Cavour-Nigra, I, 71–73.

more than 3 or 4 in that town. The most notable is M. Cousset. Before interning him I asked you for information on him; you transmitted to me very favorable information furnished you by the French Police. After that I should not have expected these unfair accusations.

Whatever the Emperor's irritation and the unseemliness of his behavior, we shall nonetheless do what we had decided to do to render legitimate satisfaction to France. But nothing more, and remember that. The King will do anything before he will submit to humiliating pressure. His Father died at Oporto, and he will die in America if necessary; but he will not tarnish his glorious escutcheon.

M. d'Aquin declared to me that in Paris everybody is in a rather irrational state of excitement. He repeated to me as coming from Walewski the same things that La Tour d'Auvergne said to me. He thinks that Walewski will have no difficulty in making the general request you have asked him for. This subject must be made quite clear, because if La Tour d'Auvergne should say that France has expressed its hopes but has made neither demand nor request he would be putting us in a cruel position, now that since receipt of your telegraphic dispatches we have seized six consecutive numbers of the *Italia e Popolo*. Speaking of that accursed journal, I shall tell you that by having its printing verified I have determined that there were 400 copies printed of which 200 were distributed gratis and 200 sent to subscribers. In view of these facts it is impossible to understand how France can attribute so much importance to the wretched sheet.

The ambassadors from Prussia and Russia openly condemn French conduct toward us. I maintained very reserved language with them. Still it would be useful in this regard to determine whether they are speaking on their own accounts or whether they are faithfully expressing the opinions of their governments. M. de La Tour d'Auvergne has come back to his campaign for the ejection of Bianchi-Giovini; that is really too much, considering that for the past ten days the poor man has been defending the Emperor's policies. To give you an idea of de La Tour's ill-will, let it suffice to tell you that when the Order of St. Helena, which is headed by a number of generals, celebrated with much pomp a solemn Te Deum at the Santi Martiri, La Tour, though invited in due form did not attend and contented himself with sending secretaries.

Alessandro Bixio* to Cavour

(Private)   (Paris, 18 March 1858)

My very dear friend,

I so love the Italian cause, which your government today personifies, and I have such true friendship for you, that I hesitate to tell you with what regret I have learned that the legislative proposal has just been rejected by the committee.**

Sardinia is obliged to rely either on Austria or France. Any alliance with Austria would be odious and impossible, so that you are obliged to lean on France, whatever her government is.

The present question is of more importance than is imagined in Turin. Nobody here will ever believe that if M. de Cavour had chosen to make this into a question of confidence in his cabinet, it would have been rejected; and there is a rancor here against the Sardinian government and against M. de Cavour which will very soon be translated into deeds. If on the other hand M. de Cavour makes it a confidence question, the liberal majority will probably realize that to turn power over to the clerical party for the sake of needling the Emperor of the French would be a deplorable maneuver. If they should be obstinate about it, fine; M. de Cavour would resign power, and surely that would not be for long.

But if I were in M. de Cavour's place I should wish, before undertaking this kind of campaign, to learn from the French government what it would give me for the Italian cause, in case I burned my boats this way.

Such importance is attached here to the passage of that law that I am persuaded full guarantees against Austria would be given. If M. de Cavour spent 48 hours in Paris this question could be better handled by him than by anybody else; in default of a trip, which the adjournment of the Congress† makes impossible, I am convinced the question could be handled by correspondence.

Let me summarize.

The law, to which the French government attaches an importance much more concerned with pride than security, does not violate the principles which you and I have always defended; I should make it a

*An acquaintance of Cavour's who moved in high circles in Paris, notably in the entourage of Prince Napoleon.

**The proposal for stiffening the Sardinian press laws, called the "De Foresta law."

†Discussing the disposition of the Danube principalities, at Paris.

Il carteggio Cavour-Nigra, I, 81.

confidence question; but I should not get into a battle with the mis-
informed but general sentiment of my country until after assuring
it in return certain compensations. If I can help you in any way, indicate it frankly.

Yours from the heart

Villamarina to Cavour

My dear Count,   Paris, 28 March 1858
Day before yesterday the Emperor let me be sent by way of our excellent friend C . . . the original of the letter written to H. I. M. by
Orsini on 11 March, along with the original of his testament. Our
friend C . . . told me that the communication of these two items to
me was done in a confidential manner so that I could if need be
guarantee their authenticity. The excellent C . . . did not fail to make
me understand that while it was impossible for the Emperor to give
publicity to these two items in France at this time, he had a *lively* desire to see them receive it in our country.

After reading the letter, and Orsini's testament, I answered with
extreme delicacy that first I needed something written which proved
the Emperor's authorization; then that while the Orsini letter seemed
to me of a kind to have a good effect at home, I should still have to
ask you about it; and that when you had answered, I should hasten
to inform the Emperor of your decision.

No sooner said than done. . . . the next day I received *exact*
copies of the two items in question, sent to me by C . . . at the Emperor's orders. In transmitting them to you herewith I am only carrying out the promise I gave, with no intention of exercising the slightest influence on your mind, which remains free to take whatever
line it finds appropriate; still, if in order to comply with the Emperor's
wish you should in your wisdom see nothing inconvenient in letting
these two items be published at home, I think you would be doing
something which would be agreeable here by letting them appear,
at least the letter without testament, in the unofficial part of the
Piedmontese Gazette, saying *purely and simply* that they come from
an authentic source, which will be enough to assure that they will not
be considered apocryphal; and as it goes without saying that all the
other journals will hasten to publish these documents in their turn,
it would perhaps be wise with regard to those papers which correctly

Il carteggio Cavour-Nigra, I, 82–83.

or incorrectly are considered friendly to the government, such as the *Opinione,* the *Espero,* and the *Indipendente,* to let them be published there with the following introduction, which, I assure you, if it does not come from the Emperor's pen, certainly emanates from his thought. Here is the introduction:

> Italian patriots can be well persuaded that they will not attain their just ends by crimes abhorred by all civilized Society, and that conspiracy against the life of the single foreign Sovereign who nourishes sentiments of sympathy for their misfortunes, and who alone can still do something for the good of unhappy Italy, is a conspiracy against their own fatherland.

Considering the impatience manifested to me on this matter in high places, I should be very obliged to you, dear Count, if, should your decision conform with the desire that has been expressed to me, you were by telegraphing me the simple word *Yes* place me at once in the position of rendering myself agreeable to the Emperor and advancing another degree in the confidence with which he is good enough to honor me. . . .

Alessandro Bixio to Cavour

Paris, 31 March 1858

Thank you for your good letter,* my dear friend; you have chosen the best path and if the left is so unintelligent as to league itself with the right against you in this question of the De Foresta law, so much the worse for the left, so much the worse too, alas, for the country; but at least you will have nothing to reproach yourself for. I could only wish that you had not been too chivalrous on that occasion. When you so courageously raised the cry of the crusade against the Russians, you made no conditions and so people were disposed to accord you a great deal.

You succeeded in making Sardinia enter the congress of great nations, but you did not acquire the smallest village, not even Mentone and Monaco. France and England showed you great deference in the way of recognition but Sardinia was not given any guarantees for the event of a war with Austria; she was given no assurances for the case of a rearrangement of the map of Europe.

*The letter alluded to seems not to have been published, and may no longer exist. Ed.

Il carteggio Cavour-Nigra, I, 83–84.

I repeat, my friend, you have obtained much but you would have obtained much more if you had had better knowledge of what some were willing to give you to get your cooperation against the Russians.

It is my conviction that the same applies in the present question. Great store is set by the De Foresta law; if you stipulate in exchange advantages for Sardinia you must get them from France. But for this to succeed you must not negotiate through ordinary channels. Your excellent Villamarina will get nothing out of Walewski; you must deal directly with the Emperor, outside diplomacy. While you yourself could manage these negotiations in three days, in one day perhaps, still you could get agreement in the absence of yourself, whose presence in Turin is so useful; I do not know your personnel well enough to hazard advice. Only bear in mind that everything depends on the choice of the Negotiator.

And now what shall I say to you?

They say here that the Tory ministry finds your Ambassador d'Azeglio too thick with Lord Palmerston and with his daughter-in-law and that they intend to show you their teeth if you do not sacrifice him to them.

They say too that Naples is going to hand the *Cagliari* and your sailors over to you. Your firm note must have accomplished its purpose; I should rejoice.

Your utterly devoted friend

Cavour to Doctor Conneau*

Most honored Sir,   6 May 1858

A few days ago communications of supreme importance for the future of our country reached me, in the name of Prince Napoleon. I was given to understand these were matters not foreign to the Emperor's thinking. These communications hinted at propositions which cannot be discussed either in a letter of by means of diplomatic agents, however trustworthy they may be.

If matters were more advanced, if they rested on solid bases, perhaps the best thing would be for me to go to Paris myself for an interview with the Emperor. But in the present European situation, such a step would arouse immense suspicions, would occasion dangerous comment, could hurt the goal we hope to attain; it seems

*Napoleon III's personal physician, and a friend of Cavour's since 1856.

Il carteggio Cavour-Nigra, I, 85.

to me therefore that this ought not to be done until the conclusion of a definite accord seems probable, if not certain.

If however the Emperor consents to Your Excellency's coming to Turin, with the pretext of one of your customary visits to Italy, the proposition could be discussed with maximum secrecy.

I beg you to place these considerations before His Imperial Majesty and inform me of his august intentions.

This letter will be brought you by my private secretary, Sig. Nigra, whom I am sending to Paris to take to the Marquis Villamarina instructions relative to the coming conference.

Sig. Nigra enjoys my entire confidence.

"Conventional Phrases" for Telegraphic Correspondence Between Cavour and Nigra

May 1858

1. Conneau is informed of the project.
   —I pray Your Excellency let my wife know I have had a good trip.

2. Conneau is not informed of the project.
   —Let my family know that I have arrived in Paris without difficulty.

3. The Emperor confirms the propositions.
   —Would Your Excellency let my wife know that I am well.

4. The Emperor does not confirm the propositions.
   —Let them know at my house that I am well.

5. Doctor Conneau is coming to Turin.
   —I expect to leave soon.

6. The Emperor insists that you come to Paris.
   —I await your instructions.

Il carteggio Cavour-Nigra, I, 86.

Alessandro Bixio to Cavour

My dear friend,   Paris, 9 May 1858
You promised me two letters. One was to be delivered to Castelli: its purpose was to introduce my nephew, *Master Giulio Roberti,* to M.

Il carteggio Cavour-Nigra, I, 86.

de Brême and to commend him with as much warmth as your relations with M. de Brême permit. At the time I write you, you must already have sent it to him, and I thank you with all my heart. This letter, by calling M. de Brême's attention to a composer [*compositeur*] of real merit can decide my nephew's future. You will have made two people happy at the same time: him and me. A thousand thanks. Nothing you could do could please me more.

The second letter was for me, my dear friend; it was supposed to let me know whether your hope soon to visit Paris would be realized. All your friends in Paris would be happy to see you; I speak not of myself, for I fear I shall be deprived of that pleasure. I leave 17 May for Spain and shall not return until 4 June; I beg you to write me about what your plans are on the 14th at the latest.

Adieu, my dear friend; whatever happens you may count on my lively affection and my entire devotion.

Dispatches from Nigra to Cavour, Paris, 9 May 1858

Received at 10:20 a.m.

Count Cavour—Turin
Let my family know that I have arrived in Paris without difficulty.

Received at 5:55 p.m.

Count Cavour—Turin
Would Your Excellency let my wife know that I am well; I expect to leave soon.

Il carteggio Cavour-Nigra, I, 87.

Nigra to Cavour

(In cipher, with the deciphered form superimposed in Cavour's hand)

Paris, Hôtel du Louvre, Sunday, 9 May
This evening I presented letter Doctor as he was ignorant of project I refrained from complete explanation. I got him to promise read letter to the Emperor at three. Doctor communicated response Emperor said nothing was more serious than this proposition he confirmed his three points i.e. marriage, war with Austria, and Kingdom

Il carteggio Cavour-Nigra, I, 87–88.

of Upper Italy. But he added the war must be justified in the eyes
of the peoples it is therefore indispensable that the motives given for
it be plausible. Emperor did not enter into details he will send Doctor
to Turin at the end of the month to treat with Y. Excellency absolute
secrecy indispensable my presence has aroused no suspicion.

Paris, Hôtel du Louvre, Monday, 10 May 1858
I continue the letter of yesterday interrupted by the departure of the
courier for the execution of our projects Emperor believes cooperation of Russia useful he urges us in consequence not to offend sympathies of Czar for Court of Naples in Cagliari question he advises
us to be conciliatory he believes a war between two Italian governments would be harmful to our interests it appears that the intention
of the Emperor would be to divide Italy into three states i.e. Upper
Italy, Central Italy, and kingdom of Naples which would be left as is
same idea expressed to Doctor by Empress. Emperor greatly pleased
by the conduct of the King's government.

Paris, Hôtel du Louvre, Wednesday, 12 May
I confirm my two preceding enciphered notes and I add the Emperor
would not like the pretext of the war to be a question of émigrés.
Doctor told me yesterday he will leave the twenty-fifth unless you
give contrary orders.

P. S.   The next cipher can, without inconvenience, be deciphered by
a Cabinet Clerk.

Cavour to Alessandro Bixio

My dear friend,   14 May
Yesterday your nephew gave me your letter of the 9th of this month.
I think he will have told you that our friend Castelli has put him in
touch with Brême; I shall devote all my efforts to seeing that his
wishes are granted, though there is no hiding the fact that Theater
Directors are difficult people to manage.
    I have had to postpone my travel projects. The chief of the Great
House you spoke to me about having desired to have a person who
has his entire confidence visit the spots upon which the operations are
to be carried out, before negotiating. If this visit has the results I

hope for, it is probable I shall go to Paris next month. I shall be glad of this delay if it gives me the advantage of finding you in Paris.

Believe, my dear friend, in my devoted sentiments.

Doctor Conneau to Cavour

Palais Royal—216 Rue St. Honoré, 15 May 1858

Excellency,

I received your most esteemed letter from the hands of Sig. Nigra, and spoke immediately to the Emperor about the communication sent Your Excellency by the Prince Napoleon. His Majesty has confirmed everything, and expressed to me the greatest desire to make himself useful to Italy not only with words and advice, but with direct actions as well. Nevertheless, he said to me, he would not be able to do so if the occasion be not of a kind to attract general approbation. It is necessary, he said, to have this point clearly understood, not however to decide on what pretext to provide, but to establish only as a basis the conditions under which his cooperation could not be obtained. 1st: If it is a question of a war against purely Italian powers; 2nd: if the occasion of the war were to sustain a Mazzinian insurrection, or any such similar insurrection; 3rd: if it have as its purpose the support of Lombard subjects who have become Sardinians.

From what I have enumerated note that if it were subjects of Sardinian origin that were to be supported and defended the cause would be good. If one had to defend a population against unjust Austrian aggression. In the event of infractions of conventions and treaties, and he cited me as an example the fortifications built at Piacenza in defiance of the treaties, all that would be good pretext [*sic*. Dr. Conneau for some reason wrote in Italian, of which he was not master.] But he leaves it to your wisdom to find the pretext, provided that ere acting you come to agreement and accord. In any case there must be preparations, no wish to start things, and a wait until the spring of the coming year. Meanwhile allow no reconciliation. The Emperor for his part will start promptly, will avoid as best he can any reconciliation with Austria on the points under discussion, try meanwhile to send a fleet to the Adriatic under pretext of the Montenegrin difficulties, etc. But what he asks Your Excellency to have the greatest care for above all is not to jar Russia, which

Il carteggio Cavour-Nigra, I, 89–90.

Y. E. well knows has decided sympathy for Naples. The Emperor told me one must not from this take offence at that power which it it most useful to have in our favor; that if afterwards, as is probable, events require and lead to a sacrifice of Naples, the thing will seem to have come by itself and not preconcerted. Russia does not realize that a war in Italy with Austria cannot take place without the rest of Italy getting involved, and it is useless and even harmful to disabuse Russia on this point.

The Emperor would much have liked to talk with Your Excellency, but he sees that such a meeting would give material for many conjectures it is well to avoid. I shall be in Turin about the end of the month, and shall bring confirmation of what I tell you today briefly, and all that will be entrusted to me by the Emperor for the King or for Y. E.

Meanwhile may Your Excellency receive attestations of my profound respect and my high consideration. Most dev.

Cavour to the Marquis S. di Villamarina at Paris

My dear Marquis,   Turin, 2 June 1858
I saw Dr. Conneau as he passed through Turin. He told me some very friendly things from the Emperor. It seems that the bad impressions caused by the events of the past year and aggravated by the good offices of *our friends* have been entirely erased. From certain words which the doctor said to me I have reason to believe that the Emperor would not be displeased to have a chat with me about the state of Italy. He said repeatedly that as the Emperor was going to spend a month at Plombières, he would be close to our frontier during that time.

This geographical error does not diminish the import of the political hint. I told him that for my part I expected to take a few weeks vacation in Switzerland, and that if I had a few days available, I should be quite happy to spend them in paying a visit to the Emperor. It is probable that the doctor will report our conversation to Paris and that the Emperor will next charge you with informing me of his intentions. You understand that it is of the greatest importance that neither Walewski nor anybody else suspect what passed between the doctor and me.

Believe, my dear Marquis, in my devoted sentiments.

Cavour, *Lettere*, II (2d ed.), 556–57.

Alessandro Bixio to Cavour

Paris, 8 June 1858

Here I am back from my trip to Spain, my dear friend, and I want you to learn from no other person but me of the coming marriage of my daughter Helen, who will marry M. Camille Deprit, businessman of Moscow. I would be the happiest of fathers, for this marriage fulfills everything I could desire, but it will take four or five years before her husband has *finished his time* in Moscow and four or five years will seem to me a long time.

And the other marriage, my dear friend, just tell me where it stands and whether I can hope that my friend will be agreeable. There is apathy and I am counting on your precious cooperation, for a word from a man like you will clearly be decisive. I urge you not to make me wait for your answer. If in your opinion the marriage cannot be made, better to say so clearly; I should be as desolated as my friend, but nothing is worse than uncertainty.

Have you been so good as to expedite the matter of the *Imperial* Insurance Company whose request I sent to you? Should any justification or any explanation become necessary, let me know; you shall be immediately obeyed.

Adieu, my dear friend; I await your reply with anxious impatience.

Your completely devoted

Il carteggio Cavour-Nigra, I, 91.

Cavour to the Marquis S. di Villamarina at Paris

Turin, 19 June 1858

I send you Boyl with the boxes you ask for. Their official destination is The Hague, but you are authorized to keep them in Paris for as long as the conferences last.

I have received your message of the 17th which I found of great interest. I agree with you that despite all the protocols the question of the Principalities* will become an apple of discord, which is entirely consistent with our interests. I am very satisfied with the role you have played. Without putting yourself too much forward, you have succeeded in stating in a clear way the position of Sardinia.

*Agreement had just been reached on the organization of the Danubian Principalities.

Cavour, *Lettere*, II (2 ed.), 560.

I am impatient to know if the Emperor will follow up Conneau's insinuations, by inviting me to go see him at Plombières.

Still we must avoid forcing any explanation whatever on this subject. If occasion to see the Emperor does not arise quite naturally it must not be sought. Should the Emperor let something be said to you *by the Doctor,* you would not send it to me by telegraph, but rather you would let it be known by sending Mr. Minetti to Chambéry. Try to see Count Orloff and make sure he is still as anti-Austrian as ever. Believe, etc.

Cavour to Alessandro Bixio

My dear friend,   Turin, 14 June 1858
I felicitate you on the marriage of your daughter Helen. I hope this assures her happiness. The separation from the paternal household and even from one's country are often things which render marriages happier.

I am astonished that you ask for information on the affair which you brought about the month past at Turin. I thought you would have been told that the head of the house to which your friend belongs had sent his agents to Turin, and I have met them frequently. Although this agent was well-satisfied with what he saw, he told me that we could conclude nothing without his chief's having spoken directly with me. He has taken it upon himself to let me know when and where this interview will take place. As he did not return directly to Paris, he has not yet been able to send me the information in this regard which he has promised me.

I have sent the request of the *Imperial* Insurance Company to the Ministry of Finance with my recommendation. I shall solicit the expediting of the authorization which is necessary for its operations in the country. Believe, etc.

Il carteggio Cavour-Nigra, I, 91–92.

Conneau to Nigra

Most Illustrious Sir,   Florence, 28 June 1858
On the day after tomorrow I shall leave Florence for Corsica. For at least a month and a half I shall be at the *Porta Arrond.t de Bastia.* I have sent a letter to H. I. M. in which among other things I an-
Il carteggio Cavour-Nigra, I, 92.

nounced that H. E. Count Cavour, who is planning to go to Switzerland, will have written the aide-de-camp of the Emperor at Plombières to obtain from H. I. M. the honor of coming to pay his respects, meeting him at an agreed place.

I think H. E. must already have written and that the answer, if it has not already arrived, will not be long in coming. In any case I should like to assure H. E. of my devotion and my service.

Receive, most Noble Sir, attestation of my high esteem and consideration.

Alessandro Bixio to Cavour

Paris, 7 July 1858

I had always hoped, my dear friend, that you would come to Paris in the first days of July and that you would assist as a witness to the marriage of my daughter. Events have ordained otherwise, and I have really regretted it as has Prince Napoleon, my other witness, who would have been happy to have you as *second* and who has had to act without you.

Today all the papers announce your coming journey to France; but it would be very good of you to let me know with a word at what exact time we can expect you here. Our friend is as impatient as I for your arrival. I have learned from him all the details of the affair you have told me a few words about and all I know gives me hope and confidence.

You were kind enough to tell me that you had sent to the chief of the division of your finance ministry which has to do with insurance the request of the *Imperial* Society which I had relayed to you.

My brother* went to see him, and he answered that he had not received this file; did something get misdirected? Tell me, I pray you, which is the competent employee to whom my brother can address himself?

Your very affectionate friend.

*Nino Bixio, if this allusion really is to him, was a well-known Italian patriot-nationalist who had fought under Garibaldi in 1849.

Il carteggio Cavour-Nigra, I, 93–94.

Cavour to Countess Anastasia de Circourt at Celle-St.-Cloud

Turin, 7 July 1858

. . . If I were free to follow my sentiments and my desires, I should certainly make use of my vacation to ask your hospitality at Bougival; but as I am yoked to the political chariot, I cannot turn off assigned paths. . . . If I were in France at the moment when diplomats were vainly arguing in search for the solution to a problem they have rendered insoluble, my trip would give rise to all sorts of comments. . . . As soon as the session is closed, I shall go to Switzerland to breath the fresh mountain air, far away from men who think only of politics. I expect to stay over in Pressing a few days; nobody will suppose I am conspiring against the peace of the world with my good friends the De La Rives. . . . We shall speak often of you, and more than once we shall transport ourselves in spirit to that delicious hermitage which you have made into a terrestrial paradise for your friends. . . .

Cavour, *Lettere*, II (2d ed.), 561–62.

Adjutant of Napoleon III to Cavour

Monsieur le Comte,   Plombières, 11 July 1858

I receive at Plombières the letter which Your Excellency has done me the honor of addressing to me, and which has just been given me by the son of Monsieur le Marquis de Villamarina.

I immediately received the orders of the Emperor, and His Majesty charges me to have the honor of informing you that He will be charmed to receive you at Plombières, and that He leaves to Your Excellency all dispositions over the timing of your visit, provided it be before the 24th of this month, the day fixed by the Emperor for his departure from the Waters and his return to Paris.

Please accept, Monsieur le Comte, the expression of my very high consideration.

Aide-de-camp to the Emperor
Général Baron de Béville.

Il carteggio Cavour-Nigra, I, 98.

Cavour to General Alfonso La Marmora, Minister of War and Marine, at Turin

Dear Friend,   Geneva, 14 July 1858

Beville's reply reached me here. He says the Emperor will be *charmé* to see me at Plombières. The drama is approaching its climax. Pray heaven inspires me to make no blunders in this supreme moment. Despite my bold front and my customary self-confidence, I am not without grave uneasiness.

As La Tour d'Auvergne has a colleague close to the Emperor, I have written Salmour to tell him confidentially of my journey there. If he speaks to you about it, I think you should attribute little importance to it and treat it as a private act of courtesy.

Villamarina has come to pay me a visit. He has brought me no important news. But the details he reported show that Walewski is no greater a man today than he was two years ago.

Prussia, when all was settled, felt obliged to make a protest in favor of the principle of union [of the Danube principalities], as she has not supported it in the discussion stage. New proof of a debility and an uncertainty little worthy of a great nation.

We are reasonably satisfied with the work on the tunnel. Though the work is not being pushed with the feverish energy which pleases Bona and even me, yet it seems to me to be carried out with much intelligence and without useless expenditure of money.

I was also very satisfied with the work on the railroad from Aix to Culoz, now coming to completion. The bridge on the Rodano is a monumental work. This route will be a great help if our plans work out.

At Chambéry I saw Castelborgo and the Intendant. Both seemed to me dissatisfied with the regiment stationed there. . . .

I wrote Lanza of my journey to Plombières, so that he will not be offended when he reads about it in the papers.

Addio, Your aff.

Cavour, *Lettere,* II (1st ed.), 317–19.

Diverse Notes Taken to Plombières by H. E. Count Cavour

[First summary page]

1st. question
What will be the aim of the war.

2nd. question
What will be the causes or pretexts upon which the declaration of war will be based.

3rd. question
Mode of cooperation with France.
Immediate dispatch of an army.
To what points must the French forces be brought?

4th. question
In what proportions shall the costs of the war be distributed?
France will clear the channels for Piedmont to float a loan. Aid from the Italian Provinces delivered from Austria or from Austrian Princes in the burdens of the war.

. . .

What will be the conduct of the allies at the beginning of the war toward:

> The Duchess of Parma
> The Duke of Modena
> Tuscany
> The Pope
> The King of Naples?

. . .

Marriage of Princess Clotilde.

[Second, more developed page]

Questions which should be discussed with the Emperor, or which he may raise.

1. What will be the aim of the war?
2. What will be the causes or pretexts motivating the declaration of war?
3. Mode of cooperation with France: importance of land and sea forces employed in the war in Italy.
4. What will be the operational base of the French army? What will be its initial assembly-points?

Il carteggio Cavour-Nigra, I, 98–102.

5. In what proportions will the costs of the war be supported by France and by Piedmont?
6. How to organize the provinces delivered from the Austrian yoke?
7. What will be the conduct of the allies at the beginning of the war toward:

> The Duchess of Parma
> The Duke of Modena
> Tuscany
> The Pope
> The King of Naples?

8. Should there be a treaty and a military convention?
9. Marriage of the Princess Clotilde with Prince Napoleon.
   How to answer if the Emperor makes this a *sine qua non* condition of the alliance?
   If the marriage is decided upon in principle, what conditions should be attached to it?

[*Third page, on military questions*]

1. What will be the importance of the army corps which France will send to Italy.
2. What system will be used for provisioning the army.
3. Will the provinces liberated from the Austrians cooperate in the maintenance of the French army.
4. Employment of the fleet.
5. What will be the bases of operations, depots, magazines.

[*in pencil*:]

Horses
Arms for insurgents.

[*in pencil, Lamarmora's hand*:]

80 thou. French
80 thou. Piedmontese
Spezia base of operations for the French army.
Necessity of sending a general who has the confidence of the Emperor for coordinating preparations and making a convention.

• • •

[*Notes of Cavour after the first and second conversations at Plombières*]

Practically settled on the first point.
Found for the second a solution which seems to me quite satisfactory.
For the third general cooperation sufficing to go all the way to Vienna.

Fourth point not yet settled.
Fifth point not yet settled, but satisfactory exchange of ideas.
Sixth point agreed.
Seventh point agreed.
8 and 9 not yet considered.

Postscriptum—11 o'clock in the evening: In a second conversation
the Emperor excessively preoccupied with condition 9. Did not press.
Would wait a year. I said that Y. M., not knowing the Emperor's
intentions, gave me no positive instructions. Promised make his desires known and give answer at Paris.

[*Final page on the results of the meeting at Plombières, in the hand
of Nigra*]

Art. I
Defensive and offensive alliance.

Art. II
For the purpose of cementing the alliance, marriage.

Art. III
In the event that war should break out in Italy between Sardinia and
Austria, whether it be declared by Sardinia for grave and just causes,
or whether it be declared by Austria, H. M. the Emperor of the
French engages to come to the aid of H. M. the King of Sardinia by
putting at his disposition an army corps and a fleet, in a manner that
will be determined by a special convention.

Art. IV
Considered to be adequate causes for a declaration of war against
Austria would be the occupation by Austrian troops of any part of
Italian territory apart from that subjected to occupation by the Vienna
treaties of 1815, Austrian violation of existing treaties, and other
things of a similar kind.

Art. V
The French army corps mentioned above would be placed under the
command of H. M. the King of Sardinia.
Sardinian fleet joined to that of France and placed under the command of a French admiral.

Art. VI
Once the war is under way, the H. C. P.'s engage to prosecute it
until Austrian troops have left Italian soil.

Art. VII

The country conquered in Upper Italy and along the Po valley, including Venice, the Duchies, and the Legations, will be annexed to the Kingdom of Sardinia, which will assume the title of Kingdom of Upper Italy.

Art. VIII

Once the Kingdom of Upper Italy is constituted, the population of Savoy will be called upon to vote by universal suffrage on the annexation of that Duchy to France or to Upper Italy.

Art. IX

No separate treaties.

Equal treatment for the respective plenipotentiaries at the peace conferences.

Il carteggio Cavour-Nigra, I, 98–102, 114–16.

V
THE OUTCOME

Cavour to La Marmora

Dear friend,   Baden, 24 July 1858

I thought it my duty to make known to the King without delay the results of my conference with the Emperor. I therefore drafted a very long report (about 40 pages) which I am sending to Turin by an attaché to the King's legation at Berne. I should very much like the King to have it read to you, because I think I reported in it everything of importance in what the Emperor said to me in a conversation that lasted scarcely less than eight hours.

I do not have the time to repeat everything; but I shall tell you in outline that it was settled

1st.   That the State of Massa and Carrara would be cause or pretext of the war;

2d.   That the purpose of the war would be to drive Austria out of Italy: the establishment of the kingdom of Upper Italy composed of the whole valley of the Po and of the Legations and the Marches.

3d.   Cession of Savoy to France. That of the County of Nice undecided.

4th.   The Emperor is confident of the cooperation of Russia and of the neutrality of England and Prussia.

Nevertheless the Emperor does not deceive himself on the military resources of Austria, on her tenacity; on the need of rendering her prostrate if we are to obtain the cession of Italy. He said to me that peace could be made only at Vienna itself, and that to get there we would have to put together an army of 300,000. Ready to send 200,000 combatants to Italy; expects 100,000 Italians.

Il carteggio Cavour-Nigra, I, 114–16.

The Emperor entered into many particulars on the problems of the war, which it is my duty to tell you about, and which I shall report to you orally. He seemed to me to have studied the matter rather better than his generals, and to have sensible ideas in that regard.

He talked of direct command questions—of how to manage the Pope—of the administrative system for stabilizing the occupied countries—of methods of finance. In a word of all the essential things for our grand project. We were in accord on everything.

The only undefined point is that of the marriage of the Princess Clotilde. The King had authorized me to agree to that, but only in the case that the Emperor had made it a condition *sine qua non* of the alliance. The Emperor not having pushed his insistence to that extreme, I did not, as a gentleman, undertake pledges. But I remain convinced that he lays very great importance on the matrimonial question, and that on it depends, if not the alliance, then its final outcome. It would be an error and a very grave error to commit oneself to the Emperor and at the same time to give him an affront which would never fade. There would then be immense danger in having at his side, in the bosom of his Council, an implacable enemy, so much the more dangerous because Corsican blood flows in his veins.

I have written strongly to the King not to risk the finest undertaking of modern times out of sour aristocratic scruples. I beg you, if he consults you, to join your voice to mine. Perhaps this enterprise should not be attempted, in which the crown of our King and the fate of our people are jeopardized; but if it is attempted, then for the love of heaven let nothing be neglected which could decide the final outcome.

I left Plombières in very serene spirits. If the King consents to the marriage I am confident, let me say almost certain, that within two years you will enter Vienna at the head of our victorious columns.

Still, so as to make sure of the bases of the hopes manifested to me by the Emperor concerning the probable stances of the great powers in the event of a war with Austria, I thought I would come take a cure in Baden where the run-down kings, princes, and ministers of the various countries of Europe are to be found. That was a good inspiration, for within twenty-four hours I had talked with the King of Württemberg, the Prince Regent of Prussia, with the Grand Duchess Helena, with Manteuffel, and with various other Russian and German diplomats. Appropos, both the G. D. Helena and M.

Balan, one of the most cautious Russian diplomats, told me that we could rely on the certain armed cooperation of Russia. The G. D. told me that if France joined us, the Russian nation would force its government to do as much. Balan said to me, "Si vous avez à l'un de vos côtes un chasseur de Vincennes, comptez que de l'autre vous aurez un soldat de notre garde."

Respecting Prussia I think that although she may feel a great antipathy for Austria, she will remain doubtful and uncertain until events force her irresistibly to take part in the game.

I have no time to go on. But what I have said so far will prove to you that I have not wasted my time, and that my trip cannot be called a real vacation.

Addio. I hope still to see you at the frontier.

Cavour to La Marmora at Turin

Dear Friend,   Basel, 25 July 1958

I write you a few lines from here to tell you I am very well-satisfied with the Prince of Prussia and his diplomats. It is doubtful whether Manteuffel will retain the post he now occupies or whether he will be replaced by someone more decisive; but either way it is the universal opinion that Prussia will seek to vindicate her moral defeat of 1850, which made her lose almost all her influence in Germany.

Austria is relying on the support of the secondary German powers, especially Bavaria and the Kingdom of Saxony, which now are very loyal to her in the continually recurring struggles in the Diet. But if it came to cases, and were a matter of taking up arms, it is unlikely they would declare themselves against France in Prussia's face.

It was really a happy inspiration to come to Baden-Baden. Better than if I had gone to Berlin.

This evening I shall be in Zurich; tomorrow on Lake Constance and the day after at Coire. I shall let you know from there what my itinerary to Turin will be.

Addio. Your aff.

(PS) At Baden-Baden I met an old chamberlain of the King of Württemberg who said he had known you at Paris and much admired your skill at riding when you were only a captain of artillery.

Cavour, *Lettere*, II (1st ed.), 327–28.

Cavour to Napoleon III

Sire,   2 August 1858

As soon as I arrived in Turin, I hastened to repeat to the King, my august Master, what Y. M. charged me to say to him on the subject of the marriage of the Prince Napoleon with his daughter the Princess Clotilde.

The King directs me to inform Y. M. that, desiring to please you in all things, he had no objections whatever to make to a project destined to draw closer the relations which sympathy, affection, and sincere admiration have formed between Himself and Y. M.; that he was all the more disposed to give his consent because after having had occasion last year to know Prince Napoleon in an intimate way, he has been able to appreciate those qualities of heart and of mind which distinguish him; and that thus the impressions which certain talk, to which he had given an inexact or exaggerated importance, had left in his mind had been completely erased.

Yet the King cannot pledge his word in a definitive manner without the free consent of the Princess his daughter to the union. Now it is certain that his daughter, whatever her disposition to second the intentions of her father and to do a thing agreeable to Y. M., for whom she professes a respectful liking, will not consent to a formal engagement until after she has come to know personally the Prince to whom she must unite her destiny. For that reason and also because the King wishes that the Prince, before engaging himself irrevocably, should have seen his daughter from close at hand and should have judged whether she conforms to the idea he has formed of her, he proposes to Y. M. to urge the Prince to come to Piedmont upon his return from Algeria, on the pretext of fulfilling the promise made a year ago to visit our country.

Should Y. M. approve this proposition, the King would inform his daughter, at present in the country in a château situated in a high Apennine valley, of the Prince's visit, not leaving her ignorant of its purpose; and if the result is what I hope for, the marriage would be arranged in a definitive way to take place in the course of the following year.

After leaving Plombières, I went to Baden-Baden, where I spent 48 hours. During that short stay I had the occasion to see on several occasions the Prince of Prussia, the Grand Duchess Helena of Russia, and to have long conversations with several Russian and Prussian

statesmen and diplomats. At that time I became convinced of how
accurate the opinion was which Y. M. had formed of the sentiments
of the two great Northern powers with regard to Austria. The Grand
Duchess, a woman of high intelligence who appears to me to inspire
to a certain extent the policies of the Tsar her nephew, concluded by
saying to me that she was persuaded that if war broke out between
Y. M. and the Emperor of Austria over the Italian question, the Emperor of Russia, even though he might not be disposed to do so,
would be obliged to take part in it by the pressure exerted upon him
by the unanimous opinion of the country.

M. Fonton, diplomat of the first rank and well advanced in the
good graces of the Emperor his master, expressed to me in more
reserved terms very nearly the same opinion.

The facts confirm these words. The fact is that Russian diplomacy
in Germany is devoted to maintaining and fomenting the irritations
between Prussia and Austria, caused by their divergence on various
German questions. I was able to ascertain e. g., that M. Fonton was
engaged in pouring vinegar on the bleeding wound which Austria's
success in the Rastadt matter* has inflicted on Prussia.

The Prussians are more reserved; but it is evident from the language of the diplomats and statesmen who surround the Prince of
Prussia, both those who are trying to achieve power and those who
are trying to keep it, that both the one and the other think the best
way to succeed is to flatter the anti-Austrian sentiments of the Prince
and of the country.

Among all the Prussian politicians it is also easy to perceive,
through a more or less nebulous phraseology, the ardent wish to aggrandize Prussia at the cost of the secondary German states and even
of Austria.

From Baden I travelled across German Switzerland to Coire, where
I had to inspect the Luckmanier pass, ostensible purpose of my
journey.

Throughout Switzerland I found great sympathy for the Italian
cause and sentiments very hostile toward Austria.

[Here follows a long crossed-out passage: "In Coire itself, at a
dinner accorded me by the magistrates and attended by M. de Toggen-
berg, first cousin of the Minister of Commerce of the Emperor Franz

---

*Rastadt (or Rastatt) was the site of a fortress of the German Bund, and
control over it was the subject of frequent contention among German states.

Josef, there was a toast to the independence of Italy, without the cousin of the Imperial Councillor making the faintest grimace.

"I think it will not be impossible to exploit these popular sentiments in the event of war with Austria. I have not forgotten that Y. M. thinks we could get along without this cooperation, which would require serious monetary expenditures. Y. M. is absolutely right. If the struggle does move outside Austrian territorial limits. But if the Cabinet at Vienna succeeds in enlisting in its cause (a goal to which all its efforts tend) a portion of the states of the German Confederation and especially of the South German states, upon which she exercises considerable influence, then Switzerland could render very great services to our cause by menacing the frontiers of those states, which touch Switzerland's at so many points. If Y. M. thinks it well to keep this eventuality in mind, a possible if not a probable one, we could start preparing Swiss public opinion for it, acting of course with immense prudence and great reserve.

"In that case, I should dare submit to Y. M. the question whether it would not be opportune for France to have a new representative in Switzerland, who, uncompromised by conflicts with any of the parties which divide that country, could more easily exercise a more effective influence on men and opinions."]

I have read, by the way, the letter which the Emperor of Austria addressed to the Archduke Maximilian on the concessions he plans to make, on his own initiative, to the Lombard-Venetian provinces. That is a really ridiculous action. To a people which complains that the land-tax has been almost doubled, and that the annual military conscription has been raised from 8,000 to 14,000 men, the government responds by appointing a commission which will need, even if it goes at it with extraordinary good will, several years to accomplish the mission entrusted to it; and by giving the Governor General the power to excuse from military service some few university students who have given proof of unusual capacity.

I have no doubt that these measures, done for the single purpose of making an impression on that portion of the English press that supports the Anglo-Austrian Alliance, will produce the greatest irritation in Lombardy and Venetia, and dispose active minds there more and more toward opinions favorable to Y. M.'s projects.

In accordance with the authorization Y. M. was kind enough to give me, I attach a note on the points agreed upon at Plombières. If

I have made some slight error, I beg Y. M. to let me know of it, for it is essential that I know Y. M.'s intentions in the most precise manner.

In a few days I shall have the honor of sending him several notes from General Lamarmora.

As Doctor Conneau may not return to Paris until toward the end of the month of August, I take the liberty of sending this letter to Y. M. by way of M. Mocquart, as though it were a simple letter of thanks for the kind reception accorded me by Y. M. at Plombières.

I cannot end this letter, though perhaps it is already too long, without evincing to Y. M. the profound recognition which pervades me of the so noble, so generous, so magnanimous sentiments which animate Y. M. toward my country. Let Y. M. accomplish the glorious task which his noble heart and his strong intelligence have conceived, and the sentiments I express to him with all the ardor of which I am capable will be forever shared by all Italians who will owe Y. M. what is more than life: the resurrection of their unfortunate country.

Résumé of points agreed upon at Plombières [sent to the Emperor on 3 August 1858]

1.

To the end of the deliverance of Italy from the Austrian yoke and of consecrating the great principle of Italian nationality, a treaty of offensive and defensive alliance will be concluded between the Emperor of the French and the King of Sardinia.

2.

War once declared between Sardinia and Austria—France would intervene immediately by sending an army corps to Spezia and one or two divisions to Genoa which would operate with the Sardinian army against the Austrian forces concentrated on the Po and on the Ticino.

The military forces of the allies in Italy would be rapidly brought to 300,000 men, that is to say 200,000 French and 100,000 Sardinians and Italians.

A [crossed out: "large"] fleet in the Adriatic would support the operations of the land armies.

3.

Preparations for war, and the mode of immediate action, will be concerted in advance between France and Sardinia. To that end the Emperor will decide whether he wishes to send to Turin an officer

enjoying his entire confidence, or whether he prefers General La
Marmora to go to Paris.

4.

The military convention to be formed on the basis of these pre-
liminary agreements will regulate the way in which the costs of the
war must be met by the two Nations and the allocation of resources
to supply the countries successively occupied.

5.

France will facilitate for Sardinia the floating of a loan in Paris.

6.

The Italian provinces successively occupied will be declared in
state of siege, and placed under martial law. Administration will be
entrusted to persons named by the King of Sardinia. There will be
an immediate attempt to make use [crossed out: "Immediate use
will be made"] of the active forces of the country, either by recruit-
ment or by a call for volunteers.

Recruits and volunteers will be incorporated into the Sardinian
army.

7.

The war having as its goal the complete deliverance of Italy, it
will be pursued until [crossed out: "Austria renounces"] that goal is
attained.

8.

With peace, the Kingdom of [crossed out: "Italy"] Upper Italy
will be constituted. This will include, in addition to the present states
of the Kingdom of Sardinia:

The Austrian provinces in Italy;

The duchies of Parma and Modena;

The Papal States this side of the Apennines.

9.

The conduct of the Grand Duke of Tuscany and of the King of
Naples *vis à vis* the allies and the political events consequent upon
the war will determine the destiny of those states in the peace.

Meanwhile it is established in principle that the seat of Catholicism
will be preserved at Rome, and that the Pope will continue to exercise
sovereign authority there, also over the territory that will be annexed
to it; and that the part of Italy not included in the Kingdom of Upper
Italy will be divided into two states.

10.

The several States of Italy will constitute a confederation.

11.

It remains to be seen whether, should the throne of Tuscany become vacant, one might dispose of it in favor of the Duke of Parma.

12.

As the war will take place by virtue of the grand principle of nationality, the population of Savoy [crossed out: "will be consulted to see if they wish"] can be reunited to France. Sardinia retains nevertheless the fortress of Esseillon situated at the foot of Mont Cenis.[2]

The nationality of the inhabitants of the County of Nice being in doubt, the question regarding them is reserved.

Separate Article

[crossed out: "To bring about war"] If between now and next spring no occasion presents itself which might bring about war with Austria, the Sardinian Government will no longer oppose addresses from the populations of Massa and Carrara, long subjected to a most oppressive rule, pleading for her aid and protection. It will permit a formal address from the inhabitants of those countries asking the annexation of these two small duchies to Sardinia.

King Victor Emmanuel, without granting this petition, would take them under his protection by addressing to the Duke of Modena a forceful and threatening remonstrance.

The question, being thus engaged not only with Modena but also with Austria her natural protector, would necessarily lead to a declaration of war. Sardinia could if necessary occupy Massa and Carrara.

2. An Alpine pass connecting Piedmont proper with Savoy.

Cavour to Alessandro Bixio

(3 August 1858)

My dear Bixio,

I was not in a position to give you a definite answer before seeing the Emperor at Plombières; that is why I did not write sooner.

Now I am happy to tell you the King consents whole-heartedly to his daughter's marriage; and that the Princess has no prejudicial ob-

Il carteggio Cavour-Nigra, I, 125–26.

jections to it, but that before giving a definitive *yes* she wishes to become personally acquainted with the Prince who is destined for her.

This desire will seem quite natural to the Prince, and he will have no difficulty accommodating himself to it; he has too much intelligence and too much heart not to prefer to treat his marriage otherwise than as a contract of sale or purchase.

Besides I think that handled this way, the marriage will be concluded under better auspices than if negotiations were confided entirely to diplomats, for, permit me to say so, the Prince gains infinitely from being known from close at hand. All who come near him (women included) like and appreciate him; if he has detractors, they are among those who know him from afar.

The King would propose to the Prince that he come to Piedmont upon his return from Algeria, on the pretext of keeping his promise of a visit to go hunting with him. The reason he does not invite him sooner is that his sons and daughters will stay until the middle of October in a château in a high Apennine valley. As long as they are there, it will be impossible either to take the Prince there or to summon the Princess to Raconis and to Turin without breaking the secrecy which it is highly important to keep regarding this affair.

I could not have been more satisfied than with the reception I had from the Emperor at Plombières and with the sentiments he manifested to me on that occasion. I should have many things to tell you about that, except that I have not the time to do so, being overwhelmed with business and work of every kind. Besides, I hope to see you soon, and then we shall talk out everything that touches on the great cause to which I have devoted my life and which interests you scarcely less than me. Believe, etc.

P.S. Naturally, not only the bearer of this letter but the whole legation at Paris is ignorant of any hint of the affair in question.

Princess Clotilde to Cavour

Casotto, 12 August 1858

My dear Count,

I thank you a thousandfold for the devotion you have shown in all things to the King my Father and to me, and now that he has just spoken to me of a matter as important as my marriage, I think of you with redoubled gratitude. I know all you have done in these recent affairs and I have even seen the papers you sent to the King. I have already thought a great deal; but my marriage to the Prince Napoleon is a very serious thing, and one which above all is quite contrary to my hopes. I know too, my dear Count, that it could, perhaps be advantageous to a nation like ours and above all to the King my Father.

I have already said that I have been thinking; I shall go on thinking and I hope Our Lord will guide me with His infallible sustainment; I am placing everything in His hands for now and I cannot decide anything. We will be able to see afterwards.

Do, my dear Count, keep for the King and for me an affection as dear to us as yours.

Cavour to the Princess Clotilde

Turin, 15 August 1858

Madame,

I feel the need of expressing to Your Royal Highness the profound appreciation which fills me for the benevolent expressions She has deigned to address me, and to manifest to her at the same time my admiration and my sympathy for the noble sentiments which animate her toward the King her Father, and her country.

Even if I had not been sure of it in advance, the letter which Y. R. H. was good enough to write me could have left no doubt that, whatever her decision, it will be worthy of the grand-daughter of that great-spirited King who sacrificed his throne and his life to the glory of his people, and to the daughter of the generous Monarch whom Europe admires as a model of constancy and loyalty.

The kindness of Y. R. H. toward me encourages me to address a prayer to Her: that She permit me, as soon as She has returned to Raconis, to present myself before Her so that I can, with the permission of the King her Father, describe to Her the motives of my conduct in a matter which touches Y. R. H. so intimately and upon which may depend the future of her August Family and of her country.

I beg Y. R. H. receive kindly the sentiments of profound and respectful devotion with which I am, Madame, Y. R. H.'s very humble and very obedient servant.

Il carteggio Cavour-Nigra, I, 127.

J.A.R. Marriott on the War of Italian Independence

The Union of North and Central Italy

In January 1859 Europe was startled by the news that Napoleon, at his New Year's Day reception, had addressed the Austrian ambassador as follows: "Je regrette que les relations entre nous soient si mauvaises." It was a bolt from the blue. Still more startling were the words of Victor Emmanuel when, on 10 January, he opened Parliament at Turin:

> Our country, small in territory, has acquired credit in the Councils of Europe because she is great in the idea she represents, in the sympathy she inspires. The situation is not free from peril, for, while we respect treaties, we cannot be insensible to the cry of anguish (*grido di dolore*) that comes to us from many parts of Italy.

The significance of the words was instantly apprehended: "A rocket falling on the treaties of 1815," was the vivid description given by Sir James Hudson, the English Minister at Turin. Massari, an eyewitness of the scene in the Chamber, declares the effect of it to have been simply electric.

> "At every period," he says, "the speech was interrupted by clamorous applause and cries of *Viva il Rè!* But when the King came to the words, *grido di dolore,* there was an enthusiasm quite indescribable. Senators, deputies, spectators all sprang to their feet with a bound and broke into passionate acclamations. The ministers of France, Russia, Prussia, and England were utterly astonished and carried away by the marvellous spectacle. The face of the ambassador of Naples was covered with a gloomy pallor. We poor exiles did not even attempt to wipe away the tears that flowed unrestrainedly from our eyes as we frantically clapped our hands in applause of that king who had remembered our sorrows, who had promised us a country. Before the victories the plebiscites and the annexations conferred on him the crown of Italy, he reigned in our hearts; he was our king!"

Europe was aghast at the prospect thus suddenly opened of another war. Diplomacy did its utmost to avert it. England, and especially the English Court, left no stone unturned to maintain peace. "Be reserved," wrote Lord Malmesbury, the English Foreign Secre-

From J. A. R. Marriott, *Makers of Modern Italy* (London, Oxford University Press, 1931), pp. 105–36, footnotes omitted. Reprinted by permission of the publishers.

tary, to Hudson. "We shall not support any party that begins the strife." On 4 February 1859 Queen Victoria wrote a personal letter to the Emperor Napoleon, in terms unusually direct even for her.

> "Your Majesty," she wrote, "has now an opportunity either by listening to the dictates of humanity and justice, and by showing to the world your intention to adhere strictly to the faithful observance of treaties, of calming the apprehensions of Europe, and of restoring its confidence in the pacific policy of your Majesty, or, on the other hand, by lending an ear to those who have an interest in creating confusion, of involving Europe in a war whose extent and duration it is scarcely possible to foresee, and which, whatever glory it may add to the arms of France, cannot but interfere materially with her internal prosperity and financial credit . . . if anything could add to the sorrow with which I should view the renewal of war in Europe, it would be to see your Majesty entering upon a course with which it would be impossible for England to associate herself."

The Emperor's reply, couched, of course, in the most courteous terms, contained an elaborate disavowal of any intention, on the part of France, to break the peace of Europe and an assurance—technically accurate—that he had discouraged Victor Emmanuel from "an aggressive line of conduct and had promised to support him only if he were unjustly attacked."

No party in England contemplated the possibility of English intervention. Lord Palmerston had long ago formed the opinion that Austria would have best consulted her own interests by withdrawing from Italy.

> "Her rule," he wrote in 1848, "was hateful to the Italians and has long been maintained only by an expenditure of money and an exertion of military effort which left Austria less able to maintain her interests elsewhere. Italy was to her the heel of Achilles, and not the shield of Ajax. The Alps are her natural barrier and her best defence."

Nevertheless, Palmerston, when in power, consistently pressed counsels of patience and moderation upon Sardinia. Lord Malmesbury, now at the Foreign Office, sent Lord Cowley on a mission of mediation to Vienna, and the Queen addressed a letter in a similar sense to the Emperor Francis Joseph.

It was all to no purpose. The treaties between France and Sardinia were definitely concluded in January 1859. On the 30th of that month Prince Napoleon, the son of Prince Jerome Bonaparte, was

married to the Princess Clothilde of Sardinia. The "deposit" stipulated in the contract was thus paid. Would Napoleon complete it?
That he was still assailed by doubts and hesitations is certain; the
dangers in the path along which Cavour was luring him were painfully obvious to him; he was acting in defiance of the public opinion
of Europe; he was endangering his alliance with the French clericals;
the Empress looked coldly on his adventure; Walewski's sympathies
were, and always had been, wholly with Austria. Might he not, even
at the eleventh hour, draw back? To Cavour he insisted that unless
Austria attacked, Sardinia must expect no help from France.

The strain imposed upon Cavour during the last three months had
been terrible. That Italy could ever be either liberated or united without recourse to arms was, in his judgement, impossible. War with
Austria was, as Mazzini had long ago maintained, inevitable. But in
desiring it Cavour stood, among the statesmen and rulers of Europe,
absolutely alone. The responsibility was crushing, and at the eleventh
hour he so far yielded to the combined pressure applied by France
and England as to promise that, if Sardinia were admitted to the
proposed Congress on equal terms, he would, though "foreseeing
the disastrous consequences this measure would have for Italy," consent to disarmament. On 19 April his consent was made known, and
produced an excellent effect in Europe at large. But would Austria
be satisfied? Cavour was in a fever of apprehension lest she should
be; but at the very last moment Austria played Cavour's game.
France, it is true, had absolutely refused the proffered mediation of
England; Austria accepted it, only on condition of the unconditional
disarmament of Sardinia; and on 19 April Count Buol dispatched an
emissary to Turin with a demand for the immediate and unconditional disarmament of Sardinia. On 23 April Cavour summoned an
emergency meeting of the Chamber of Deputies, informed the
members that the Austrian ultimatum was on its way, and asked that
full powers should, during the crisis, be conferred upon the King to
provide for the defence of the country.

His speech was hardly finished when the arrival of the Austrian
messengers was announced. As Cavour left the Chamber to meet
them he remarked: "I leave the last sitting of the Piedmontese Parliament; the next I attend will be the Parliament of the Kingdom of
Italy."

The Sardinian reply to Austria was delivered on 23 April. It was
a categorical refusal. The Austrian troops thereupon crossed the
Ticino. The war of Italian independence had begun.

Lord Derby, speaking in the City, described Austria's action as "hasty, precipitate, and (because involving warfare) criminal." Queen Victoria, writing privately to "Uncle Leopold," commented that the rashness of Austria had "placed them in the wrong," but at the same time reported "one universal feeling of anger at the conduct of France, *and of great suspicion*." Nor did the suspicion lack justification; yet candour compels the admission that if Napoleon was a willing prey the tempter was in Turin.

Any way, the thing was done; *alea jacta est,* as Cavour remarked. "We have made some history," he added, "and now let us have some dinner."

King Victor Emmanuel promptly issued the following proclamation to his people:

> People of Italy. Austria assails Piedmont because I have maintained the cause of our common country in the councils of Europe, because I was not insensible to your cries of anguish. Thus she now violently breaks the treaties she has never respected.
>
> So to-day the right of the nation is complete and I can with a free conscience fulfil the vow I made on the tomb of my parent by taking up arms to defend my throne, the liberties of my people, the honour of the Italian name. I fight for the right of the whole nation. We confide in God and in our Concord; we confide in the valour of the Italian soldiers, in the alliance of the noble French nation; we confide in the justice of public opinion. I have no other ambition than to be the first soldier of Italian Independence. *Viva l'Italia.*
>
> Victor Emmanuel.

On the 13th May the King met at Genoa the Emperor of the French, "his generous ally," who had come to "liberate Italy from the Alps to the Adriatic."

The welcome accorded to the Emperor was, naturally, enthusiastic. "It was roses, roses all the way," writes one of Cavour's biographers, "as befitted that May afternoon and the Maytime of hope in every Italian heart. Then, if ever, Napoleon might believe himself to be a benefactor of mankind." Exactly nine weeks later he started home again. "Thank God he's gone," was Victor Emmanuel's exclamation after bidding his ally farewell.

The campaign which intervened was represented at the time as a triumph of French arms. Superficially it had that appearance. For a month the allies carried all before them: on the 4th of June they won a great victory at Magenta; on the 8th they entered Milan; on the 24th they won the double battle of Solferino and San Martino;—and then, the "magnanimous ally" suddenly stopped short; the victor sought an armistice from the vanquished; Napoleon met the Emperor Francis Joseph at Villafranca, and personally negotiated with him, without the concurrence of Victor Emmanuel, the terms of an armistice.

Italy was to be free not to the Adriatic but only to the Mincio; Austria was to retain Venetia and the Quadrilateral; Lombardy up to the Mincio was to be handed over to Napoleon, who would, of course, transfer it to Piedmont. Leopold of Tuscany and Francis of Modena were to be restored to the thrones from which they had been driven by their respective subjects, "but without the use of force"; Parma and Piacenza—being Bourbon not Hapsburg principalities—were annexed to Piedmont; Italy was to be united in a confederation under the honorary presidency of the Pope.

To King Victor Emmanuel and Cavour, to the peoples of Venetia, Tuscany, Modena, and above all of the Romagna, who had looked for the speedy termination of Papal rule, the news of the Armistice came as a terrible shock. Cavour could, at the moment, attribute its conclusion to nothing but deliberate treachery on the part of Napoleon.

On learning, not directly, but by way of Paris, of the negotiations for an armistice Cavour immediately set off for the front. On his arrival he had a stormy interview with King Victor Emmanuel, he denounced the treachery of Napoleon; begged his own Sovereign to refuse Lombardy; to carry on the war alone; to abdicate—to do anything rather than accept terms which involved a surrender of all the objects for which Piedmont and her Italian allies had taken up arms; which left Austria in possession of Venetia and the Quadrilateral and in a commanding position as a member of an Italian confederation; which denied the hegemony of Piedmont, which dissipated all hope of liberty for the States of central Italy; which thrust the Romagna back under the heel of the Papacy; above all, which frustrated all hopes of Italian unity.

Cavour's impeachment of the terms of the armistice was substantially accurate; but Cavour had for the moment lost his head, and when (12 July) he proffered his resignation, the King accepted it. Yet he bitterly resented his minister's desertion.

> "For you gentlemen," he said, "things always come right; for you settle them by resignation. I am the one who cannot

get out of a difficulty so nicely. . . . I cannot desert the cause.
We work together until there comes a difficulty, then I am left
alone to face the music. I am the one who is responsible before history and the country."

The reproach was not undeserved; yet Cavour was right, in the interests not less of his country than of himself, to retire.

Nevertheless, to Europe as to Victor Emmanuel, his resignation
seemed an attempt to evade responsibility. He himself justified his
action partly on the ground that being the "bête noire of diplomacy"
Piedmont would be much stronger in the peace negotiations without
him; partly because his retirement "was necessary to attenuate the
unhappy consequences of the peace."

> "You know," he wrote to his friend Emmanuel d'Azeglio
> the Piedmontese minister in London, "that the policy of the
> Cabinet has been frankly national; that it had in view, not
> the enlargement of Piedmont, but the emancipation of Italy;
> the establishment of a wise liberal system throughout the
> Peninsula. If the present peace leads to the return of the old
> régime in Central Italy it will do more harm than good to
> the national cause. I could not take the responsibility for it."

Cavour was right. Yet at this supreme moment in their country's
fate the judgement of the King was sounder than that of his minister.

Victor Emmanuel, though not less deeply chagrined, looked at the
matter more calmly, and estimated more justly the benefits likely
to accrue to Italy. "The political unity of Italy," he said, "since Novara a possibility, has become since Villafranca a necessity."

Napoleon's motives in concluding the armistice have been endlessly
canvassed. Cavour's bitter comment contains an element of truth:
"He was tired; the weather was hot." Tired he was, and horrified
by the awful carnage which he witnessed at Solferino. But there were
other reasons; nor is it now disputed that they were substantial.
French financiers were already grumbling at the enormous cost of
the war; the politicians saw no adequate recompense in sight; the
Austrians, though driven back behind the Mincio, were not really
beaten, and the military outlook was less encouraging than Napoleon's critics have imagined; above all the diplomatic situation was
difficult, and the attitude of Prussia was dubious not to say menacing.
To his own disgust Napoleon found himself abetting the Revolution
in Italy; to the dismay of the Empress and the French clericals his
success in the north was endangering the position of the Pope; the

courts of England, Belgium, and Prussia were regarding with increasing suspicion the Italian adventure of the French Emperor; Prussia was actually mobilizing with a view to an offer of "mediation." The last-named development was not less alarming to the Austrian Emperor than to Napoleon. It was, indeed, the determining factor alike in the offer and in the acceptance of the armistice. "The gist of the thing is," wrote Moltke to his brother, "that Austria would rather give up Lombardy than see Prussia at the head of Germany."

Napoleon's own explanation, given on his return to Paris, was concise and conclusive: "To serve Italian independence I made war against the wish of Europe; as soon as the fortunes of my own country seemed to be endangered I made peace."

The attitude of England, at this critical juncture, was of the greatest moral assistance to the Italian cause, and is still gratefully remembered in Italy. The British Government declared and maintained the strictest neutrality during the war, and made every effort to localize it; but public opinion, though profoundly mistrustful of the Emperor Napoleon, was unmistakably on the side of the Italians. Queen Victoria shared to the full her subjects' mistrust, and was now, as always, unrelentingly opposed to the disturbers of the peace of Europe. So long as the responsibility for war seemed to rest on Napoleon and the Italian "revolutionaries," she was undoubtedly "pro-Austrian"; on the other hand, when Austria's "rashness" precipitated the rupture she unhesitatingly condemned it. In June 1859 Lord Derby's ministry was thrown out and Lord Palmerston, at the age of seventy-five, again became Prime Minister. Lord John Russell insisted on having the Foreign Office, and Lord Clarendon, whom both Palmerston and the Queen would have preferred, modestly stood aside.

The Prime Minister and the Foreign Secretary were, however, completely in accord in disapproval of the terms arranged at Villafranca. They were well calculated, so Palmerston insisted, to drive Italy to despair. *L'Italie rendue à elle-même,* he bitterly declared, must now be read, *L'Italie vendue à l'Autriche.* Lord Palmerston had already refused a suggestion made to him by Napoleon, before the conclusion of the armistice, that England should take the lead in proposing an armistice upon terms suggested by the French. Palmerston would have none of it.

If the French Emperor is tired of his war and finds the job tougher than he expected, let him make what proposals he

> pleases, and to whomsoever he pleases; but . . . let him not
> ask us to father his suggestions and make ourselves answer-
> able for them.

Thus to Lord John Russell (6 July). To the Duc de Persigny he
wrote (13 July), after learning the terms of the armistice, that England could never be a party to the creation of an Italian Confederation, in which Austria would have a place in virtue of Venetia. That,
he declared, would be "to deliver Italy, bound hand and foot, to Austria." England, so far from acquiescing in such an arrangement,

> might well deem it her duty to protest most emphatically and
> in the face of Europe against such an enslavement of the
> Italian peoples. Austria ought, on the contrary, to be strictly
> excluded from all interference, political or military, beyond
> her own frontiers. If that is not done, nothing is done, and
> the whole business will, in very short time, have to begin all
> over again.

Perhaps something less than justice has been done to Napoleon
in regard to his Italian policy. Since 1870 there has been no party in
Europe concerned to vindicate his memory. That his motives were,
even more than usually, mixed is true; but that he had a real sentiment for Italy is unquestionable. What he desired to see, however,
was Italy liberated but not unified. When urged by the Marquis Pepoli, just after the signature of the armistice, to allow the Central
States to unite with Piedmont he retorted:

> If annexation should cross the Apennines, unity would be
> accomplished, and I will not have unity; I only want independ-
> ence. Unity would make trouble for me in France, on account
> of the Roman Question; and France would not be pleased to
> see on her flank a great nation that might diminish her pre-
> ponderance.

With the determination thus expressed his whole policy, precedent
and subsequent, was consonant. A victory over Austria was popular
in France; the destruction of the Papal power would have been profoundly unpopular. What Napoleon aimed at, accordingly, was a
Confederation over which the Pope would preside, in which Austria
as well as Piedmont would find a place, in which there would be a
place also for a Central Italian Kingdom. The crown of that kingdom the Emperor hoped to place on the brows of his cousin Prince
Napoleon.

Plainly, the key of the situation was to be found, not for the moment at Turin, but in the States of Central Italy and primarily in Florence. What was the situation in those States?

The attitude of Pope Pius IX was entirely uncompromising. He firmly refused, though urged by Napoleon, to become the Honorary President of an Italian Confederation, or to abate one jot or tittle of his claims on the allegiance of the Romagna, or any other portion of the Papal States. After Napoleon's victories in Lombardy the Austrians had evacuated the Legations and the Papal representative followed suit. A Provisional Government was then set up in Bologna, and not only the Romagna but the Marches adhered to it. At Perugia, also, a Provisional Government was set up for Umbria. The Marches and Umbria were, however, soon re-occupied by Papal troops, the re-occupation of Perugia being followed by an indiscriminate massacre of men, women, and children.

The Romagna, on the contrary, maintained its independence, declared its adherence to Piedmont, and shortly afterwards united itself with Modena and Parma, under the dictatorship of L. C. Farini, one of the stoutest supporters of Cavour and an ardent Italian patriot.

After the defeat of the Austrians at Magenta (4 June) Duke Francis V had withdrawn from Modena and his subjects placed themselves under the protection of Victor Emmanuel, who sent Farini to administer the Duchy as Piedmontese Commissioner (19 June).

Parma showed more hesitation, but the Duchess, after more than one feint, finally withdrew on 10 June, and the Parmesans accepted as governor Cavour's nominee Count Pallieri. The union of Parma and Modena with Piedmont was part of the bargain struck by Cavour with Napoleon at Plombières; but after the armistice their fate, still more the fate of Tuscany and the Romagna, hung for some time in the balance.

On this question the English Government had very decided views, and the language employed by Lord Palmerston in correspondence with Lord Cowley, British ambassador in Paris, contained a very nasty hint to Napoleon, as well as to other recently crowned heads. "The people of the Duchies," he wrote (22 August 1859), "have as good a right to change their leaders as the people of England, France, Belgium, and Sweden; and the annexation of the Duchies to Piedmont would be an unmixed good for Italy, and for France and for Europe."

Lord John Russell's language was not less emphatic and even more picturesque: "The disposal of the Tuscans and Modenese as if they were so many firkins of butter is somewhat too profligate."

It was Tuscany that held the key of the position, and fortunate it was for Tuscany and for Italy that at this critical moment they could command the services of so strong a man, so disinterested a patriot, as Baron Bettino Ricasoli. To get rid of the Grand Duke was not difficult. On the outbreak of the war he had declared his intention to remain neutral; but the Florentines were bent on co-operation with Piedmont, and on 28 April Leopold was compelled to withdraw from his Duchy—never to return to it. A Provisional Government was promptly set up and offered the Dictatorship to Victor Emmanuel, but, with the approval of Cavour and to the satisfaction of Napoleon, he declined it. Carlo Boncampagni, Piedmontese Minister at Florence was, however, nominated by Victor Emmanuel to act as "Commissioner Extraordinary for the war of independence." He presently appointed a ministry which included Ricasoli.

After the armistice the Piedmontese Commissioners were officially instructed to withdraw from the central Duchies, but Farini (privately urged thereto by Cavour) remained at Modena, and governed as dictator Parma and the Romagna as well, now consolidated with Modena under the title of Emilia. Ricasoli, on the withdrawal of Boncampagni, was similarly dictator of Tuscany.

For all the States of Central Italy the problem was a difficult one; not least for Tuscany, though most of all for the Romagna.

In Tuscany, autonomist sentiment still remained strong, and in the absence of the Grand Duke there might have been some support for a Napoleonic kingdom. But in the breast of Ricasoli there burned the fire of a wider patriotism, and his influence sufficed to secure from the Assembly a unanimous resolution, not for annexation to Piedmont, but in favour of Tuscany forming "part of a strong Italian kingdom under the constitutional sceptre of King Victor Emmanuel" (20 August).

The resolution was conveyed to Victor Emmanuel on 3 September, but the Peace Conference was still in session at Zürich, and the King's formal reply to the request for union was consequently guarded. In private, however, he used very different language to the delegates, who received an enthusiastic welcome from the populace both in Turin and Genoa. Emilia followed the example of Tuscany, and to the Emilian delegates Victor Emmanuel made a similar reply, promising to support their wishes at the Council Board of Europe, but uttering no word of annexation.

The Treaties of Peace were signed at Zürich on the 10th of November, the terms embodied therein being virtually identical with those agreed upon at Villafranca.

Almost simultaneously, however, the Central States elected as "Regent" Prince Eugenio di Carignano. His election conveyed a threefold hint: the old rulers were not to be restored; Napoleon was not to create a Central Italian kingdom for his cousin; and the "Regent" would presently give place to a king—Victor Emmanuel. The French Emperor, however, vetoed the appointment, and suggested that the settlement of the whole Italian question, including the future of the Papal States, should be referred to a European Congress. This suggestion was reinforced by a pamphlet which, issued towards the end of December under the title of *The Pope and the Congress,* was certainly inspired if not actually written by Napoleon. The main proposal was that the Pope, while retaining the Patrimony of St. Peter, should surrender the rest of the Papal States, which in their recalcitrance were a source rather of weakness than of strength to the Holy Father. The Pope indignantly repudiated the suggestion; England saw in the proposed Congress one more attempt on Napoleon's part to induce Europe at large, and England in particular, to pull the chestnuts out of the fire for him; Austria would have none of it. The idea of the Congress dropped, and Napoleon's policy took yet another turn: Central Italy should be allowed to unite with Piedmont, but France must have its pound of flesh—Savoy and Nice.

Such was the situation by which on his return to office (20 January 1860) Cavour found himself confronted. "Let the people of central Italy themselves declare what they want and we will stand by their decision, let the consequences be what they may." Such was Cavour's inflexible determination as regards Tuscany and Emilia. As to Savoy and Nice, if Italy were freed from the Alps to the Adriatic, the price would have to be paid. But the inevitable blow to Italian pride must be softened by the application of the same device as that invoked in the case of central Italy: the populations concerned must express their own wishes by means of a plebiscite. It was a highly ingenious suggestion. The rumour that Napoleon was to get Savoy and Nice had roused bitter indignation in England. "In the opinion of Her Majesty's Government the King of Sardinia will besmirch the arms of the House of Savoy if he yields to France the cradle of his ancient and illustrious House." So Lord John wrote to Sir James Hudson. But Lord John was notoriously more apt at homilies than at action: his words were generally braver than his deeds. Suppose that

Cavour, in reliance on English support, had defied Napoleon, would England have supported him in arms? Those who recall the part subsequently played by the same Whig ministers in relation to the Danish Duchies will hesitate to give an affirmative reply. Any way, Cavour felt himself bound by the bargain of Plombières. The price must be paid.

There was the King to be considered. To surrender to France the "cradle of his race" was for Victor Emmanuel "the sacrifice most painful to his heart." But he had already sacrificed his daughter to the French alliance. As "the child had gone, why not the cradle too?": such was his bitter comment on the transaction.

Garibaldi and Mazzini regarded the cession of these provinces as a characteristic instance of Cavour's diplomatic chicanery. To them Cavour was a "low intriguer"; Napoleon nothing better than a "vulpine knave." Garibaldi, a Nizzian by birth, particularly resented the cession of Nice. "You have made me," he complained, "a foreigner in the land of my birth." But Cavour had no option. To defy France would be to invite attack from Austria. Only with the assent of France could northern and central Italy be united; but the assent of France had to be purchased by the sacrifice of the trans-Alpine Provinces.

On 11 March a plebiscite in the central States declared for union with the kingdom of Italy; on the 24th Cavour signed the Treaty for the cession of Savoy and Nice; on the 25th elections were held for the Italian Parliament; on 2 April the first Parliament, representing no fewer than 11,000,000 Italians, met at Turin.

> "The last time I opened Parliament," said the King in his first speech to the new Parliament, "when Italy was sunk in sorrows and the state menaced by great dangers, faith in Divine justice comforted me and augured well for our destinies. In a very brief space of time an invasion was repelled, Lombardy liberated by the glorious achievements of the army, Central Italy freed by the marvellous merit of her people; and to-day I have here assembled around me the representatives of the rights and of the hopes of the nation. . . . In turning our attention," he concluded, "to the new order of affairs we invite all sincere opinions to a noble emulation that we may attain the grand end of the well-being of the people and the greatness of the country. It is no longer the Italy of the Romans, nor that of the Middle Ages; it must no longer be the battle-field of ambitious foreigners, but it must rather be the Italy of the Italians."

Then came the one discordant note:

> In gratitude to France, for the good of Italy, to consolidate
> the union between two nations that have a common origin,
> principles and destinies—and finding it necessary to make
> some sacrifice, I have made that which has cost my heart
> dear. Subject to the vote of the people, the approbation of
> Parliament, and the consent of Switzerland, I have made a
> treaty for the reunion of Savoy and Nice to France.

Three weeks later the "vote of the people" was taken in Savoy and
Nice; the vote was almost unanimous in favour of union with France.
At the end of May the Italian Parliament, by an overwhelming ma-
jority ratified the Treaty.

Thus the curtain falls on the first act of the drama of Italian unification: Cavour's work was half done. The Scene of the next Act
was in the south. Three days after the meeting of the Italian Parliament at Turin an insurrection broke out in Sicily.

The Union of North and South

Garibaldi, Victor Emmanuel, and Cavour

FOR the next act of the drama the stage was set in Sicily and Naples.
The leading part was played by Garibaldi; though had it not been
for the wise and prudent diplomacy of Cavour the act might well
have ended not in triumph but in tragedy. As the action becomes at
this point exceedingly complicated, it may be well at the outset to
disentangle some of the main threads, and indicate, very briefly, the
attitude of some of the leading actors.

The first scene of the act was laid in Sicily, which, as we have seen,
had long been restless under the rule of its Bourbon kings, and ardently desired autonomy and independence. In the Italian drama the
Sicilians had little interest, and none whatever in the fate of the
Neapolitans, whom they detested. The attitude of the Neapolitans
cannot be indicated so simply or briefly. No worse government, except perhaps that of the Pope, was to be found in Italy than that of
the Bourbon kings of Naples. But their rule, though infamous according to our standards, was not wholly intolerable. A more pitiable
creature than Francis II, the last of the Neapolitan Bourbons, who
succeeded his father, "Bomba," in May 1859, has rarely occupied a
throne. But his queen, a youthful Bavarian princess, was as spirited
as she was beautiful. The Neapolitan peasants were too far sunk in

superstition and ignorance to be conscious of political degradation;
the army was loyal to the end. Discontent was, however, rife among
the more educated middle classes, upon whom the hand of the tyrant
pressed most heavily. But their aspirations were rather in the direction of Neapolitan liberty than of Italian unity. None could, however, be insensible to the gross misgovernment of which they were
especially the victims.

> "Naples and Sicily," wrote Sir Henry Elliot, "were at that
> time entirely governed by an irresponsible police, uncontrolled
> by any form of law, and regardless of the most elementary
> considerations of justice. Men by hundreds were arrested,
> exiled, or imprisoned for years, not only without going through
> any form of trial, but often without being even informed of
> what, or by whom they were accused, or being allowed the
> opportunity of saying a word to explain or refute the accusa-
> tion . . . while the police connived at ordinary criminals, their
> zeal and activity knew no bounds in hunting down supposed
> political offenders. . . . Another frightful abuse was the arrest
> and imprisonment of men on secret private denunciation,
> more especially on that of the priests. . . ."

It was with the unhappy fate of the political prisoners that Mr.
Gladstone was particularly concerned when, in 1851, he addressed
his memorable letters to Lord Aberdeen.

It was with no idea of political investigation, still less of political
propagandism, that Mr. Gladstone visited southern Italy in the winter
of 1850–1. But he naturally met many of the foremost men in
Naples, and was quickly enlightened by them as to the condition of
affairs. He witnessed the trial of Carlo Poerio, a strict constitution-
alist, a leading politician and an ex-minister of the Crown, who with
Settembrini and forty other political prisoners was sentenced to lifelong imprisonment under revolting conditions. He managed to visit
some of the prisons; he saw refined gentlemen, imprisoned for no
proved offence, chained two and two in double irons to common
felons; his generous spirit was roused within him, and he was moved
first to indignation then to vehement remonstrance. He was himself
a Conservative, an ex-minister in a Conservative Government. He
could not condone the misdeeds of an established government. He
could not keep silence. For the step, admittedly unusual, which he
was impelled to take he adduced three reasons:

> First, that the present practices of the Government of
> Naples, in reference to real or supposed political offenders,

are an outrage upon religion, upon civilization, upon humanity
and upon decency. Secondly, that these practices are certainly
and even rapidly doing the work of republicanism in that
country: a political creed which has little natural or habitual
root in the character of the people. Thirdly, that as a member
of the Conservative party in one of the great family of European nations I am compelled to remember that that party
stands in virtual and real though perhaps unconscious alliance
with all the established governments of Europe as such; and
that according to the measure of its influence they suffer more
or less of moral detriment from its reverses and derive strength
and encouragement from its successes. This principle . . . is
of great practical importance in reference to the Government
of Naples, which from whatever cause appears to view its
own social like its physical position as one under the shadow
of a volcano, and which is doing everything in its power from
day to day to give reality to its own dangers and fresh intensity together with fresh cause to its fears.

"It is not," he goes on to say—"it is not mere imperfection,
not corruption in low practices, not occasional severity that I
am about to describe; it is incessant systematic deliberate violation of the law by the Power appointed to watch over and
maintain it. It is such violation of human and written law as
this, carried on for the purpose of violating every other law,
written and eternal, temporal and divine; it is the wholesale
persecution of virtue when united with intelligence, operating
upon such a scale that entire classes may with truth be said
to be its object; . . . it is the awful profanation of public
religion, by its notorious alliance in the governing powers
with the violation of every moral law under the stimulants of
fear and vengeance; it is the perfect prostitution of the judicial
office which has made it under veils only too threadbare and
transparent, the degraded recipient of the vilest and clumsiest
forgeries, got up wilfully and deliberately by the immediate
advisers of the Crown for the purpose of destroying the peace,
the freedom, and even if not by capital sentence the life of
men among the most virtuous, upright, intelligent, distinguished and refined of the whole community; it is the savage
and cowardly system of moral as well as in a lower degree of
physical torture through which the sentences extracted from
the debased courts of justice are carried into effect. The effect
of all this is total inversion of all the moral and social ideas.
Law instead of being respected is odious. Force and not affection is the foundation of government. There is no association
but a violent antagonism between the idea of freedom and

that of order. The governing power which teaches of itself that it is the image of God upon earth, is clothed in the view of the overwhelming majority of the thinking public with all the vices for its attributes. I have seen and heard the too true expression used, 'This is the negation of God erected into a system of Government'."

It is impossible to follow in detail the minute evidence upon which the English statesman based this appalling but not exaggerated indictment. It may be read, together with an examination of the official reply put forth in the name of the Neapolitan Government, in the volume already cited.

The publication of these Letters, written by a man in Mr. Gladstone's position, caused an immense sensation, not merely in England, but throughout Europe. Lord Aberdeen was somewhat embarrassed, but Lord Palmerston gave his unequivocal support to Mr. Gladstone, and in 1856 both the British and French Governments took the unusual step of withdrawing their ministers from Naples as a protest against King Ferdinand's misgovernment. Three years later Bomba so far yielded to the storm as to liberate more than sixty of his prisoners with a view to their deportation to the United States. They managed, however, to get control of the ship in which they were sent off to America, and diverted its course to England, where a cordial reception awaited them.

That Cavour ardently desired the complete unification of Italy is undeniable. But he was too great a statesman to wish to see the process hurried. On the contrary, after the union of northern and central Italy, he would have called a temporary halt. That both the Two Sicilies and Rome would ultimately form part of a unified Italian kingdom he never doubted; but neither Italy nor Europe was, in his judgement, yet ready for this further move.

Austria, needless to say, was strongly opposed alike to the further aggrandizement of Piedmont, and to any further weakening of the principle of "legitimacy" as represented by the Pope and the Neapolitan Bourbons. The Emperor of the French, less concerned about "legitimacy" was equally anxious, for domestic reasons, to maintain the Temporal sovereignty of the Papacy and to prevent the union of southern and northern Italy. As late as July 1860 the French minister at Turin pressed Cavour to grant the eleventh-hour appeal of Naples for an alliance with Piedmont, while at Naples the French minister declared definitely that France would not allow annexation. But to the Neapolitan royalists Napoleon had himself declared a

month earlier (12 June) that they must not look to him for active
help against Garibaldi or against Piedmont. "We French," he declared, "do not wish for the annexation of south Italy to the kingdom
of Piedmont, because we think it contrary to our interests." He would
be delighted, he added, if the Neapolitan Royalists defeated Garibaldi; but they must do it themselves. The victor of Solferino and
the liberator of Lombardy could not oppose in arms the cause of
Italian nationality in Naples. Rome was a different matter. "The
French flag," he pointed out, "is actually waving on the Pope's territory, and then there is the question of religion." If the Italians attacked Rome, he would be compelled to act; but Naples must defend
itself—preferably by alliance, if they could still get it, with Piedmont.

Could they still get it? In May 1859 Victor Emmanuel had held
out the hand of friendship to the young King of the Two Sicilies. It
had been rejected. So late as 15 April 1860, on the very eve of
Garibaldi's departure from Genoa, the offer was renewed—on terms.

> "Italy," so Victor Emmanuel wrote to his "dear Cousin"
> of Naples, "can be divided into two powerful States of the
> North and the South which, if they adopt the same national
> policy, may uphold the great idea of our times—National In-
> dependence. But in order to realize this conception, it is, I
> think, necessary that your Majesty abandon the course you
> have held hitherto. The principle of dualism, if it is well estab-
> lished and honestly pursued, can still be accepted by Italians.
> But if you allow some months to pass without attending to
> my friendly suggestion, your Majesty will perhaps experience
> the bitterness of the terrible words—*too late.*"

Cavour must have been well aware, when he approved this letter,
that the "friendly suggestions"—internal reform and cordial alliance
with Piedmont—would not be attended to. He and his master were
cognizant of the fact that for months past Naples had been negotiating with the Papacy, Austria, and the exiled rulers of Parma and
Modena, for a combined attack on Piedmont and for the restoration
of the Romagna to the Pope, if not for the reinstatement of the
former rulers in the Duchies.

Nevertheless, the preference for dualism expressed by Victor Emmanuel may have been sincere. Cavour doubted whether the pear
was yet ripe; so did foreign friends of Italy. Italian unity had no
more ardent well-wishers than Sir James Hudson, the English minister
at Turin, and Mr. Henry Elliot, who represented us at Naples. The
attitude taken up by England in July and August 1860 was decisive;

it gave Naples immediately to Garibaldi, and ultimately to Italy; but not until and after Garibaldi's conquest of Sicily were Hudson and Elliot converted to the idea of Italian unity. So late as 18 May Hudson had argued strongly against the fusion of north and south Italy; contending that the intervening Papal territory would make it difficult to rule Naples from Turin or Florence, and that the corruption of the Neapolitans was so abominable that "their junction with north Italy, where honesty is the rule in public affairs, would merely produce a social decomposition, and then a political petrifaction." No one was in closer touch both with the King and Cavour than Hudson, and in this passage he probably speaks their mind. Elliot wrote from the Neapolitan angle:

> "At that time" [i.e. summer of 1859], writes Elliot, "the strongest of the Neapolitan Liberals would have been found unanimous in repudiating with indignation the notion of their absorption into the comparatively small northern kingdom of Sardinia . . . it was not until after the extraordinary success of Garibaldi that all parties united in regarding incorporation with Piedmont as the only issue left open to them."

Garibaldi's Sicilian expedition was indeed the deciding factor, and to the story of it we now turn.

The sequence of events is important, and even at the cost of repetition must be recalled. On 11 March the Central Provinces decided by plebiscite on union with Piedmont. On the 22nd Victor Emmanuel accepted their decision and appointed the Prince of Carignano as Viceroy, with Baron Ricasoli as Governor-General. On the same day Cavour learnt from Villamarina, his trusted agent in Naples, that a Papal envoy had visited Francis II with a view to promoting Neapolitan intervention in the Romagna. Three days later the elections were held for an Italian Parliament, which met for the first time at Turin on 2 April. On 5 April an insurrection, stimulated by Francesco Crispi—destined to play a great part in the politics of United Italy—and Rosalino Pilo, broke out in Sicily. On 15 April Victor Emmanuel wrote to Francis II of Naples the second of the two warning letters already referred to; on the 18th and 22nd the plebiscites, approving union with France, were taken in Nice and Savoy, and on the 26th the Parliament at Turin ratified by an overwhelming majority the Treaty which embodied the agreement for the cession of those provinces.

Meanwhile, Garibaldi having denounced in the Chamber a treaty which involved "human traffic," and made him an alien in the city of his birth (Nice), sailed with his "Thousand" volunteers for Sicily.

Garibaldi waited for no leave from the Piedmontese Government. On 29 September 1859 he had written to the Sicilians:

> My brothers, the cause fought for by me and my comrades in arms is not the cause of a parish, but the cause of our Italy, from Trapani to the Isonzo, from Taranto to Nice. Therefore the work of the redemption of Sicily is the work of our own redemption, and we will fight for it with the same zeal with which we fought on the Lombard battle-fields.

He kept his word. On the eve of his embarkation at Genoa he wrote to the King:

> I know that I embark on a perilous enterprise. If we achieve it I shall be proud to add to your Majesty's crown a new and perhaps more glorious jewel, always on the condition that your Majesty will stand opposed to counsellors who would cede this province to the foreigner, as has been done with the city of my birth.

The Piedmontese Government was, as a fact, in complete sympathy with the objects of the expedition, though had it been possible, they would have postponed it. On 30 March Cavour wrote to Villamarina at Naples:

> Evidently events of great importance are preparing in the south of Italy. . . . You know that I do not desire to push the Neapolitan question to a premature crisis. . . . It would be to our interest if the present state of things continued for some years longer. But . . . I believe that we shall soon be forced to form a plan which I would like to have had more time to mature.

Cavour was right; but he could control neither events nor Garibaldi. Cavour, indeed, understood Garibaldi better than Garibaldi understood him. Victor Emmanuel, even better than Cavour, understood him, and did all in his power, consistently with loyalty to his minister, to assist him. He contributed 3,000,000 francs out of his private pocket towards the expenses; the public also subscribed generously; the *National Society* supplied guns and ammunition, though not in adequate amounts; and the Government turned a blind eye to the enlistment of volunteers and other preparations which went on busily, almost ostentatiously, at Genoa.

Cavour had a difficult game to play, but he played it with consummate skill; so skilfully, indeed, that the Mazzinians, despite all the evidence to the contrary, have always asserted that he spared no pains to frustrate the objects of the expedition. Lord Acton describes his conduct as "a triumph of unscrupulous statesmanship," and evidently regards Garibaldi as his catspaw and dupe. Lord Acton's verdict seems to be as far from the truth as that of the Mazzinisti. Mr. Trevelyan summarizes the facts with judicial impartiality: "Mazzini and his friends instigated the expedition; Garibaldi accomplished it; the King and Cavour allowed it to start, and when it had begun to succeed, gave it the support and guidance without which it must inevitably have failed mid-way."

The "Thousand" embarked at Quarto near Genoa on 6 May; on the 11th, after a very narrow escape from Neapolitan cruisers, they landed at Marsala. On the 15th Garibaldi defeated the Neapolitan forces at Calatafimi, and on the 27th successfully assaulted Palermo, which was finally evacuated on 6 June. There was some desperate fighting at Milazzo (20 July), but by the end of July Garibaldi was master of the whole island, except the actual citadel of Messina and a few of the Sicilian ports. The Neapolitan garrison was allowed to retain the citadel of Messina, but under a pledge of neutrality, which averted all danger to the future plans of Garibaldi, as far as the island was concerned. Soon after landing at Marsala Garibaldi had accepted the dictatorship of the island, immediately decreed conscription for the islanders, and imposed stern discipline alike on them and upon his own volunteers. Cavour attempted to induce Garibaldi to annex the island at once to the kingdom of Italy, but Garibaldi definitely declined to do so. His obstinacy served Cavour and Italy well. Had Victor Emmanuel become responsible for Sicily in July, Garibaldi would never have been allowed by the Powers to cross the Straits. The conquest and therefore the annexation of Naples might have been indefinitely postponed.

As it was, the diplomatic situation was intensely critical. The English Government alone made no secret of its sympathy with Garibaldi's enterprise; Napoleon III would do nothing to offend England. But the attitude of the eastern Courts was very different. "A horde of pirates," "bandits," "desperadoes," "dregs of the human race"— such were the least opprobrious of the descriptions applied to Garibaldi and his followers. Cavour had to bear the brunt of the attack, but he was not dismayed. "Here things do not go too badly," he wrote from Turin to La Farina, his agent in Sicily. "The diplomatists do not molest us overmuch. Russia made a fearful hubbub—Prussia less": Cavour could write in this light vein; but his responsibilities were heavy. When, a few months later, he sped his king and the Italian army on the expedition to the south, he knew not whether they might not, on their return, find Turin in the occupation of the Austrians—or it might be the French. But courage, combined with prudence, earned its appropriate reward. We must not, however, anticipate events.

Cavour had failed, fortunately as it now appears, to get Sicily annexed to Piedmont. He was determined that if he could help it, Garibaldi should not be in a similar dictatorial position on the mainland. Down to the middle of July he was endeavouring to stir up an insurrection in Naples which would forestall Garibaldi's intervention. Before the end of July he had realized the hopelessness of doing this, and had changed his plans to meet the changed situation. Garibaldi must on no account be prevented from crossing to the mainland. But Napoleon was determined to stop him, if England would join in a blockade of the Sicilian coasts. The English Government were disposed to agree that Garibaldi had already been allowed enough rope, and must not be permitted "to cross the Straits."

On 27 July Garibaldi received two letters from his Sovereign. In the first, intended for publication to the world, Garibaldi was reminded that the King had *not* approved his expedition to Sicily and was advised "to renounce the idea of crossing to the mainland . . . provided the King of Naples pledges himself to evacuate the island and leave the Sicilians free to decide their own future." In a second and secret communication Garibaldi was bidden to refuse, with every expression of devotion, to obey his Sovereign. Garibaldi duly replied in the terms dictated (secretly) by the King. Meanwhile (25 July), Lord John Russell was induced to decline Napoleon's invitation, and to allow Garibaldi to cross to Calabria. Napoleon was dumbfounded, as well he might be, by England's *volte face*, but he was unwilling to take any action of which England disapproved; Garibaldi, with a handful of followers, crossed the Straits (18-21 August) and took Reggio by storm.

Meanwhile, Francis II, in deference to the advice of Napoleon, and anxious also to conciliate English opinion, had (25 June) published a Liberal Constitution for Naples and promised to grant autonomy to Sicily under a prince of the Royal House. He also made humble suit at Turin for an alliance with Piedmont. It was too late. Carlo Poerio and other Neapolitan exiles were in Turin, and endeavoured to convince Cavour that Bourbon promises were made only to be broken; that Francis II was likely enough to stage anew the blasphemous farces performed by his predecessors in 1821 and 1848.

> "The Neapolitan Government," said Poerio, speaking in the Chamber at Turin, "has the tradition of perjury handed down from father to son. . . . I trust that the Ministers of Victor Emmanuel will not stretch out their hands to a Government which certainly is the most declared of the enemies of Italian independence." (29 June.)

Cavour was placed in a cruel dilemma. His sympathies were all with the Neapolitan liberals; but he had the Powers to consider. France had suggested the alliance; England officially supported France; Austria, Russia, and Prussia would have welcomed anything which would save legitimacy in Naples. "If we consent to the alliance," wrote Cavour, "we are lost. If we reject it what will Europe say? I was never, in my life, more embarrassed." He endeavoured, as we have seen, to stir up revolution in Naples, until his agents there convinced him that only Garibaldi could do that. So Garibaldi must be allowed to cross the Straits.

Garibaldi crossed; and in the first week of September was marching on Naples. On 6 September Francis II and his Queen quitted the capital and sailed for Gaëta. On the following day Garibaldi, hurrying on in advance of his army, entered Naples, proclaimed himself Dictator, and demanded confirmation of his Dictatorship from the Piedmontese Government. The Parliament at Turin had already, at Cavour's instance, approved the annexation of the Two Sicilies to the Italian Kingdom. Would Garibaldi respect that decision?

Garibaldi declared that he would not permit annexation until he could proclaim Victor Emmanuel King of Italy in Rome. Everything was now at stake: the life-work of Cavour; the life-work of Mazzini; the life-work of Garibaldi himself. To suggest that "called upon to face an awful moment to which Heaven had joined great issues" Cavour was "happy as a lover" would be affectation. He was distraught with anxiety; yet he was "equal to the need." By a masterly stroke of policy the control of the movement was taken out of the rash hands of the impetuous crusader, and confirmed in those of sober statesmanship. Cavour decided to dispatch a Royal army to the Roman Marches with the twofold object of warding off from the Romagna the attack threatened by the Papacy, and of obstructing, if necessary, the advance of the Garibaldians on Rome. "If we do